Missed It by That Much

Missed It
by That Much

*Baseball Players Who
Challenged the Record Books*

by
VICTOR DEBS, JR.

McFarland & Company, Inc., Publishers
Jefferson, North Carolina, and London

Front Cover: Jimmie Foxx (both photographs courtesy of National Baseball Library & Archive, Cooperstown, N.Y.). **Back Cover:** David Cone.

British Library Cataloguing-in-Publication data are available

Library of Congress Cataloguing-in-Publication Data

Debs, Victor, 1949–
    Missed it by that much : baseball players who challenged the record
books / by Victor Debs, Jr.
      p.   cm.
    Includes bibliographical references (p.) and index.
    ISBN 0-7864-0508-2 (sewn softcover : 50# alkaline paper) ∞
    1. Baseball players — Rating of — United States.   2. Baseball
players — United States — Statistics.   3. Baseball — Records — United
States.   I. Title.
GV865.A1D374   1998
796.357'0973 — dc21   98-7486
                                                    CIP

Manufactured in the United States of America

McFarland & Company, Inc., Publishers
  Box 611, Jefferson, North Carolina 28640

To the memory of
Sala Saba and Emile Kashou,
who are missed very much

Acknowledgments

My thanks to the following people and organizations for making this book possible:

ElRoy Face, George Kell, Joe Moore, Bill Lohrman, and Harry Danning for generously taking time to speak with me.

Researchers at the National Baseball Library for providing biographical material on some of the players.

Bill Burdick of the National Baseball Library & Archive, and Jocelyn Clapp of Bettmann, for their help in obtaining photos.

The staffs at the microfilm departments of the New York Public Library, main branch, and the St. George Public Library, Staten Island, for their patience and diligence.

Thanks, as always, to my loving wife, Lola, and my precious daughter, Jackie, whose love and support inspire all that I do.

Table of Contents

Introduction

The continued popularity of baseball in America may result from its fans' fascination with records. In no other sport do such diligent statisticians keep followers so well informed of every aspect of the game. Fans of the national pastime are quickly made aware anytime an active player's performance approaches an existing record. Subsequently, the athlete becomes the object of increasing attention by the media until he either surpasses the old mark or falls short.

The resulting publicity can be a blessing or a curse to the would-be record-breaker. Roger Maris detested the attention while he was setting a new homerun record in 1961, but Rickey Henderson seemed quite comfortable with it when he was breaking Lou Brock's stolen-base mark years later. Had Maris played at a time when million-dollar endorsement opportunities were available, perhaps he would have shown more tolerance toward the persistent press.

What is true of both players is that, though their skills were transitory, the memory of their record-setting feats survives. Ballplayers can perform with excellence season after season, but the ones remembered best are the record-smashers. Babe Ruth was the greatest player of his (or any) era, but his 60 homers in 1927 and career homer total of 714 are what fans recall. When Hank Aaron surpassed the Sultan of Swat, he ensured that his other achievements, such as a lifetime batting average of .305 and slugging average of .555, would be virtually ignored.

With so much importance placed on breaking records, the feats of those who came *close* to breaking them are often forgotten. Few fans are unaware of Maris' mark; yet how many recall that Jimmie Foxx was the first to approach the Babe's 60 homers? Fans talk about Nolan Ryan's no-hitters, but not many realize he had a dozen one-hitters. Experts will quickly name Rudy York as the player to hit the most homers in a month (18), but how many are aware of Willie Mays' 17 in August of 1965?

Missed It by That Much will review some of the sensational performances of various players in baseball history. That their achievements fell short of the mark makes their efforts no less meritorious. After all, record-holders wouldn't be as highly regarded without the subsequent failures of others. As an old proverb advises, "Look down if you would know how high you stand."

Vince Lombardi should have stopped after stating that winning isn't everything. There is honor in giving the good try.

One

Terry Ties

Nineteen thirty was a year that tested America's confidence. Its economy had taken a dive with the crash of 1929, the prelude to a decade characterized by low wages, high unemployment, and the government's initial experiment with socialism. Some who were out of work at times broke the law, rationalizing that incarceration might be preferable to freedom, only to discover later that they were mistaken. Attempts to break out of jail or prison were frequent and usually resulted in death. Being a model prisoner didn't ensure safety either. In April of 1930, over 300 inmates were killed in a fire; this incident incited a riot that wasn't completely subdued until a week later.

Good news was usually accompanied by troubling news. The *New York Times* reported in July that the nation's death rate from disease had been halved since the beginning of the century and cited medicine's control of diphtheria and typhoid as the main reason. That article on longevity would have brought little comfort to a pair of black Alabamans, who that same day were running from a revenge-seeking posse for allegedly killing two whites. As the *Times* indicated, their fleeing was futile; one was shot to death and the other hanged. In August, President Herbert Hoover proudly declared fifty-year-old Philippines commander Douglas MacArthur to be the new chief of staff, unaware of the Old Soldier's future significance to America's fight against aggression and injustice. But as Mac was accepting his post, the nation's farmers were fighting a depressing battle against a drought which saw Nebraskans lose thirty percent of their corn crop and states such as Ohio and Missouri suffer damage estimated in the hundreds of millions.

Historians point out that baseball reflects societal attitudes, an idea which applies, at least, to the magnates of 1930. Major-league attendance had been 9,120,000 in 1920, a forty percent increase from the previous year, but it surpassed that amount in only five of the following nine seasons. By

3

1929, owners were concerned over unstable gate receipts, and they became frantic when the stock market plunged two weeks after the 1929 World Series. Thinking that increased run-production was commensurate with increased attendance, owners resolved early in 1930 that A. G. Spalding's horsehide, whose alteration prior to the twenties resulted in the demise of the "dead-ball era," was in need of further adjustments. Consequently, even livelier baseballs were produced.

One batter who required no assistance was Bill Terry. Born in Atlanta fourteen months prior to the turn of the century, Terry left home at age 13 shortly after his parents' divorce. He supported himself by unloading freight cars while learning his future hardball skills playing for a semipro team in Georgia. After several years of pitching in the minors, Bill landed a job with the prestigious New York Giants, who were impressed not with his arm, but his bat.

A reliable but not outstanding hitter early on, the first baseman roared to superstardom in the late twenties. The lefty-swinger averaged .342 from 1927 to 1929, peaking to .372 in 1929. During a decade of increased power-hitting, the 6' 2", 200-pounder adopted the more traditional style of "spray-hitting," reaching the 20-homer plateau only once in his first seven seasons covering 1923–1929. Yet he exceeded the 30 mark in doubles four times and had more than ten triples two times.

Former Giant catcher Harry Danning recalled for this author in 1994 an incident which exemplified Terry's skill with the bat. "We were in Philadelphia once, and the shortstop and second baseman were playing Terry both as a righty and lefty pull-hitter, playing towards the corner bags. He said to me after his first time up, 'How do you like what they're doing?' Then he hit three balls right past the box for hits his next three times up."

Still, the new ball wouldn't impede Terry's proficiency for propelling long drives, as he proved with a pair of homers, one to left, the other to right, in his final exhibition games. His power must have perked up New York's irascible manager, John McGraw. Little Napoleon had become increasingly ill-tempered in the five years preceding the Giants' last pennant in 1924. Offense was not his worry. Cleanup batter Mel Ott's power perfectly complemented third place hitter Terry's ability to reach base.

Ott, who first put on a fielder's glove at age five and at seven was used as a batting-practice pitcher while team bat boy for his father's semipro club, had a look-see in 1925 by Mr. McGraw. (Players always showed proper respect when speaking to or about their skipper.) The 16-year-old joined the Giants as a part-timer the next year, belted 18 homers in 1928, and was league runner-up with 42 in 1929. Wrote *New York Times* sportswriter John

Drebinger in regards to Ott's explosive power and complacent personality, "It may just be his way to drift along for twenty more years and crack all records." Indeed, upon his retirement in 1947, Ott had hit more homeruns than any other National Leaguer, with Babe Ruth and Jimmie Foxx the only big-leaguers to have exceeded his 511 round trippers by then.

Pitching shouldn't have been a concern for McGraw either. The staff included southpaw Carl Hubbell and righty Freddie Fitzsimmons, who between them won 34 games in 1929, along with the league leader in ERA, Bill Walker. But the defense-minded McGraw wasn't satisfied and pushed his pitchers to the limit during spring-training workouts, forcing them to go all-out in batting practice sessions. As McGraw explained to reporter Bill Brandt, "If a pitcher is careless in practice, he will find himself up against it when he gets in a tight place in some close game."

At noon of April 15, 1930, the gates at the Polo Grounds opened, and despite cold temperatures which made it feel, as Drebinger wrote, "like Knute Rockne's Notre Dame horsemen would come galloping on the field any moment," over 50,000 paid their way in. New York's dapper mayor Jimmy Walker probably entered free-of-charge, though he certainly could afford the price of a ticket, as would become glaringly evident in the months ahead. While the smiling ex-showman was throwing out the first ball to inaugurate the season, charges of corruption in his administration were being leveled by Republicans. After a year of intensified attacks, Walker's smile began to fade. He found no friend in fellow Democrat, Governor Franklin Roosevelt, who demanded an explanation for Walker's swelling bank account. Hizzoner resigned in 1932.

Baseball broadcasting was still in its infancy in 1930. The Old Redhead, Red Barber, was just beginning his distinguished career, spinning records and giving news reports at the University of Florida's WRUF. His idol, Graham McNamee, must have felt like a veteran by then, having done the first World Series broadcast with Grantland Rice in 1923. McNamee was on Station WJZ for the 1930 Polo Grounds opener, describing Walker's toss and the flag-raising ceremony and continuing with the play-by-play account when the Boston–New York battle began.

And a splendid battle it was. The Giants wasted little time in scoring, pushing a run across in the first and another in the third, but the Braves fought back heroically with a pair in the fourth. New York considerately provided McNamee with a climactic finish, scoring the game-winner with two outs in the ninth. Not only did the two-hour struggle end in success for the Giants, but for Terry as well, his two hits both resulting in runs.

In contrast to the frigid New York weather of April which would force several postponements, Terry remained hot in the early part of the season.

Not until the Giants' tenth game on the final day of the month, when Brooklyn fireballer Dazzy Vance stopped them on five hits, did Terry fail to get a safety. He had 2 or more hits in 6 of his first 9 games, and his batting streak generated 16 hits in 38 plate appearances, including two doubles, a triple, and three homers. It was a productive first month for the line-drive specialist, but even the most ardent admirer couldn't have expected Terry's torrid pace to continue, a pace which would have left him with 274 hits and a .421 batting average at the conclusion of the 154-game schedule. Nevertheless, Terry's 1930 stats would be remarkably near those projected figures.

As grand as it would be, Bill Terry's season would have been more glorious had he succeeded in surpassing one of the most prestigious batting marks — most hits in a season. Not only did he come excruciatingly close to George Sisler's record 257 of 1920, but he needed only one more to break the National League mark set a year earlier by the Phils' Lefty O'Doul. Terry's 254 hits in 1930 was good for a senior-circuit tie, but no more.

After enduring record cold temperatures and snow the week before, New Yorkers were donning bathing suits on May 2 as the mercury reached a humid 82 degrees. The Giants weren't around to sweat out the weather, having traveled west to play Cincinnati. Terry stayed hot in his first game of the month, drilling a single and his fourth homer. It wasn't enough to save his team, which lost a 9–8 slugfest, their fourth straight defeat, following a 7–0 start.

Bill Terry, whose nickname Memphis Bill derived partly from his working for the Standard Oil Company in the Tennessee metropolis, stroked singles in each of his next two games, giving him 20 hits and a .377 average after 13 games. Yet he wasn't among the league's top ten in batting or hits. Former batting champ Paul Waner was atop the NL leaderboard with a .500 average, and Babe Herman was leading the hit pack with 29. As productive as he had been, Bill would have to improve to be the best in the year of the hitter.

Terry responded with a streak as troublesome for pitchers as Mohandas Gandhi and his civil disobedience followers of India were for the British that year. His streak began on May 5 when he outhit Waner three-to-two, helping New York coast to a 9–1 laugher in Pittsburgh. It was the first of seven consecutive multiple-hit games for Terry. The streak ironically ended in a slugfest in Chicago on the twelfth. His single that day was dwarfed by nine homers, five doubles, and thirty total hits. That the Giants had a 14–0 lead in the fifth and then barely escaped with a 14–12 decision is an indication of how dangerous Wrigley Field was for pitchers in 1930 when they were compelled to cast a juiced ball into the wind.

During the seven-game stretch, Terry accumulated three doubles, two triples, and two homers. He had a pair of three-hit games and banged out four hits in another. His 18 hits in 32 at-bats gave him a .563 average for the seven games and raised his seasonal mark to .447, good for second in the league. And for the first time that year, Bill led the National League in hits with 38. Even in that illustrious season for hitting, Terry was beginning to attract attention.

And it wasn't that his stats were misleading in terms of helping his team win games. The Giants had the best record in the league by mid–May, and not coincidentally, Terry led the club in runs-scored and RBIs. Unquestionably, Ott was a significant force as well, and his batting behind Terry helped Bill see better pitches. Despite Terry's spectacular season, he would receive only 57 passes. Ott gathered twice as many in 1930 and probably wished on more than one occasion for a switch with Terry in lineup positions.

As dictator Benito Mussolini pounded his fist to emphasize that might makes right in justifying his weapons buildup to thousands listening in Florence, Italy, Terry continued pounding baseballs, his bases-loaded two bagger on May 14 driving in all three Giants runs in a 7–3 loss to the Cardinals. Gallant Fox won the Kentucky Derby on the seventeenth, and Terry was as heroic with five hits in a twin bill that day, including a double and a homer. His two bagger in front of Ott's sixth homer was the difference in a 3–2 Giants victory the next day.

Terry was stymied by the Braves' Ben Cantwell on May 20, ending a 17-game hitting streak which would be his longest of the season. It marked only the second time in 28 games that he had gone hitless. His oh-for-five dropped his average 17 points to .410, and Herman's five hits put him in a tie with Terry for most in the majors with 50.

Worst of all for the team-minded Terry, his futility at the plate hurt the ballclub, which lost a squeaker when former American Leaguer Sisler singled home the winning run in the tenth. The setback dropped New York to fourth in the standings, but the race was close, with the fifth place, defending-champ Cubs only two games behind league-leading Brooklyn.

Although heartbreaking defeats in September are the ones to remember, games lost in April and May are equally meaningful. Losing an extra-inning affair at home to a club which finished last or next to last in eight of the past ten seasons wasn't conducive to capturing flags, especially after the Giants had lost three of the first four of the series. McGraw, who had been absent from the dugout until the finale, may have wished he had stayed away.

If the Giants hoped for a reprieve against Philadelphia, the cellar-

Hall-of-Famer Bill Terry, whose finest season came in 1930 when he hit .401 and nearly broke Lefty O'Doul's NL mark for most hits in one season (National Baseball Library & Archive, Cooperstown, N.Y.)

dwellers provided none. The terrible twosome of Terry-Ott displayed their hit-then-homer act in a trio of games, but the Phillies prevailed in three of four, thanks to their gifted pair of lumber-wielders. O'Doul, the best batter of 1929, had a homer and five RBIs for the series, and slugger Chuck Klein, who was leading the league in ribbies (though Hack Wilson would eventually explode and take the crown with 191), belted two doubles, a homer, and five RBIs.

The Phils' Leo Sweetland hadn't made Terry happy in the finale of the series, collaring him in four trips to the plate. The Robins' Cuban right-hander Dolf Luque did the same the next day, marking the first time in 1930 that Bill was held hitless in consecutive games. The drought was stretched to three straight when Vance dazzled Terry for the second time that year. In the midst of his first slump of the season, the hit man may have been wondering when his next one would come.

Brooklyn's Jumbo Elliot provided the answer. The hefty lefty surrendered a first-inning single to Terry, ending his oh-for-eleven slide. Bill finished with two hits that day, had another pair the next, and lengthened his latest, more propitious streak to five by drilling two hits in the final three games of May. As a result of his brief lapse, however, the man who would be king was forced to settle for a below .400 batting average and runner-up honors in hits entering the season's third month.

The Giants would gladly have settled for runner-up position in the standings. Instead, the red-faced McGraw and his embarrassed players held sixth place after again losing to the Braves in the final game of May, and they retained that position none too securely. The Reds were a game away, and even the floundering Phils weren't bolted in the basement, having lost only one more than New York. And with Ott now out with a leg injury and team captain Travis Jackson and equally reliable Freddie Lindstrom unavailable as well, things would probably get worse before getting better. As Terry stated in early June, "That's like taking three wheels off an automobile and expecting it to run."

But New York took a giant leap forward in Boston on June 2 by twice trouncing its nemesis by scores of 9–4 and 16–3. The team's heavy hitters, Ott and Lindstrom, returned the next day, as did their heavy hitting, punishing the Reds 9–1. New York plated six in the opening inning on the fourth and coasted to a 8–5 win; they then completed the sweep of the Reds' dead machine with a 7–4 victory, leaving the field as hot as the 90-degree temperature. No longer concerned with their rear, the Giants owned third place, a .500 won-lost percentage, and a five-game winning streak. The Polo Grounds residents brimmed with confidence. Boasted Terry, "We've got the best club in the league, man for man."

Terry had three hits in the Cincy finale, raising his hit total to 73, one better than Herman's, and boosting his average to .397, fifth best in the league. He belted his ninth homer against the Cards on June 8, and though rain forced postponements of the next two games, it did little to cool him off. He resumed his rampage with another three-hit day against the Pirates on the eleventh, helping the Giants extend their winning streak to nine and stretching his hit string to 14.

The Bucs' Ray Kremer put a halt to both streaks on June 12. The tall righty, whose 20 victories in 1930 would be the league high, scattered nine hits in going the distance. With the oh-for-four, Terry's average again dipped below .400, and despite swinging at a pace of 1.67 hits per game for nearly a third of the season (nearly the same as his 1.65 rate by year's end), his lead in hits over rival Herman was only one.

Even with the competition, Terry's latest streak had been grand. He batted .483 for the fourteen games, averaging precisely two hits per contest, and raised his season's average thirty-one points. In only three of the fourteen games did he get fewer than two hits, and he had three three-hit games. The streak was his second long one in a little over a month. Had his fourteen and seventeen game strings not been separated by the trio of hitless games in late May, Terry would have faced Kremer with a 31-game hitting streak and a league-leading .429 average.

The second place Cubs came to the Polo Grounds in mid–June, hoping to stave off the Giants and move closer to the Dodgers (then called the Robins), who were leading the pack. Hurler Pat Malone held Terry hitless and defeated New York in the opener. Terry rebounded with two hits to help his club square the series the next day. His sole hit in the closer wasn't enough, however, as Chicago prevailed 8–5. Terry then banged two safeties in Pittsburgh in a 4–3 Giant win on the eighteenth, was collared by Kremer again the next day in an 8–4 loss, but spanked a pair of singles to lead the Giants past the Bucs in the decider. The trend of the team's winning when Terry hit, losing when he didn't, wasn't isolated to those two series but would be indicative of the entire season.

Listed in the chart on the following page is the Giants' 1930 record broken down according to games in which Terry had one, two, three, and four-or-more hits, as well as the team's record when he was held hitless. The Giants' record gets progressively better for games in which Terry accumulated more hits: a .531 percentage in games he had one hit, .583 for two-hit games, .714 for three-hit games, and .909 for games where Terry had four-or-more hits. Compare these statistics with New York's dismal .320 in games in which he was collared. The club's 79–50 record (.612) in games Terry stroked at least one hit compared to its overall season mark of 87–67 (.565) offers further evidence of his value to the club in 1930.

Terry's and Giants' 1930 Performance

Terry	Number of Games	Club Record
No Hits	25	8–17 (.320)
One Hit	49	26–23 (.531)
Two Hits	48	28–20 (.583)
Three Hits	21	15–6 (.714)
Four-or-more Hits	11	10–1 (.909)

Terry picked up two RBIs in the Pirate finale, both coming on sacrifice flies, and since it would be a year later that the sac-fly rule was abolished (it was reestablished in 1939), Terry's average wasn't adversely affected by the fly-ball outs. By game's end, it stood at .390, sixth best in the league and a distant thirty points behind league-leader Klein, but he trailed the Phillie phenom by only one in total hits.

The Giants then traveled to Cincinnati to play a June 23 game against Dan Howley's cellar-dwellers. Howley joined the Reds in 1930 after a three-year stint with the St. Louis Browns. It was a classic case of jumping from the frying pan into the fire. From 1927 to 1929, the Browns never contended, finishing as far behind as 50 games in 1927. Yet Howley would find no comfort in Cincy. Although the Reds climbed out of the bottom berth to finish seventh in 1930, they sank to their more accustomed position the next two seasons. By the end of 1932, Howley decided he had seen enough and put an end to his managing career, probably reflecting ruefully in retirement on those unfounded rumors of 1927 which claimed he would be replacing crony Ty Cobb as manager of the Tigers.

The Giants and the weather offered no relief for Howley on June 23. In temperatures that approached the three-digit mark, Bill Walker scattered six hits in blanking the Reds and attaining the club's first shutout of 1930. Walker rested between innings by lying on his back on the bench while teammates swung towels to revive him. Terry helped on offense with a pair of singles and an RBI but almost paid the price for hustle on the field. Considered by experts to be one of the finest fielding first basemen in history, Terry was sure-handed with the glove, had a strong accurate arm, and had better range than most of his peers. In the seventh inning, that ability to cover ground almost cost him. Chasing a foul fly, Bill collided with muscular 240-pound catcher Shanty Hogan and, as the *New York Times* reported, "finished second in the crash." Sprawled on the grass for several minutes, Terry appeared seriously injured, but he returned to his position and, in the next inning, "whaled the game's hardest drive, a whistling single to center," plating the Giants' third and final run.

It is a safe bet McGraw wasn't doing much whistling after the Giants laid down for the Reds the next two games. It had been a productive month prior to those defeats, with New York taking 15 of the first 19 games, moving from five games below .500 at 17–22 to six games over at 32–26, moving from sixth in the standings to third. New York rebounded by taking the next two from St. Louis but again faltered by dropping the final four of the month, including a doubleheader to the Cards on June 29. By July 1, they were seven-and-a-half away from league-leading Chicago.

Terry was held hitless in that doubledip disaster in the Gateway to the West, the first time he had been collared in a twin bill. Doubleheaders would actually hurt Terry's stats in 1930. In the 42 games played in the 21 twin bills, Terry had 67 hits in 169 at-bats for a .396 average, compared with his season's mark of .401 and his single-game average of .403. His average of 1.60 hits per game during doubleheaders was also lower than his season mark of 1.65 and his single-game average of 1.67.

Doubleheaders drain a player's energy, and Terry was no exception. Those who point to today's players as being superior might keep in mind that doubleheaders, ostensibly absent in contemporary baseball, were a detriment to a player's stats in past decades. If indeed modern ballplayers are better, which is not necessarily true, part of their success may arise from the superior conditions they enjoy — better fields, better equipment, an easier (though not lighter) schedule, and more comfortable road accommodations.

Terry began July with a three-hit assault off Cubs pitching, good for two ribbies and a Giant victory. His hit the next day was his 107th of the season, the major-league high going into the Fourth of July, and Bill's average stood at .389, third in the senior circuit.

There were a million people packed onto the Coney Island beaches on Independence Day, but enough of New York's baseball fans remained to fill over 45,000 seats at the Polo Grounds to watch the Giants battle Brooklyn in a morning-afternoon doubleheader. By evening, both clubs had reason to rejoice — the Giants taking the first game with a run in the eleventh, the Robins rebounding with a 5–2 win and retention of their first place position. Terry had no reason to celebrate. For the second straight twin bill, he was held hitless in both games. Dazzy Vance, Terry's toughest foe in 1930, collared him for the third time that year, and Watty Clark stopped him in the second game.

But Terry was valuable for more than his bat, as Robins manager Wilbert Robinson pointed out to sportswriter John Kieran during fielding practice the next day. "Lookit Bill Terry," Robinson barked. "That's the way to start double plays. See how neat he does it — no effort." Uncle Robby would get no argument from Kieran. Two weeks later, after watching Terry perform magic with his glove in Philly, he explained his reasons for picking the Giants first sacker as the best in the majors. Wrote Kieran, "Gehrig and Foxx are great hitters but so is Terry and he is the best of the three in a pinch. Foxx is only a fair fielder. In addition, Memphis Bill is one of the fastest men in either league getting down to first base and can step at a lively pace after turning that corner."

Harry Danning confirmed for me Terry's all-around ability, labeling him "a great hitter, good runner, and as fine a defensive first baseman as you'll ever see." But Kieran's comparison was premature. Foxx's best years were still ahead of him, including a Triple Crown and a 58-homer season, and two MVPs. Gehrig was at his prime and had already won an MVP, but, like Double X, would go on to win the Triple Crown and take another MVP.

Still, the remarks by Robinson and Kieran and retrospection by Danning indicate the respect that was shown Terry by players and writers. Wasn't Bill correct, then, to wonder aloud at Cooperstown in 1954 why his induction into the Hall of Fame came 18 years after his retirement? Of course, Kieran's comments in 1930 preceded by several years Terry's sarcastic query at the start of the 1934 season, "Is Brooklyn still in the league?" a question which came back to haunt him when the Dodgers eliminated the Terry-managed Giants on the last day. Terry never forgave the press for reporting his tactless pronouncement, and the mutual antagonism intensified. Yet selection into the Hall of Fame should not be based on popularity, and it is difficult to defend writers who, for so many years, ignored a .341 lifetime batter.

Terry followed his anemic holiday hitting with a two-hit attack on July 5 and then had a more productive twin bill the next day. He complemented his brilliant fielding in the aforementioned game against the Phils with a double and inside-the-park homer and then had a single in the nightcap to cement the sweep for the Giants. Terry cracked a pair of hits on July 7, two more on the eighth, and two more on the tenth. He had a double in the following game which would have been another inside-the-parker had he not missed the first-base bag and been forced to retrace his steps from second. Terry punished Cincy hurlers with four hits on July 13 and three the day after. Riding a ten-game batting streak which included three doubles, three triples, a homer, and twelve ribbies, the NL hit leader seemed unstoppable.

Terry's tomahawking ceased abruptly with a hitless game against the Reds' Red Lucas on July 16, marking the 13th time he had been collared in 81 games. Although he would need to improve his hit output to catch Sisler and O'Doul, since his 127 in 81 games put him on a pace to collect 241 by season's end, Terry was also threatening to match Rogers Hornsby's record of the most games with at least one hit — 135 in 1922. If Bill could avoid the collar in fewer than seven of the remaining 73 games, he would match the Rajah's mark.

Terry put only one in the hit column on July 17, but it carried significance. His opposite-field, upper-deck homer brought three runs, that being the difference in the Giants' 12–9 victory. They came close to blowing it in the ninth, and Terry came close to becoming goat rather than hero. His dropped ball of a two-out throw to first kept the game alive. It was followed by a homer, two walks, and a single. With the go-ahead run at the plate, McGraw called on Hubbell to end the trouble, which he did.

It was the Giants' turn to stage a late-game rally, which they did the next day, and unlike the Cards, they were successful. The Cards distanced themselves from New York by four runs going into the final frame, thanks mostly to their captain, former Giant Frankie Frisch, who homered twice and drove in five. Frisch hadn't been as respectful of McGraw as were others, and after eight years had been traded to the Cards for the even more outspoken Rogers Hornsby in 1927. Not surprisingly, Hornsby's stay in the Big Apple lasted one year. Frisch not only starred for Sam Breadon's club for eleven years but also managed the highly spirited Gas House Gang for six of those seasons.

Despite his heroics, Frisch's antagonist had the last laugh that day. In the final frame, the McGrawmen fought back with a pair and had the bases filled for Terry. St. Loo skipper Gabby Street brought in spitballer Burleigh Grimes, one of the few remaining hurlers still permitted to "load one up" since the spitball was banished in 1920. (A grandfather clause had been added in 1921.) Burleigh's wet ones weren't slippery enough, as Terry cracked a single to tie the game, and Travis Jackson ended it with a one-base blow to left.

The Giants took the field the next day in stifling humidity and 93-degree heat, which would reach a record 96 by midafternoon. If their manager was confident following the consecutive victories against the Cardinals, his team's play in the doubleheader did little to reinforce that feeling. New York managed only seven hits in the opener, two by Terry in a 4–1 loss to the Cards' ace, Jesse Haines, and then fell in the nightcap when St. Louis scored five in the last two innings. The Giants remained in third place, five behind the Robins and Cubs, the exact position they had held at the beginning of July and would hold at month's end. Giant players were beginning to hear it from McGraw.

Friction between Terry and his skipper had always existed, but their hard-headed feud may have intensified in 1930. Terry's heavy hitting and deft defense made his value to the club obvious to all, including himself, thus emboldening him to rebuff harsh, critical comments emanating from the tyrannical boss. At the same time, McGraw felt threatened by a player who was well liked and respected by teammates and thus a logical candidate to replace the aging helmsman. Terry wasn't the first talented ballplayer he had managed, but McGraw had been a winner with the likes of Christy Mathewson, Rube Marquard, Larry Doyle, and Frankie Frisch. He had always received an inordinate share of credit for past championships. Now, with the team losing despite having Terry, Ott, Hubbell, et al, who else could take the blame? If McGraw was becoming paranoid, his panacea should have been the five-year deal offered by Giants' president Charles

Stoneham in September. Despite the signing, however, McGraw remained nervous about running a ballclub in failing health (his doctor banned him from the bench throughout much of the latter part of the 1930 season) and with a more capable leader in full view.

Terry continued to give McGraw as little to complain about as possible. In a 3–1 win on July 25, he singled and doubled, scoring both times, and walloped a homer into the Polo Grounds' right-field stands. On the twenty-eighth, Drebinger summed up the victory of the day before by writing, "Ostensibly the Giants defeated the Phillies 5–4, but actually it was nothing more than a personal triumph for William Terry." It was praise well deserved because Terry scored three runs and drove in as many, the last on a game-winning, ninth-inning sac fly. The other ribbies had come on solo homers off the upper-deck facade in left. If such opposite-field power in 1930 seems an anachronism, it must be pointed out that the distance to that protruding target was only 250 feet. Yet for those advocates of modern play quick to squawk over that advantage, consider the other park's dimensions: 450 feet to left-center, 505 feet to center, and 445 feet to right-center, before coming back to 250 feet in right. As former Terry teammate Jo-Jo Moore reminded me in 1994, "In the Polo Grounds, it was tough to hit homers if you were a straightaway hitter. Terry wasn't really a pull-hitter. He'd hit the ball to all fields. But he'd still hit his share of homers."

After Terry's fly ball sent home the winning run, 5,000 fans rose from their seats to cheer, nearly half of them women. The Giants were trying something new that year — Ladies' Day, when women were permitted to attend for free, a gimmick used by other clubs beginning in the 1920s.

Terry was stopped by Boston's Bob Smith on July 30, ending a 16-game hitting streak. During the stretch, Terry batted .460, averaging better than two hits per game, and had six doubles, a triple, and five homers while scoring 20 runs and driving in 15. Had his 10-game hitting streak not been interrupted by his collar of July 16, Terry's streak would have run to 27 before being snapped by Smith.

Terry rebounded with three hits and three ribbies in the final game of the month, boosting his average to .397, still 14 points behind league-leader Klein and 6 points shy of O'Doul, though he was ahead in hits with 169. In a *New York Times* article, Terry was paid the ultimate compliment by a suggestion that he would rival Ruth's power-hitting if his batting style was altered to that of a pull-hitter. Probably concerned that his batting average would suffer, Bill continued spraying the ball throughout the remainder of his career.

Terry had some measure of revenge against Dazzy Vance on August 3,

Bill Terry and John McGraw seem amiable enough here, but this was not always the case (UPI/Bettmann).

cracking three singles, though his efforts didn't prevent the hard-throwing righthander from registering a 1–0 whitewash. Bill made it six hits in eight at-bats with another trio the next day. One was labeled by sportswriter Roscoe McGowen as "one of the hardest drives seen in Ebbets Field." It carried to the deepest part of the park and one bounced into the center-field bleachers for his 17th homer. (It wasn't until the following year that the rule was changed, making balls bouncing in seats ground-rule doubles.)

Bill might have had four hits that day had it not been for an exceptional play by Brooklyn shortstop Glenn Wright. Wright scampered toward the left-field foul line to corral Terry's blooper. In all likelihood, the ball would have dropped foul, so that Wright's play didn't assure Bill of another safety. By game's end, Terry was undoubtedly content with his single, double, homer, and two ribbies, but the catch did deprive the would-be record-setter of another try. That lost opportunity would seem more significant by season's end.

In spite of Wright's athleticism, the Giants took the game and a two-to-one lead in the series, but they lost a heartbreaker in the closer. Trailing by five going into the ninth, New York rallied for a pair and had their most productive player at the plate representing the tying run. Terry took aim at Ebbets Field's enticing (and slanted) right-field wall 296 feet away and muscled a Dolph Luque delivery over it to knot the score at six-all. In the tenth, Freddie Lindstrom nearly did the same, his drive off the wall still good enough for two ribbies and the lead. With darkness approaching and the first Brooklyn batter retired in the tenth, it appeared a lost cause for the never-say-die Brooklyn fans. Then a hit brought hope, a misjudged fly-ball turned double brought heightened interest, a single brought everyone to their feet, and when a nervous Lindstrom booted a potential game-ending, double-play grounder, it brought the tying run home. The field was showered with straw hats and confetti.

It was left for pinch-hitter Eddie Moore to perform the coup de grace. His fly ball was sufficiently deep to tally the game-winner, whereupon Lindstrom, cognizant of his abrupt hero-to-goat transformation, heaved his glove nearly as far into the stands. For old-timers at the ballpark, the battle may have been reminiscent of one played sixty years before in what *Baseball Anecdotes* regards as the "first truly great game," when, in the dusk, Brooklyn yielded two runs in the top of the twelfth, then rallied for three in its half to hand Harry Wright's Reds their first defeat as a pro team in 92 games.

For the Giants, the loss was the toughest yet. A victory would have put them within four of the high-flying Robins. Instead they were six out, with still another 16 games to play on the road before returning to the Polo Grounds near month's end. Their third place position seemed secure, with the Cards and Pirates well back, but McGraw wasn't interested in a good showing. He would take it all or know the reason why.

The reason would have nothing to do with Terry. In the Brooklyn finale, he was retired only once in six official trips, taking the league lead in both hits and batting average for the first time. His best game to that point left him with eleven hits in his last fourteen at-bats, including two doubles, two homers, four runs-scored, and five RBIs. His eleven hits in three games fell one shy of the still-standing National League record for the century.

Terry was stopped in Steel City by a combination of three Pittsburgh hurlers, a formidable feat considering he rebounded with a four-for-five performance in game two and that his average for the previous four games, if the hitless game is excluded, was an unreal .789. It appeared a group of Buc pitchers had Terry collared again the next day. After failing his first four tries, he drilled a double which ignited a four-run outburst and a Giants victory. He had three hits on August 11, including a game-tying homerun, two more on the thirteenth, one coming in the ninth to help tie a game the Giants eventually won in extra innings, three more on the fifteenth, including a double and mammoth homerun, and three more on the sixteenth in a doubleheader sweep of the Reds. New York now had won seven of the last eight games following the painful loss to Brooklyn, keeping them within five of the Cubs in the topsy-turvy battle for first.

Despite his hot stick, Terry could shake neither Babe Herman nor Chuck Klein, who were tied with the Giant first sacker for the hit lead with 189. Terry pulled away with five in a doubleheader split with the Cards on August 17, but one week later, his 198 hits were only three better than Klein's total, six more than Herman's, despite his averaging 1.7 hits per game in 118 played to that point. It was an enviable pace for any modern ballplayer but not enough to ensure Terry's capturing his first hit crown in a season marked by more hits than any other prior to baseball's first expansion year of 1961.

New York lost the getaway of its 20-game road trip, a heartbreaker which saw Terry single and score the tying run in the ninth, only to have speedster Danny Taylor steal home with two outs to win it for the Cubs, who thus distanced themselves from their second place challenger by five games.

While the Giants returned home haunted by the nightmarish effects of Taylor's legs, New York's most notorious gangster was legging it out of the country. Newspapers reported that Jack "Legs" Diamond was running from either Chicago mobster Al Capone or the law, which had recently uncovered in his house "an arsenal of gangsters' weapons unprecedented in the history of the police department." In fact, Diamond was using a cruise to Europe to escape heat from rival New York hoodlum Dutch Schultz, with whom he had been feuding, and to set up drug deals in England and Belgium. His anatomical sobriquet had been derived from a propensity for cheating death, but Diamond's uncanny knack for narrow escapes would end with three point-blank shots to the head delivered a year later by either a Schultz accomplice or another revenge-motivated gunman.

The Giants had troubles of their own, which intensified following back-to-back losses to third place Brooklyn at the Polo Grounds. Terry managed only one hit in the two games and was held hitless again on August 29. He rebounded with one of his most productive games of the year the next day, smashing five hits off three different Robin hurlers, including a triple which, according to newspaper accounts, must have traveled about 450 feet on the fly before skipping on the deep center-field grass. Although Terry's hold of the batting lead had solidified in August, with his .408 mark 21 points higher than Klein's by the thirtieth, both lefty swingers had the same number of hits as the final dog day approached.

Terry stroked a pair of singles in the nightcap of the August 31 twin bill after being held hitless in four tries in the opener. It was indicative of his final month's work — splendid one game, less than mediocre the next. Terry collected two or more hits in 11 of 28 September games, but had as many one-hit performances. He had four four-hit games but was collared in six. His 44 hits in 116 plate appearances, a .380 mark, actually lowered his average four points, but he would still manage to finish over the .400 mark, albeit barely.

Of greater consequence were Terry's six unproductive games in September. Had one of the collars been averted, the league hit record would be his today. Braves hurlers were Terry's greatest nemesis, holding him hitless in three straight games early in the month, ending his chance at Hornsby's record for the most games with at least one hit. (Ironically, Rajah's still-standing mark was equaled by Klein that year, despite Terry's outhitting him by fifteen points.) Following an 11-game hitting streak which boosted his hit total by 18, Terry was collared by the Cubs' Pat Malone on September 18 and by the Reds' Ray Kolp and Eppa Rixey two days later.

Nevertheless, going into the final game on September 28, Terry had tied O'Doul's league record of 254 hits and was three away from George Sisler's major-league mark. Ten thousand were in attendance at the Polo Grounds, most of whom were there principally to cheer for Terry. The Giants had been eliminated from the race a few days earlier, a result of a 15–13 record in the final month which left them three games shy of Chicago. Yet the Cubbies lost the flag as well when the red-hot Redbirds flew from the middle of the pack to the top with a 21–4 September.

Terry entered the finale with a six-game hitting streak, 13 hits in his last 25 at-bats, and a .403 average. The mound opponent was Phils righty Ray Benge, whose 5' 9", 160-pound frame, 11–15 record, and 5.70 ERA couldn't have made Terry feel pessimistic. Indeed, Benge surrendered seven Giant hits that afternoon in as many innings, but he stopped Terry in three official at-bats.

Terry was walked in another plate appearance and had a sac fly in the bottom of the ninth, the game-tying ribby keeping alive his chance at surpassing O'Doul. Unfortunately, the contest wasn't extended quite long enough. The Giants won it in the tenth when, with two outs, Freddy Leach pulled southpaw John Milligan's slant into right for the game-winner. Had Leach made an out, Terry would have batted second the next inning.

The last of Terry's two dozen collars in 1930 was the most dramatic cause for his failure to establish a new hit record, but underlying factors appear when one analyzes the entire season. His subpar performance against certain starters was perhaps the most significant. Brooklyn righthander Dazzy Vance's 17–15 record doesn't seem overly impressive, but his leading the league with a 2.61 ERA and limiting opposing hitters to a league-

low .246 batting average in a year in which major leaguers set still-standing records for runs (7,025) and hits (13,260) necessitates ranking his 1930
performance as one of the all-time greatest. Not the least of Dazzy's accomplishments that year was his success in stopping the league's best hitter. In
seven starts against the Giants, Vance held Terry to an incredibly meager
.192 average. Terry's 26 at-bats against the hard-throwing Hawkeye were
more than he had against any other pitcher that year, but he managed only
five hits and was collared in four of the seven games. It may seem absurd
to suggest that Vance's work in 1930 deserves equal recognition with that
of a near record-setter, but consider that Terry's .401 was merely eight
points better than runner-up Babe Herman's average and that the top five
batters all had averages above .375, whereas Vance was the only regular
starter to attain an ERA of under 3.00, with Carl Hubbell's 3.87 a distant
second.

There were other NL starters besides Vance who troubled Terry in
1930. Lefty Watty Clark wasn't quite as effective as teammate Vance, but
his holding Bill to a .296 average in seven starts against the Giants and
shutting him down in two, is noteworthy nonetheless. Buc righty Ray Kremer wasn't unnerved by Terry's plate appearances and held him to a minus-
cule .227 in five starts while also collaring him twice. Terry fared even
worse against Ray Benge, averaging .214 in the four starts by the Phillie
righty, which included his season-ending collar. Boston's Socks Seibold
gave Terry problems in five outings; he averaged only .286 in those games.
Terry did not do well against Sheriff Blake either, averaging .261 in the Cub
righthander's five starts.

Of course, Terry had his share of pet pitchers. He batted a healthy
.526 in Phillie righthander Claude Willoughby's four starts. The sight of the
euphoniously named Buc hurler Heine Meine must have delighted Terry,
who averaged .429 in the righty's five appearances. Pat Malone pitched with
distinction in 1930, leading the league with 20 victories, but he had little
success against Terry, who batted .455 in his six starts. Burleigh Grimes'
wet ones weren't moist enough when facing Memphis Bill, resulting in a
.533 mark in four starts. Perhaps the pitcher most abused by Terry was
Pittsburgh's Erv Brame who, despite leading the league in complete games,
finished only one of four against the Giants, due in no small measure to
Terry's 11 hits in 17 at-bats (.647).

Comparison of Terry's home and road performances show why he was
probably the league's most dangerous batter in 1930. Unlike Klein and Wilson, who took advantage of cozy ballparks (as well as a juiced ball) to accumulate impressive power stats that year, the Giants slugger was a .401 hitter at home, an even .400 hitter on the road. Yet he did have ballpark

preferences. Listed below are Terry's stats in each of the road ballparks in which he played in 1930.

Terry's 1930 Averages at Opposing Ballparks

Park	Games	At-Bats	Hits	Average
Forbes Field	11	47	21	.447
Baker Bowl	11	48	21	.438
Crosley Field	11	46	20	.435
Wrigley Field	11	51	22	.431
Ebbetts Field	11	47	19	.404
Sportsman's Park	11	39	13	.333
Braves Field	11	46	14	.304

There undoubtedly occurred instances in 1930 in which Terry was robbed of hits by outstanding fielding plays that ultimately prevented his setting the league hit-record. At times, game summaries would include descriptions of such thefts. On September 7, *New York Times* reporter Roscoe McGowen was sufficiently impressed with Dodgers center-fielder Johnny Frederick's running, one-handed catch of Terry's deep drive to mention it the next day. Other superb snares probably occurred which went unreported.

Yet despite Terry's difficulties in hitting against certain pitchers and teams and at particular ballparks and despite occasional potential hits taken away by inconsiderate glovemen, the fact remains that he had a shot at the record on the final two days, with the odds heavily in his favor, and blew it. Did Terry choke? Considering he went hitless in his final six at-bats of the season (oh-for-two following a fifth-inning single in the next-to-last game, then hitless in four tries in the finale), while needing only one more hit to surpass Lefty O'Doul, it's difficult to believe otherwise. Perhaps no Polo Grounds observer was more surprised at Terry's failure in the final game than O'Doul, who, upon viewing Leach's tenth-inning, game-ending single from the Phillie bench, probably did some celebrating of his own, thinking that a share of a record was better than none at all.

Terry probably felt the same prior to his death in 1989, considering the mark still stood (as of 1997, it remains unbroken). And if his season-ending failure was a disappointment in 1930, Terry's major-league-leading .401 average offered solace. He was the last senior-circuit star to reach the unreachable .400, the only one in the century besides Rogers Hornsby to do it. It would be the sole batting crown captured by the player with the ninth-highest career average in the century. Not that Terry's bat was silent in forthcoming seasons. He followed up with 213 hits and a .349 average in 1931, the year of the dejuiced ball, topping the league in runs-scored and triples. Failing to lead in any offensive categories thereafter, Terry nevertheless averaged a combined .343 from 1932 to 1935, stroking over 200 hits in three seasons, while batting .350 or better twice. In half-a-season's work in 1936, Terry batted .310 in 229 at-bats, including 6 hits in 22 pinch-hit appearances.

Terry's success following the 1930 season wasn't limited to his stick-work; he led all first basemen in fielding average in 1934 and 1935 and led his team as manager. Despite three-and-a-half years remaining on his five-year deal with the Giants, McGraw retired in midseason of 1932. Failing health, an unimproved showing in the standings the year before, and a poor start in 1932 were the reasons for his terminating a 33-year managing career. Allowed to choose his successor, McGraw picked Terry, and his decision was, as author Donald Honig notes, "almost as surprising as the old man's departure," considering the mutual antagonism that had increasingly grown between them. Honig's explanation is that McGraw was dedicated to winning for the Giants, making the equally conscientious Terry the logical choice. However, McGraw biographer Charles Alexander points out that the capable Cardinal Frankie Frisch was Little Napoleon's premier pick but was rendered unavailable by Cards exec Branch Rickey, and Alexander hints that Mac might also have settled for Giants coach Dave Bancroft had owner Stoneham not objected.

Whatever his reasons, McGraw did his former players a great favor with his selection. Terry proved the antithesis of his stern, uncompromising predecessor. Rules were relaxed, practices shortened and made less frequent, coaches made less dictatorial. Although the players for the most part welcomed the change, success on the field was not immediately forthcoming. Terry inherited a last place club with a 17–23 record and a .425 percentage in early June. They finished the 1932 season in sixth place, having attained a 55–59 record and a .482 percentage under Terry. The Giants won the pennant and Series in 1933 and took flags in 1936 and 1937 as well. In Terry's ten-season managing career from 1932 to 1941 (the first five as player-manager), the Giants won 823 while losing merely 661 and finished third or better six times.

Of course, Terry's players had something to do with his success as manager. The club's improvement coincided with Carl Hubbell's blossoming into the best pitcher in baseball; he won over twenty in each season from 1933 to 1937, including a still-standing record 24-game winning streak from 1936 to 1937. Ott had some of his finest years during the midthirties, taking five homerun crowns from 1932 to 1938. Jo-Jo Moore, who was labeled by Honig "one of the team's steadier hitters in the 1930s,"

Bill Terry had many memorable moments following the 1930 season. Here, he is shown crossing home plate after connecting for the second time in the Phillies' home opener at Baker Bowl in 1932 (National Baseball Library & Archive, Cooperstown, N.Y.)

had five .300-plus seasons from 1932 to 1938. As shown previously, Terry continued as one of the top hitters in the league during the decade until he quit in 1936 rather than "wait for the bums to yell, 'Why don't you drop dead, you bum?'"

Jo-Jo Moore played under McGraw and Terry and recalled in a 1994 interview his experiences with both:

> At the end of the Texas-League season in 1930, the San Antonio club sold me to the Giants. Mr. McGraw was still the manager, and I guess I didn't fit in with his system because I played very little that year. I went to spring training in 1931 but I still didn't make the club. Then, when I had a chance to lead the International League in hitting, Mr. McGraw called me up towards the end of the season. The sad thing is that they didn't need me. They weren't going anywhere that year. Then in 1932, Mr. McGraw sent me to Jersey City after spring training. I played there until McGraw was out and Terry became manager. I was called up and played the very next day.
> Terry was as good a manager as ever lived. He used good judg-

ment, and he had the personnel to be able to do things with. As far
as I know, he was fair with everyone.

Harry Danning had a similar assessment of Terry as a manager, declar-
ing, "I thought Terry was a great manager. The press didn't like him, but
we sure did. I talked to him years later after we both retired, and he told
me that he always let us do what we wanted on the field because we were
major-leaguers. We were supposed to know what to do."

Both Danning and Moore played for Terry during the winning seasons of the thirties. When the club began to sour, finishing fifth in 1939,
sixth in 1940, and fifth in 1941, Terry's attitude may have soured with it,
as is suggested by Bill Lohrman, a righty, sinkerball pitcher who played for
Terry from 1937 until his final year as helmsman in 1941. Lohrman somewhat tarnished Terry's reputation as a player's manager when he spoke with
me in 1994.

> Terry was a good manager, but I didn't like him too much. He
> was pretty tough. I think he got his toughness from McGraw. When
> some of his good players like Hubbell, Ott, and [Hal] Schumacher
> started going downhill, Terry kind of took it out on the younger
> guys.
>
> We were in Pittsburgh one day, I think it was in 1938. Terry was
> talking to all of us in the clubhouse. He turned to me and said, "I'll
> pitch you against the Pirates because you wouldn't be able to get
> anybody out anyway." He said that right in front of all the players. It
> wasn't right. He used to be the first to holler about McGraw doing
> that stuff to him when he was a young player.
>
> One year, he said he'd fine any player he saw with a glass of beer.
> Well, in those days we used to take a train from St. Louis to
> Chicago. We used to eat together in the dining car. Terry would
> walk in with his coaches holding a couple of bottles in his hand.
> Right in front of us. It was a fine if we drank beer, but it was alright
> for him to drink. The guys used to hate that.
>
> There was another time at the Polo Grounds. The team played a
> bad game, and Terry was sore. He fined the whole club for not hus-
> tling, including the guys who were in the bullpen. They weren't even
> in the game.
>
> I was pleased when Ott took over the club in 1942. I don't know if
> it was a coincidence, but I had my best season that year.

Lohrman's comments cast doubts on whether Terry was always as fair-
minded and popular with players as has been suggested in the past, but they
also serve to emphasize the difficulty any manager, past or present, has in
pleasing everyone on his ballclub and how even the most capable and previously successful manager may act differently when the pressure to pro-

duce a winner intensifies. Such was the case with McGraw, who, though always tough-minded, became increasingly hostile towards his players as they consistently failed from season to season. A Jekyll-to-Hyde transformation may have occurred with Terry for the same reason.

Few who have played the game wouldn't envy Terry's career, which was climaxed by his .401 in 1930. Still, to come so near to breaking a record and then fail in his final attempt put a damper on the season. To be sure, Terry wasn't the first player to barely miss the mark, nor would he be the last. Two years later a Maryland muscleman would challenge the Great Ruth's cherished homerun record and come tantalizingly near, only to fall short in the end.

Bill Terry's 1930 Season

Date	Opponent (H/A)	AB	H	Avg.	Starting Pitcher
4/15	Boston (H)	4	2	.500	Seibold*
4/19	Philadelphia (H)	3	1	.429	Koupal*
4/20	Philadelphia (H)	3	2	.500	Alexander
4/21	Philadelphia (H)	5	2	.467	Willoughby
4/26	Philadelphia (A)	4	1	.421	Koupal
4/26	Philadelphia (A)	5	3	.458	Sweetland
4/27	Brooklyn (A)	5	1	.414	Clark
4/28	Brooklyn (H)	3	2	.438	Dudley*
4/29	Brooklyn (H)	6	2	.421	Phelps
4/30	Brooklyn (H)	3	0	.390	Vance*
5/2	Cincinnati (A)	4	2	.400	Rixey
5/3	Cincinnati (A)	4	1	.388	McWeeny
5/4	Cincinnati (A)	4	1	.377	May*
5/5	Pittsburgh (A)	5	3	.397	Meine
5/6	Pittsburgh (A)	5	2	.397	Kremer
5/7	Pittsburgh (A)	4	2	.403	Brame
5/8	Pittsburgh (A)	4	2	.408	Jones
5/9	Chicago (A)	5	2	.408	Carlson
5/10	Chicago (A)	5	4	.432	Malone
5/11	Chicago (A)	4	3	.447	Root
5/12	Chicago (A)	6	1	.429	Blake
5/13	St. Louis (A)	4	1	.421	Sherdel
5/14	St. Louis (A)	4	2	.424	Grabowski
5/17	Boston (H)	5	3	.433	Seibold*
5/17	Boston (H)	4	2	.435	Smith*
5/18	Boston (H)	4	1	.429	Zachary*
5/18	Boston (H)	5	2	.427	Cunningham
5/20	Boston (H)	5	0	.410	Cantwell

*Indicates a complete game by starter

Date	Opponent (H/A)	AB	H	Avg.	Starting Pitcher
5/21	Philadelphia (H)	3	1	.408	Elliott
5/22	Philadelphia (H)	5	2	.408	Willoughby
5/23	Philadelphia (A)	3	1	.406	Benge
5/24	Philadelphia (A)	4	0	.394	Sweetland
5/25	Brooklyn (A)	3	0	.386	Luque*
5/26	Brooklyn (A)	4	0	.375	Vance*
5/27	Brooklyn (A)	3	2	.381	Elliott
5/29	Brooklyn (A)	4	2	.384	Clark
5/30	Boston (A)	4	2	.387	Zachary
5/30	Boston (A)	5	2	.388	Grimes
5/31	Boston (A)	4	2	.390	Smith
6/1	Boston (A)	4	1	.387	Brandt
6/1	Boston (A)	4	1	.384	Seibold
6/3	Cincinnati (H)	4	2	.386	Benton
6/4	Cincinnati (H)	4	2	.389	Lucas
6/5	Cincinnati (H)	4	3	.397	May*
6/6	St. Louis (H)	5	3	.402	Bell
6/7	St. Louis (H)	5	1	.397	Hallahan
6/8	St. Louis (H)	4	2	.399	Haines*
6/11	Pittsburgh (H)	4	3	.406	Meine
6/12	Pittsburgh (H)	4	0	.398	Kremer*
6/13	Pittsburgh (H)	4	1	.395	French
6/14	Chicago (H)	2	0	.392	Malone*
6/15	Chicago (H)	3	2	.395	Blake
6/16	Chicago (H)	4	1	.393	Root
6/18	Pittsburgh (A)	4	2	.395	Meine
6/20	Pittsburgh (A)	5	0	.386	Kremer*
6/21	Pittsburgh (A)	3	2	.390	Brame
6/22	Cincinnati (A)	4	2	.391	Frey
6/23	Cincinnati (A)	4	2	.393	Kolp
6/24	Cincinnati (A)	4	2	.395	Benton*
6/25	Cincinnati (A)	3	2	.398	Lucas*
6/26	St. Louis (A)	5	1	.394	Haines
6/27	St. Louis (A)	3	2	.398	Grimes
6/28	St. Louis (A)	3	1	.397	Rhem*
6/29	St. Louis (A)	3	0	.392	Johnson*
6/29	St. Louis (A)	2	0	.389	Hallahan*
6/30	Chicago (A)	4	1	.387	Blake*
7/1	Chicago (A)	5	3	.391	Bush
7/2	Chicago (A)	4	1	.389	Malone
7/4	Brooklyn (H)	2	0	.386	Vance*
7/4	Brooklyn (H)	4	0	.381	Clark*
7/5	Brooklyn (H)	5	2	.381	Luque
7/6	Philadelphia (H)	4	2	.383	Sweetland
7/6	Philadelphia (H)	4	1	.381	Elliott

Date	Opponent (H/A)	AB	H	Avg.	Starting Pitcher
7/7	Philadelphia (A)	6	2	.380	Nichols
7/8	Philadelphia (A)	4	2	.382	Collins*
7/9	Philadelphia (A)	4	1	.380	Elliott
7/10	Philadelphia (A)	4	2	.381	Willoughby
7/12	Brooklyn (H)	4	1	.380	Clark*
7/13	Cincinnati (H)	5	4	.386	Frey
7/15	Cincinnati (H)	5	3	.390	Kolp
7/16	Cincinnati (H)	3	0	.396	Lucas*
7/17	St. Louis (H)	3	1	.386	Johnson
7/18	St. Louis (H)	5	3	.389	Hallahan
7/19	St. Louis (H)	4	2	.390	Haines*
7/19	St. Louis (H)	3	1	.390	Bell
7/20	Chicago (H)	4	1	.388	Bush
7/21	Chicago (H)	3	2	.390	Malone
7/22	Chicago (H)	4	1	.389	Root
7/22	Chicago (H)	3	1	.388	Teachout
7/23	Chicago (H)	5	1	.386	Blake
7/24	Pittsburgh (H)	3	2	.388	Kremer*
7/25	Pittsburgh (H)	4	3	.392	French
7/26	Pittsburgh (H)	5	3	.395	Brame
7/27	Pittsburgh (H)	5	1	.392	Meine
7/27	Pittsburgh (H)	4	2	.393	Spencer*
7/28	Philadelphia (H)	4	4	.399	Collard*
7/29	Philadelphia (H)	4	1	.398	Benge
7/30	Boston (H)	4	0	.394	Smith*
7/31	Boston (H)	5	3	.397	Zachary
8/1	Boston (H)	5	2	.397	Brandt
8/2	Brooklyn (A)	5	1	.394	Thurston
8/3	Brooklyn (A)	4	3	.398	Vance*
8/4	Brooklyn (A)	4	3	.401	Clark*
8/5	Brooklyn (A)	6	5	.407	Luque
8/8	Pittsburgh (A)	3	0	.404	Meine
8/8	Pittsburgh (A)	5	4	.409	Brame*
8/9	Pittsburgh (A)	5	1	.406	French
8/11	Pittsburgh (A)	4	3	.410	French*
8/13	Cincinnati (A)	5	2	.409	Benton*
8/15	Cincinnati (A)	5	3	.412	Lucas*
8/16	Cincinnati (A)	5	2	.411	Kolp
8/16	Cincinnati (A)	4	1	.410	Frey
8/17	St. Louis (A)	5	4	.414	Hallahan
8/17	St. Louis (A)	2	1	.414	Grimes*
8/19	St. Louis (A)	4	0	.410	Lindsey*
8/20	St. Louis (A)	4	1	.409	Rhem
8/21	Chicago (A)	5	1	.407	Blake
8/22	Chicago (A)	4	2	.407	Root*

Date	Opponent (H/A)	AB	H	Avg.	Starting Pitcher
8/23	Chicago (A)	5	3	.409	Malone*
8/24	Chicago (A)	4	1	.408	Bush*
8/27	Brooklyn (H)	3	1	.408	Clark
8/28	Brooklyn (H)	4	0	.404	Vance*
8/29	Brooklyn (H)	3	0	.402	Clark*
8/30	Brooklyn (H)	5	5	.408	Dudley
8/31	Boston (H)	4	0	.405	Seibold
8/31	Boston (H)	5	2	.405	Cantwell
9/1	Philadelphia (A)	5	4	.408	Willoughby
9/1	Philadelphia (A)	4	1	.407	Benge
9/2	Philadelphia (A)	5	4	.411	Collard
9/3	Boston (A)	4	3	.413	Cantwell*
9/3	Boston (A)	4	0	.410	Seibold
9/4	Boston (A)	4	0	.407	Zachary*
9/5	Boston (A)	4	0	.404	Cunningham
9/6	Boston (A)	4	1	.403	Smith
9/6	Boston (A)	5	2	.403	Sherdel
9/7	Brooklyn (A)	4	1	.402	Vance*
9/9	St. Louis (H)	4	3	.405	Grimes
9/10	St. Louis (H)	4	1	.404	Johnson
9/11	St. Louis (H)	5	1	.402	Hallahan
9/12	St. Louis (H)	3	1	.401	Rhem*
9/14	Pittsburgh (H)	5	1	.400	Kremer
9/14	Pittsburgh (H)	3	1	.399	Wood
9/15	Pittsburgh (H)	5	4	.403	Swetonic*
9/16	Chicago (H)	4	2	.403	Petty
9/17	Chicago (H)	3	0	.401	Malone*
9/18	Chicago (H)	4	1	.400	Bush
9/19	Cincinnati (H)	4	0	.398	Kolp
9/20	Cincinnati (H)	5	4	.401	Benton
9/20	Cincinnati (H)	4	2	.402	Carroll
9/21	Cincinnati (H)	3	2	.403	Kolp
9/21	Cincinnati (H)	4	3	.405	Johnson
9/23	Brooklyn (A)	5	1	.404	Vance
9/27	Philadelphia (H)	4	1	.403	Collins
9/28	Philadelphia (H)	3	0	.401	Benge
Totals		*633*	*254*	*.401*	

Bill Terry's Monthly Totals for 1930

Month	Games	AB	H	Avg.
April	10	41	16	.390
May	29	123	48	.390
June	27	102	39	.382

Month	Games	AB	H	Avg.
July	33	135	56	.415
August	27	117	51	.432
September	28	115	44	.383
Totals	*154*	*633*	*254*	*.401*

Bill Terry's Home-Road Totals for 1930

	Games	AB	H	Avg.
Home	77	309	124	.401
Road	77	324	130	.400
Totals	*154*	*633*	*254*	*.401*

The Babe Prevails

On a hot July night of 1967, Jimmie Foxx was enjoying a steak at his brother Sammy's house in southwest Miami. Dinner conversation may have included Jimmie's scheduled appearance at Cooperstown two days later when Red Ruffing, Lloyd Waner, and Branch Rickey would be inducted into the Hall of Fame. Or perhaps they spoke of the old days, when a youthful Foxx would milk cows, harvest crops, plow the fields, and perform other farming chores not yet shared by a sibling eight years his junior. Sammy's unsuccessful stab at the big leagues might have been recalled, an opportunity provided by Jimmie, who convinced a reluctant Connie Mack to give the lefty hurler a tryout in the midthirties. What probably wasn't mentioned was Jimmie's past generosity towards Sammy, his gifts and loans totaling in the tens of thousands, much of which was given during the money-tight depression.

It was Jimmie's nature to be generous. During his playing days, when a substantial salary gave no hint of a future filled with financial adversity, Jimmie couldn't spend it fast enough. He would enter a bar with friends and declare, "The drinks are on the house." At a restaurant, Mickey Cochrane, Doc Cramer, Bobby Doerr, and other teammates were never as quick as Foxx in snatching the check. Hotel roommates never concerned themselves with telephone, valet, or room-service charges, knowing Jimmie would take care of it. He would tip cab drivers $5 for $2 fares, tailors $50 for $150 suits. Few looked sharper than dapper Jimmie, with his striped flannel suit, brown-and-white shoes, silk ties, felt hats, and manicured hands. "Money went through his fingers like quicksilver," as an old acquaintance reflected. Once while licking a vanilla cone, Foxx spotted a couple of empty-pocketed lads standing near the ice-cream truck, called them over, and ordered the vendor to keep the cones coming until the delighted pair had their fill.

As veteran sports columnist Arthur Daley noted, "Foxx certainly was no businessman." During his career, Jimmie had always been easy prey for opportunists seeking financial backing for risky schemes which, along with the stock-market crash of 1929, led to his financial ruin. While Jimmie chewed the fat with Sammy, he may have been ruefully reminded of a business flop situated not too far from where they sat. An avid golfer, Foxx had been persuaded into buying a Miami golf course prior to World War II. As he bitterly recalled in later years, "You'd have thought the way folks fled Florida, that they thought the Nazi U-boats were coming up the Gulf." A Foxx contemporary commented: "He knew his baseball career was coming to an end and he'd been counting on the golf course to set him up. Instead, it wiped him out. But no matter how much he was hurting in the pocket, Jimmie always grabbed the check."

The Foxx brothers probably dwelt on more pleasant times on that heat-oppressive evening of July 21. For Jimmie, that meant his extraordinary efforts on the baseball diamond during a 20-year career that ended in 1945 with his amassing 534 homers, a lifetime .325 batting average, a dozen straight seasons with 30 or more homers, including three homer titles, a Triple Crown, five slugging championships, 13 consecutive seasons with over 100 RBIs, and a reputation exceeded by none before or since for propelling the horsehide improbable distances, though Babe Ruth and Mickey Mantle may have been his match.

Lefty Gomez, a legendary Yankee hurler of the thirties, became almost as renowned for his quips and humorous anecdotes (or "Gomez Zingers," as Paul Dickson, author of *Baseball's Greatest Quotations*, calls them) as he was for his pitching prowess. Lefty's most delightful jokes are those that describe Foxx's intimidating power. Jimmie was so brawny, Gomez insisted, that "he had muscles in his hair." Facing Foxx for the first time, the bespectacled Lefty wiped his glasses, then gazed at the muscle-bound batter. "It frightened me so much I never wore them again." In another confrontation, Gomez ignored the signs of Yank catcher Bill Dickey, hoping that Jimmie would get tired of waiting and "just go away." After being tagged for a tape-measure blast by Foxx at Yankee Stadium, Gomez recalled that "it was a fastball when I threw it but it was going a lot faster when Foxx hit it." Curious as to where the ball landed, Gomez walked to the left-field upper deck, where it had obliterated one of the seats. He complained afterwards, "It took me 20 minutes to walk out to the spot where he'd hit it in a split second." Neil Armstrong's moon walk of 1969 enabled Gomez to expound further on Foxx's muscular exploits. "Armstrong and all the space scientists were puzzled by an unidentifiable white object," Gomez explained. "That was a homerun ball hit off me by Foxx in 1937."

If the humorous hurler exaggerated in describing Foxx's power, he wasn't the only one. Sportswriter Red Smith witnessed a sky-high homer by Foxx in the mid-thirties and reported, "Three days later, a small boy on the northeast fringe of town found a baseball with snow on it." Joked reliever Jim Lindsey about a ball Foxx creamed in Game Four of the 1931 World Series, "We were watching it for two innings."

More believable comments leave no less of an impression. Dickey claimed that even when blindfolded he could tell if it was Foxx making contact by the distinguishable crack off the bat, a claim verified by another respected batsman. "It sounded like cherry bombs going off when Foxx hit them," recalled Ted Williams, who played with the aging slugger for four seasons. The Splendid Splinter, who some regard as the greatest hitter of all time, paid Foxx the ultimate compliment when he added in *Ted Williams' Hit List*, "If you asked the baseball gods to design the perfect power hitter, they would probably just point to Foxx and say, 'It's already been done.'"

Hitting rival Charlie Gehringer marveled at Foxx's strength and claimed he hit the ball as hard as anyone, including Ruth. Gehringer was especially impressed with a homer Foxx hit in an exhibition game in 1934 at Tokyo's Meijii Stadium, an expansive ballpark which "goes on for miles." According to Foxx biographer W. Harrison Daniel, Jimmie claimed the belt, which traveled an estimated 600 feet, was the longest of his career.

Like Ruth, Foxx could intimidate moundsmen more than any other batter. "Don't let anybody tell you there's no difference between the 350-foot homerun and the 500-footer," Yankees righty Bob Shawkey proclaimed. "The guy who can hit it 500 feet — like Ruth and Foxx — scares the hell out of you." Wes Ferrell, prominent pitcher of the thirties, wouldn't become upset by a Foxx tape-measure wallop but would "stand out there and admire it. A man hit a ball like that? You couldn't get mad." Commented Burleigh Grimes on an errant curve leading to a Foxx four bagger in the ninth of Game Five of the 1930 Series, which crushed the Cardinals along with some concrete in the center-field bleachers, "He hit it so hard, I couldn't feel sorry for myself." (Foxx did, admitting afterwards, "I really felt sorry for Grimes. Honest, I did.")

Hurler Jack Wilson, a teammate of Foxx for eight years, told author Brent Kelley in the mid-nineties, "I wish Foxx had been in this world to hit that ball they're hitting now. There are places he hit 'em you wouldn't believe." Ted Lyons would. The right-hander faced Foxx often during a pitching career for the White Sox that endured a club-record 21 seasons. States the Hall-of-Famer, "No matter what story you hear told about Foxx's power at the bat, believe it."

Any reminiscing between the Foxxes at the dinner table must have included Jimmie's astounding season of 1932, when he won his first of a record three MVPs. Foxx led the league in homers, RBIs, runs-scored, and slugging, but the season had its share of disappointments. His club, favored to win the pennant, had to settle for the runner-up position. Foxx, too, finished a close second in the batting race, which prevented his taking the Triple Crown. Most disheartening of all was Foxx's failure to catch the Babe in the first serious pursuit of the most famous of Ruthian records — his 60 homers in 1927. Foxx missed by two, as did Hank Greenberg who poked 58 in 1938, allowing Roger Maris to dethrone the Sultan of Swat during his torment-filled season of 1961.

Ruth had been the dominating batter of the twenties and was far from being considered washed-up prior to the 1932 season. The 37-year-old Bambino had led the league in homers, slugging, and walks the previous two years, while averaging 150 runs-scored and 158 RBIs for the same period. In contrast, Foxx hadn't come close to first in any but the dubious K category, undoubtedly unhappy in unseating Ruth as strikeout king from 1929 to 1931.

Such frequent fanning normally would have assured a big-leaguer of a one-way ticket to the bushes, but Foxx had done enough when making contact to convince A's skipper Connie Mack to disregard his young protégé's hitting philosophy, one which never included timid or restrained swings. Foxx would wield three thin-handled, top-heavy bats in the on-deck circle, helping to produce quicker bat speed when at the plate. He would clutch tightly the end of a 40-ounce stick while hacking with all his might at each offering, including two-strike deliveries. "Too many batters try to protect themselves from striking out," Foxx once argued. "They'd rather ground out to the pitcher. What's the difference?"

Foxx's power was derived from a bat cocked in a low position which sank further in a slight hitch as the pitch approached. His stride was short as he snapped his wrists at the pitch, finishing with a smooth, extended follow-through. Unlike Williams, who would attempt to outthink his adversary, Foxx was an instinct hitter, rarely guessing on pitches, though at times he would observe an opposing hurler's form and velocity. According to *Big Sticks* author William Curran, "Of all the sluggers of the 1920s and 1930s, Jimmie came closest to the Babe's bruising style of hitting."

Foxx and Ruth were alike in more ways than their batting philosophy, exceptional strength, and excessive generosity. Both were well liked and respected by their peers. In contrast to some stars of the twenties and thirties, such as the cantankerous Cobb or haughty Hornsby, Jimmie, like the Babe, was down-to-earth, easy-going, and affable. No doubt his popularity was partially enhanced by being "an inveterate check-grabber," as he was labeled by writer Daley, but Foxx's pleasant nature was the main reason.

"He never bad-mouthed anybody," Ted Williams points out. The only exceptions were when he was attempting to straighten out a wayward team-mate. Williams and Foxx would become friends, but Jimmie became annoyed with the rookie's arrogant attitude in 1939, calling him a "spoiled kid." "I guess I acted like one," the Kid admits today.

Dom DiMaggio played with the Red Sox's Foxx from 1940 to 1942 and recalled decades later the Maryland Mauler's sense of humor and good-natured manner. "No one was ever nicer to a rookie than Foxx was to me," said Dom, who roomed with Jimmie in 1940. "And he never high-hatted anyone."

Philadelphia sportswriter Frank Yeutter covered the Athletics during Foxx's 11-year tenure from 1925 to 1935, and years later he wrote of Jim-mie's infectious smile and modest, unassuming personality. Foxx was gen-erous to a fault, but he also genuinely cared about people. Billy Sullivan, Jr., recalled for author Eugene Murdock in 1980 how Foxx had seen the White Sox sophomore first baseman using a small "motormen's glove" during infield practice prior to a game against the A's in 1932. "Now it's the next day, and I'm out there with my little glove. When we were through, Foxx called me over. He handed me a great big glove, just like his, all broken in and in fine shape. He said, 'Keep it, that's the kind of glove we use up here.' Wasn't that a nice thing for him to do?" Foxx's concern for others could extend beyond being nice. Later that year, Foxx and some teammates were staying in a hotel in Cleveland when a nearby apartment house caught fire, followed by a deafening explosion. Risking injury, Foxx helped rescue three girls and an adult from the building.

For all his amiable attributes, Foxx's prolific production with the lum-ber was what others most admired. Assuredly, it was what first attracted the attention of Frank "Homerun" Baker prior to his inviting Jimmie to a tryout at his Class C Easton club in 1924. The former A's and Yankees third baseman liked what he saw and on May 24 signed the 16 year old to his first pro contract.

That Foxx would make a name for himself in sports should have sur-prised no one from Sudlersville, a small Maryland village located about forty miles east of Baltimore across the Chesapeake, about five miles west of the Maryland-Delaware border. Samuel Foxx, Jimmie's father, was a poor Protestant-Irish tenant farmer. He had at one time played semipro ball, and it soon became apparent that his son was athletically inclined as well. Work on the wheat and corn fields, baling hay, and hoisting 200-pound phosphorous sacks transformed the six-foot youngster into a muscle-bound 160-pounder by the age of 14, but he became known at Sudlersville High more for his track accomplishments than for baseball. He performed well enough on the diamond, however, to earn a dollar a game playing for a semipro club during the spring. Having already won several county track events, Jimmie sprinted well enough in high school to take the gold in several state competitions and by 1923 was named Maryland's outstanding athlete. "I dreamed of becoming faster even than Charley Paddock," Foxx once reflected. Paddock had been a 1920 Olympian and was considered at the time the world's fastest human being.

But Homerun Baker helped redirect Foxx's future by signing him for $100 a month in 1924 and further affected his destiny by coaxing Jimmie towards Connie Mack's Athletics late in the season. The Yankees had also been interested in the talented 16 year old, but Foxx leaned toward the A's when Baker recommended Mack as the preferred skipper over Miller Huggins, who was balking at recruiting a green high-school senior. Connie sent scout Mike Brennan to have a closer look-see, and when Brennan returned with a favorable report, Foxx was purchased from Easton for $2,000, as Mack anticipated being accused of "robbing the cradle."

Jimmie remained with the A's in September but saw no action. His impressive hitting in the spring of 1925 included a 470-foot blast which was reportedly the longest homer ever hit at Fort Myers. Foxx made the Phillie roster, but his first plate appearance didn't come until May 1 when he pinch-hit for Lefty Grove at Griffith's Stadium and doubled sharply to left. His limited opportunities prompted Mack to ship the benchwarmer to Providence, where reporters marveled at his powerful pokes, but not enough to spell his name accurately in newspapers; their references to "Fox" helped the prominent power-hitter attain his most notable nickname — "Double X."

Foxx returned to the A's bench toward the end of the 1925 season and then worked on his father's farm and hunted ducks during the off-season. He reported to Fort Myers in the spring of 1926 with about 20 pounds more muscle than the year before. He might have landed a platoon catching position had he not suffered an ankle injury which sidelined him until mid–May. He played sparsely during the remainder of the season, finishing with 10 hits in 32 at-bats and still without his first major-league homer.

That milestone came in 1927 in a Memorial Day doubleheader at Philadelphia's Shibe Park. The blast was yielded by no less a pitching artist than Yankees righty Urban Shocker, one of four outstanding starters on a team considered by some experts the greatest in baseball history. Urban won 18 that year, none the next. Memorial Day of 1928 would find Shocker making his only appearance of the year, a two-inning scoreless stint. He had been a holdout prior to his Memorial relief effort and soon afterwards developed a serious heart condition. The Yankees released him a month later and he died in September.

Foxx finished with three homers in 1927 and became a regular the next season, playing at first and third base as well as backstop. Foxx picked up batting and baserunning tips from teammates Ty Cobb and Tris Speaker, the future Hall-of-Famers both playing in their final major-league seasons.

Although Foxx would publicly acknowledge Cobb's advice as being particularly helpful, there were others on the team that disagreed. One was Joe Hauser, who was swinging a sizzling stick in 1928 until Ty began hounding him to change his batting style. According to Hauser, Cobb had become jealous of the attention given the lefty first baseman and deliberately tried to mess with his head. Whether it was a result of the Georgian's interference or was a case of a player's limited ability finally catching up with him, Hauser's average dropped 100 points before finishing at .260, although he had had a combined .288 average in the four previous seasons. He was sold to Cleveland in the winter and was used mainly as a pinch hitter before his major-league career concluded at the season's end.

Hauser's departure solidified Foxx's position in the lineup, and the Sudlersville Slugger blossomed from 1929 to 1931. Although he was not yet considered the equal of Ruth or Gehrig by 1932, Foxx's three straight seasons with 30 or more homers and 100-plus RBIs, along with a combined average for the three years of .327, had some speculating about his potential. In 1929, Jimmie lost a ball at Fenway Park when it sailed over a nearby factory and onto the Boston & Albany railroad tracks. One eyewitness was Kid Gleason, who predicted Foxx would become the game's greatest player. In 1930, Foxx became the first to hit one out of Comiskey Park, the ball clearing the left-field upper deck and sailing over West 34th Place on Chicago's South Side. Philly fans hopeful of snagging a souvenir didn't have to purchase a ticket into Shibe Park but could instead hang out on the corner of 20th and Somerset Street, waiting for Foxx to send them a sphere. Sometimes Jimmie's missiles carried too far; once one shattered a second-story window of a house across the street.

Although further fame followed for Foxx, he hadn't done badly by 1932. In 1929 he had appeared on the cover of *Time* and had endorsed his first product, Louisville Slugger bats. His contract for that year had been $5,000, and after his wife Helen rewarded him with his first son that winter, Foxx was rewarded with a three-year deal for the 1930–1932 seasons worth $50,000. His income was supplemented by World Series shares (the A's had made it to the Series from 1929 to 1931), barnstorming trips, and commercial endorsements. (Former Senators batboy John Mitchell recalled for author Neil Isaacs in *Innocence and Wonder* how he grew up hearing "And a case of Wheaties for Jimmie Foxx!") The former farmboy was doing well for himself at a time when many fellow Americans were barely surviving.

How tragically revealing it is that in 1932 Yip Harburg's "Brother, Can You Spare a Dime?" would be the most popular song in America and Pearl Buck's *The Good Earth*, a novel about Chinese peasants struggling against the odds, the top selling book. The nation was still in desperate pain; the prosperity that had been promised by a president was still remote, seemingly unapproachable.

It had been the best of times for Americans when the Republican was elected in 1928 (labor workers or farmers may have proclaimed otherwise), but by 1932 they had had enough of the grim-faced, hands-off Hoover and would pin their hopes on a vibrant Democrat whose dazzling smile, uplifted chin, upbeat theme song, and fearless speeches bespoke a vigorous and optimistic new deal for the nation. For Franklin Roosevelt, the government was an instrument of the people, one which shouldn't remain dormant during turmoil. Many voters agreed, particularly the 13 million unemployed. Ironically, Hoover had begun to see the light toward the end of his term, approving congressional funding for public works projects, most notably the Hoover Dam, but it was too little, too late. In November the Hoover political machine was swept aside in a Roosevelt landslide that carried all but six states.

Although the depression's teeth sank deep in 1932, much would occur to detract Americans from their financial troubles. Aviator Charles Lindbergh agonized over his kidnapped son's murder in May, which precipitated the most publicized manhunt and trial in the nation's history (until the O.J. farce in 1995), and aviatrix Amelia Earhart made Americans proud by duplicating Lindbergh's trans–Atlantic crossing. American Jack Sharkey predicted in a syndicated column in June that he would defeat German Max Schmeling for the heavyweight boxing title and then won on a decision a week later. The United States took most of the gold in both the Winter and Summer Olympics.

Like the rest of the country, Foxx was hoping for a change in 1932, as injuries had prevented him from having a particularly productive season the year before. In the preseason of 1931, he suffered a torn tendon while running the bases, which kept him out of the lineup until mid–May. Towards the end of the year, he missed another two weeks when an inconsiderate Senator, Heine Manush, stepped on his foot while running to first. Foxx did well in hitting 30 homers and knocking in 120 runs in 139 games, but the figures were appreciably lower than the previous year (37 homers, 156 RBIs), and the nagging injuries also caused a 44-point drop in his average, from .335 in 1930 to .291 in 1931. Playing in the final year of his contract, Foxx needed to put up big numbers in 1932 prior to winter negotiations with the always-thrifty Mack.

The A's were looking to alter little because they were perfectly content with their success of the previous three years. They weren't joyous over their Series loss in seven to the Cardinals in 1931, but how many teams would gripe after taking two world championships in three tries? Even the disappointment of 1931 was made less painful by their record-setting regular season, in which they became the first team to win 100 games for a third straight time.

Sportswriter Fred Lieb, who had accurately picked the American League pennant-winner in 8 of the previous 11 seasons, predicted the Yankees would win in 1932. His peers disagreed, most of them giving the edge to Mack's mighty A's, and with good reason. Besides "Foxxie," as Connie called his fearsome first baseman, the Phillie lineup left little breathing room for hurlers. Left-fielder Al Simmons could have retired by then and still been assured of his place at Cooperstown. In eight seasons, Bucketfoot Al had hit lower than .340 only once — .308 in his rookie season in 1924. He hit a career-high .392 in 1927 and was entering the 1932 season as the batting champ of the past two years. Aloysius was no sissy singles hitter, having twice connected for more than 30 homers, and he had driven in over 100 runs each season, including a league-leading 157 in 1929.

Slightly less imposing were backstop Mickey Cochrane's stats by 1932. As a rookie in 1925, Black Mike hit .331, adding another four .300-plus seasons in the next six years, including a career-high .357 in 1930. Outfielder Mule Haas could go get 'em in center but was no slouch with the lumber, having hit .323 in the year before. Lefty-swinging Doc Cramer and righty Bing Miller provided a potent platoon in right. And though Jimmy Dykes, Eric McNair, and Max Bishop, along with Foxx, wouldn't collectively gain as much fame as Mack's early-century $100,000 infield Stuffy McInnis, Eddie Collins, Jack Barry, and Homerun Baker, they were probably a superior hitting combination.

The Phillie starters were anything but pushovers. Fireballer Lefty Grove was in the middle of a Hall-of-Fame career that would bring 300 wins, 8 twenty-win seasons, 7 strikeout crowns, and 9 ERA titles. The temperamental, at times grouchy, Grove entered the 1932 season as the league's top winner in three of the past four years, which included a 31-win season in 1931. Rube Walberg was a lefty as well, but Grove's equal in no other way. But neither was any other AL hurler, and Walberg had shown enough in nine seasons, including 20 wins and a league-leading 291 innings-pitched the year before, to warrant Mack's confidence in him as one of the team's top three starters. George Earnshaw was the other, looking for his fourth straight 20-win season in 1932.

The Yankees still had enough murderers on their roster to ensure that many would be crossing the dish, but Ruth, Gehrig, Dickey, Tony Lazzeri, and Earl Coombs would have to work overtime to match the A's offense in 1932, while Gomez, Ruffing, George Pipgras, Herb Pennock, and Johnny Allen needed to be equally adept on the hill. And there was the intangible factor of team attitude, which favored a club grown accustomed to winning. Author Kelley describes the devoted demeanor of that Philly team, writing, "Grove, Simmons, and Cochrane were out for blood at all times, and several of the others took the field in dead seriousness. This was somewhat tempered by the lighter hearts of Foxx and Dykes, but in spite of them the team had the air of a funeral dirge."

Philly's lack of brotherly love on the ballfield was made evident to Dizzy Dean in a March 6 exhibition game in Miami. The hard-throwing Arkansas righthander's remarks were frequently hard on the ears, and Diz had bragged before the game how he would breeze by the A's batters, despite having previously pitched in only one regular-season major-league game. Instead, the Great Dean was touched for four homers, including one by Foxx, and six runs in the opening inning before Cardinal manager Gabby Street "pulled him as an act of mercy," as noted by Dean biographer Robert Gregory. But Dean's exploits in the thirties would serve to substantiate much of his boasting.

By the time a packed audience was enjoying Helen Hayes' premiere in *The Good Fairy* playing at the Garrick Theater in Philadelphia on April 11, Shibe Park groundskeepers had already prepared the field where New York and Philadelphia played the next day in the premiere of the baseball season. On hand were 16,000 freezing diehards, nowhere near a packed audience. The weather was "as cold as an Arctic sledge dog's tongue," according to *Philadelphia Inquirer* sportswriter James Isaminger, and resulted in 17,000 empty seats. But the show must go on, and so it did, as a marching band led the Yankee and A's ballplayers to the center-field flagpole, where Phillie coach Eddie Collins and his Yankee counterpart Art Fletcher hoisted Old Glory, which waved tirelessly throughout the afternoon. Pregame ceremonies included the obligatory first-ball toss, performed by Mayor Hampy Moore, whose mind may have been dwelling on the city's mounting debt while he heaved the horsehide to Cochrane, who deftly scooped it out of the dirt. Seated next to Hizzoner was A's president Thomas Shibe, undoubtedly rankled by the weather's influence on gate receipts.

The game began at 3 P.M., and Yank skipper Joe McCarthy, who the next day admitted in a Knights of Columbus speech in Philly that the A's were the best team in the league, must have been impressed with his pinstripers after their four runs in the first. Ruth, quick to dispel any notions that he might be through, muscled an Earnshaw delivery over the right-field roof and onto a rooftop across the street, providing the team with its first three runs of the year. Babe belted another in his third at bat that was good for another two RBIs, while Gehrig, who labeled Shibe Park his "happy hunting grounds," also collected a round tripper in the 12–6 Yankee victory.

Foxx's uniform shirt, like Ruth's, bore the number three. The A's had begun sporting numerals on their backs the year before, and it's probably not a coincidence that Jimmie was given the same one as the player many believed he would someday replace as the master of the homerun. That idea was further propagated after Foxx connected off Gomez for his first of 58 four baggers, the sphere sailing over the center-field fence in the deepest part of the park.

The inclusion of numbers wasn't the only change made to the A's uniform under Mack. In the early twenties, the "A" insignia on the front of the shirt was replaced with a blue elephant and then a white one. Connie's thinking was that the alteration would alter the team's luck, which had soured with last place finishes from 1915 to 1921. (The degeneration of the A's was actually the result of Mack's selling all his star players in 1914.) When the team kept losing, Mack turned traditionalist in 1928, as the "A" reappeared and the elephant was eliminated.

"Farmer Boy," as Foxx was affectionately called by his mates, was prevented from harvesting homers the next two days, not by pitchers, but by precipitation, which caused postponements at Shibe Park. When the Yanks and A's went at it on April 15, Foxx wasted little time in crashing his second of the season. Facing Ruffing in the fourth, he pasted a fastball onto the left-field upper deck, breaking a 2–2 tie. The A's added another in the fifth, but the determined Bomber bunch plated five in the eighth, two on Gehrig's homer which carried over the amplifiers in right. Larrupin' Lou may have heaved a sigh of relief after the ball cleared the horns. The day before, he had complained to a reporter about the ground rule stipulating that a ball caroming off an amplifier and onto the field was in play. "I remember that either last season or the year before, the Babe lodged the ball into the amplifiers twice and only made a double each time."

Surrender was a word alien to these A's, who showed their mettle by tallying five times in the final three frames in conquering New York 9–8. Nonetheless, the Phillie club wouldn't blossom in April. By month's end, it occupied the seventh spot in the standings with a 4–10 record and was a game away from the basement berth held by the once-proud Red Sox. Mack wasn't worried, noting that most of the early losses had come against New York and Washington. Even though these two teams had had the better of the A's in the 1931 season series, the A's had still won the pennant by 13½ games.

Neither was baseball's opening month an exceptional one for Double X, who merely doubled his homer output after socking two in the first two games. On April 17, his blast reached the back rows of the left-center stands at Griffith Stadium, carrying approximately 450 feet for what Isaminger described as "one of the longest round trippers ever seen in the District of Columbia." The next day Foxx made it four in his first six games with a "lusty" drive over the right-field wall, but he took second honors that day to Senator Joe Judge, whose homer shattered a window across the street, to the chagrin of an irate housewife.

Foxx's fourth was his last of the month, as he went homerless in the next ten games. In spite of the late-April power failure, Jimmie collected 21 hits in 53 at-bats for a .396 average, good for third in the league behind Gehrig and Detroit's Gee Walker. Foxx gathered 13 ribbies in 14 games, and his four taters were good for runner-up honors in the junior circuit, with Babe's five leading the pack.

A young Jimmie Foxx. Note the elephant on the uniform, which disappeared following the 1927 season (National Baseball Library & Archive, Cooperstown, N.Y.).

Although he was still king of the homer-hitters, Babe had some problems in April as well. The temperature in Boston was too low on the seventeenth to enable the Yankee-Red Sox game to be played, and Ruth's temperature too high to allow him to play the next two games. He forced himself out of a sick bed on the twentieth to avoid disappointing the record-breaking 55,452 paid crowd who had squeezed through the turnstiles for the season opener at Yankee Stadium. The Sultan wasn't too weak to bang out a hit and homer off Grove, though the four bagger, as described by Phillie reliever Eddie Rommell, was "nothing more than a high, lazy fly that the wind barely carried over the right-field bleachers. It was not one of his copyrighted drives."

Although Mayor Walker was being harassed by an investigation which would lead to his resignation a few months later, he wasn't too harried to attend the opener. His energetic firing of the first ball to plate umpire George Hildebrand indicated no emotional turmoil. Nor did his attire that afternoon, described as a "Mendelssohn powder-blue suit, with a blue topcoat, a shirt of Keats blue, a Wordsworth tie and a Swineburne derby hat."

The mayor's team routed the A's that day, and the two teams split the next two. The Babe had the edge over his rival in their second series confrontation of 1931. Foxx collected no homers, but stroked five hits in eleven at-bats in the three games, including a double and two long triples. Ruth had four hits in eleven at-bats, but two were homers, and he drove in seven runs to Jimmie's two. If Ruth still reigned supreme, Foxx had gained enough respect from Yankee hurlers for McCarthy to comment after the series, "Our pitchers would rather throw to Simmons twice than Jimmie Foxx once."

After announcing toward the end of April that he would be giving up golf because "ball games are tough enough on the legs," a brazen-faced Babe remarked to reporters that he wasn't "so surprised to see the Athletics slipping" and anticipated the Yanks winning "in a walk." Mack remained confident, though frustration was evident when he complained following a rainout on the first of May: "Our hitting has been terrible. There does not appear to be any base hits in our order below Jimmie Foxx."

Not many were coming from above either. The first-through-fourth positions had combined for a .287 average, not bad, but not what Mack had expected from the top half of the order. The usually destructive Simmons had but two homers and his average was a mellow .283, though many of his hits were timely, as indicated by his dozen RBIs, one fewer than Foxx's. Cochrane's .297 was equally ordinary in a league that boasted three .400 hitters. Jimmie would need help if the A's were to repeat as champs for an AL record fourth straight time.

Foxx broke a ten-game homerless drought in Boston on May 2 with a game-winning homer in the eleventh inning, which also snapped a Phillie six-game losing streak. Several of his teammates helped provide Jimmie's opportunity. Walberg allowed the Sox to tie the score in the eighth on a two-out single and then kept the game knotted by spearing a wicked comeback liner to end the inning. Simmons had the bags jammed in the tenth but ended the inning with a double-play grounder, and Grove pitched out of trouble after surrendering a pair of hits in the bottom of the tenth. Foxx led off the eleventh against Wilcy Moore with his fifth homer and the ball carried into Fenway's center-field bleachers.

Jimmie's sixth came three days later at home against Cleveland, as a

Wes Ferrell fastball finished its flight in the left-field upper deck. Foxx also had a pair of singles and walks, four RBIs, and five runs-scored in as many plate appearances. Grove was again the beneficiary of Foxx's offense in evening his record at 3–3, though he too contributed with a pair of singles in Phillie's seven-run seventh. It was the third straight win for the A's, who made it four in a row the next day despite Foxx being held hitless for only the third time in 18 games. The collar might have been averted had the Tribe's Mel Harder not avoided pitching to Jimmie with an open base in the seventh, and had Earl Averill not made a circus catch of a Foxx drive to deep center in an earlier at bat.

Any fan optimism in Philly resulting from the modest streak of the A's soon vanished following the ceremonial raising of the club's ninth pennant the following afternoon. Collins and Indians manager Roger Peckinpaugh performed the honors, while Commissioner Kenesaw Mountain Landis and AL president William Harridge observed approvingly as the red pennant with blue border and white lettering ascended the flagpole. The Indians ambushed Earnshaw for a run in the first and three in the second and finally chased the Moose with another pair in the fifth. The Athletics fought back like champs, scoring four in the final three frames, but they eventually succumbed 10–7.

Foxx played that day with a severe head cold, as he would intermittently during a career in which antibiotics weren't yet available to offer relief from chronic sinusitis. As if his clogged noggin weren't enough of a hindrance, Jimmie was bothered by blisters on his right hand as he faced Willis Hudlin in the seventh. If a little less sawdust fell from the handle than was usual while he cocked the bat, Jimmie's vicelike grip was sufficiently tight to help propel a Hudlin heater into the upper deck in left.

With two outs in the ninth, Foxx prolonged the game with a drive off reliever Ferrell which reached the flagpole in center. It is mere speculation today whether the ex-track star might have been able to circle the bases before Averill retrieved the ball at the base of the pole some 470 feet away and threw it to the cutoff man, who relayed it to the infield. With his team trailing by three, Foxx held at third, content with an RBI triple.

Jimmie tomahawked nine triples in 1932. Considering he fell short of Babe's 60 homers by 2, the obvious question is, how many of his three baggers came close to being homeruns? Based on Isaminger's descriptions, all nine did. The two against the Yankees on April 21 were labeled "leviathan drives," both being hit to the base of the left-center wall in the infamous Death Valley at Yankee Stadium. Jimmie's triple of April 24 carried 400 feet to the wall in left at Griffith Stadium. After smashing the previously described three bagger against the Indians, his next came on the first of June when his fly ball caromed off the Shibe Park right-field wall. Two days later Jimmie tripled "to the wall in deepest center" and again might have taken the extra base if the A's weren't being routed by Gehrig and Company, who tallied 20 times that day. On July 1, Foxx lofted a fly ball that "lacked two or three inches" from clearing Shibe's right-field wall, and two weeks later his triple off Fenway's short right-field-bleacher wall "would have been a homer had it been a foot higher." On September 4, his final three bagger carried to the most remote region of Griffith Park and was described as one which "would have been a homer at Shibe Park." In retrospect, Foxx's nine triples were significant, but as we'll see, they weren't the only near-miss-homer instances, nor were they the only inhibiting factors which foiled his quest to catch the Babe.

The man who would be king was still bothered by a bruised hand and blurry head when he was held hitless in three at-bats the next day by Cleveland's Clint Brown, who fanned Foxx twice. A rainout helped Foxx recuperate, and he returned to stroke two singles and a hustling double against Chicago on May 10. Two more postponements enabled the rejuvenated slugger to register his first four-hit game of the year on the thirteenth, and while none of the singles added to his homer total, they solidified his hold of the league lead in batting. He finished the game at .458, fifty points better than runner-up Carl Reynolds. The challenge for the title by the Senators' right fielder would be brief; he finished the season, as he would his career, barely over the .300 mark.

On May 14, the nation was commiserating with its aviation hero over the murder of his kidnapped son, whose body had been discovered two days earlier. An aroused public considered the crime so heinous that kidnapping was soon made a federal offense punishable by death, and the president ordered the FBI's J. Edgar Hoover to handle the case. Luck more than Hoover's diligence would lead to the arrest of Richard Hauptmann two years later. A suspicious gas pumper wrote down the license plate number of Hauptmann's car after he paid for a dollar's worth of gas with a ten-dollar bill, not a usual practice during the depression.

Hauptmann pleaded not guilty at his trial, which began on the second day of 1935. Lindbergh was present each of the 42 days it lasted, including one on which his wife Anne was asked to identify her late son's pajamas. At 10 P.M. on February 13, a crowd of 10,000 amassed outside the courtroom awaiting a verdict which was anything but problematic. Americans would have expected nothing less than the death sentence for the German, especially when a hostile press had helped to incite the public further with cameras in the courtroom. Hauptmann maintained his innocence up to his electrocution, which took place on April 3, 1936.

As the Lindberghs agonized over the crime of the century, the Browns' Bump Hadley was feeling pain on May 14 after yielding what was described as "the longest homerun Foxx has made in his career." The ball cleared the left-center roof by "30 or more feet." It was reported that Foxx was the only player to have hit one out of Shibe Park via left field, but Jimmie contradicted this five days later after again clearing the roof, claiming he had done it for the tenth time and recalling that Detroit's Harry Heilmann and Cleveland's Ed Morgan had each cleared it once.

Two days after Foxx's bomb off Bump, Isaminger would write, "The last heard of that ball hit by Foxx was that it was seen traveling over Bucks County." Jimmie had everyone's attention. As a *Sporting News* reporter observed, "Never before, over so protracted a period, has Foxx whaled the hosshide as he has this season."

Foxx added an RBI single off Hadley in helping Grove coast to his second straight shutout victory. The Athletics then rushed to catch a 6:30 train to Detroit, Philadelphia's Sunday law preventing them from playing the first of four with the Tigers at home. Jimmie continued to impress in Motown, walloping his ninth in a 7–2 loss. Back in Philly the next day, Jimmie was limited by the Tigers' Vic Sorrell to a single to "deep left" in three at-bats. Many of Foxx's one-base hits were described in a similar fashion in 1932, attesting to the respect shown Jimmie by opposing outfielders who would position themselves near or even on the warning track, or "cinder path."

Double X was again held homerless on May 17, though he clawed Bengal hurlers for a pair of singles and a double in four tries. He hit another in the finale, the three-run blow barely staying fair while soaring towards the left-field upper deck. Despite Grove winning his fifth straight game, the A's merely managed a split with the Tigers, who retained fourth place. Below them were the Mackmen, a game under the .500 mark and eight behind the front-running Yankees after the Bombers sneaked by the Indians 3–2, with the help of Babe's seventh homer, only his second of the month.

The Red Sox visited Shibe Park on May 19, and it didn't take long for Boston's Bob Kline to wish he had remained in Beantown. Haas opened for the A's first half with a single, Cochrane pushed him to third with a double, Simmons walked, and Foxx cleared the bases with his first grand slam of the year. It was the third of his career; he had hit one in each of the previous two seasons. Jimmie would connect for two more salamis in 1932, and finish his career with 17. Only Gehrig, Willie McCovey, and Eddie Murray would accumulate more.

Following Jimmie's grand wallop, the battered Kline finally registered

Jimmie Foxx's power derived from a slight hitch, a long smooth follow-through, and a hitting philosophy which advocated taking healthy hacks at every pitch (National Baseball Library & Archive, Cooperstown, N.Y.).

his first out and was impregnable the rest of the way, as he lost 4–2. The Sox held Foxxie to two doubles and a single the next day en route to their 24th defeat in 29 games, easily the worst record in the big leagues, making the perennially pathetic Browns proud of their 15–18 mark. Jimmie's last hit came in the eighth inning when with two aboard and his club ahead by four, he surprised everyone at Shibe by bunting. At-bats would prove precious in the quest to catch Ruth, so that by October Foxx may have recalled with disgust his sacrificing another chance at a round tripper.

More likely, Foxx was regretting not having laid down a few more. At the time, the bunt hit increased to fifty his lead in the batting race, but Jimmie would finish second to Dale Alexander, whose three-point margin of victory prevented the slugger from taking the Triple Crown, a disappointment made more excruciating after he accomplished the toughest of hitting feats the following season. Had Alexander not edged him out, Foxx would today be the only player in history to win back-to-back Triples. (Some argue that Alexander, whose career lasted all of five seasons and ended in 1933, didn't deserve to win in 1932 because he gathered a mere 392 at-bats in 124 games playing for Detroit and Boston.)

For Foxx, the Babe's record was a double-edged sword. His September hits would have been more numerous had he abandoned his long-ball quest, which was a nearly impossible goal in the final weeks, and had instead concentrated on winning the batting championships. By May, opposing infielders were already "inching back, getting ready to combat something hot from Jimmie's bat." They would have been even more surprised by bunt attempts in September, which often would have been successful, given Jimmie's outstanding speed. Foxx did well to sock 10 four baggers while hitting a robust .390 in September, but his compulsion to hit homers that month resulted in a ten-day .210 slump. Had he abandoned homers for singles in only a few at-bats during that period, he would have won the batting title. But Jimmie couldn't do it. He had Babe on his mind.

Perhaps Ruth was thinking about his latest challenger to the throne when he socked numbers nine and ten of the season on May 21 in leading the Bombers past the second place Senators in the opener of a doubleheader at Yankee Stadium. One of the Babe's belts was his 15th career grand slam (he would hit one more two years later), surrendered by southpaw Lloyd Brown, who took his first loss in five decisions.

Not to be outdone, Foxx matched his adversary with a homer in each of two games played at Shibe Park that day, as the A's swept the Sox before 20,000 delighted, sun-drenched spectators. The twin wins hoisted the Mackmen to third place and pulled them to within 5½ of the Yanks prior to a series in New York. For the A's, the timing of the confrontation couldn't have been better. They had won six straight games. Besides Foxx leading the league in homers, RBIs, and batting, Cochrane and Simmons seemed aroused from their batting slumber. Grove, who would face the Yankees in the series opener, owned a five-game winning streak and had been scored on but twice in the past 30 innings. True, McCarthy's crew wasn't struggling either, but they had just finished a hard-fought, five-game series with the difficult Senators, while the A's had been breezing by Boston.

Yank owner Ruppert must have had one eye on the standings as the A's entered Yankee Stadium on May 21 and the other on the gate, hoping the three-game matchup would attract the nearly 120,000 who had attended the Senators series. By day's end, the sizable crowd of 40,000 helped assuage the Colonel's pain resulting from a 4–2 loss, courtesy Grove's six-hit pitching (Ruth had two) and homers by Cochrane, Simmons, and Foxx. But the pinstripers rebounded with a 6–5 nailbiter the following afternoon, snapping the A's seven-game winning streak, and Gomez hurled a 3–1 masterpiece in the finale. Lefty fanned 10 in the first five frames and finished with 13 which, at the time, was 3 shy of the major-league mark.

Foxx, who would hit Gomez well throughout his career, was whiffed once and had one of a trio of A's safeties. In another at-bat, Jimmie drove the ball to Death Valley, where Ben Chapman was able to make a leaping grab at the wall only because he had played Foxx on the warning track, "expecting just this kind of a drive from the broadback. It should have been a homer in any other park." Ruth took advantage of the more inviting right-field target by belting number 11 off Walberg in the opening inning.

Philadelphia found easier pickings in Boston, defeating the struggling Sox in the first two games at Fenway prior to finishing the series in a twin bill at Braves Field on May 29. Curiously, a Sunday law still prevented Boston's AL park from being used, even though the ordinance prohibiting ball on the Sabbath had been dropped in Boston in 1929. Perhaps historian Harold Seymour offers a clue in *Baseball— The Golden Age* when he states that city officials imposed a license fee on clubs offering Sunday baseball. While Braves owner Judge Emil Fuchs complied, indebted Red Sox president Bob Quinn may have balked at the notion of another expense for the sake of attracting a few thousand to watch his reeling Red Sox on the Sabbath. Whatever the reason, the doubleheader with the A's marked the last time the Sox played at Braves Field on Sundays, the Fenway ban being abandoned immediately afterwards.

The issue of the Fenway Park prohibition is significant in regards to Foxx's 1932 season. Having belted his 15th homer in the rain-shortened series opener at Fenway, Foxx hit another one two days later in the doubleheader at Braves Field. (Only 6,000 showed up, with the chilly weather, sickening Sox record, and foreign ballpark being obvious reasons for the sparse crowd.) Since by season's end Foxx would hit at least one homer in each ballpark, including the two in Beantown, he may be the only player in the pre-expansion era to connect in nine different ballparks. In fact, Jimmie had a chance to make it ten. After finding the seats three times in a game at League Park in July, he returned to Cleveland later in the season to play several games at the Indians' spanking-new Municipal Stadium, but he failed to connect.

Seventy-year-old Arlie Latham had been one of the 6,000 fans at Braves Field on May 29. The former baseball clown became famous for his late-nineteenth-century antics on the field, but he may have been wondering if his act had ever been as humorous as the Red Sox's play that year. After the twin bill, a story circulated that the club was up for sale. Owner Quinn brushed aside queries, which might have served as a confirmation of the rumor. By the end of the year, when the Sox had accumulated 111 losses, a still-standing club record for futility, Quinn found a buyer in Tom Yawkey, who in his four-decade reign would transform the team into a competitive, if not world-championship, franchise.

Memorial Day is a time America pays tribute to those who died for their country. On May 30, 1932, a thousand living war veterans preferred cash over commemoration. They had gathered in Washington the day before to demand payment for bonus certificates received from the government, which was stalling in making good its pre-depression promise. By June, other veterans from across the country arrived, swelling the "Bonus Army" to over 17,000, all refusing to leave before Uncle Sam coughed up. Although the House passed a bill authorizing payment, it was killed by the Senate, and the veterans were told to return home. When a couple thousand refused, coercion replaced conciliation as federal troops headed by General Douglas MacArthur drove them out.

Memorial Day in America also meant baseball doubleheaders (note use of the past tense). Some owners took advantage of the fans with morning and afternoon affairs, as was the case with Thomas Shibe, who felt no aversion to twice collecting gate receipts. (Shibe's father Benjamin had been half-owner of the club until his death in 1922, and the ballpark was named for him.) Fifteen thousand gathered to watch the A's humble Walter Johnson's Senators 13–2 in the first engagement, and another 25,000 witnessed Foxx's seventh-inning, three-run blast which erased the Washington 6–4 lead. Jimmie's game-winner offset a poor plate performance in the morning, when he fanned three times in hitting for the collar.

The Senators rebounded by taking the finale of the month in a thriller that ended with back-to-back triples in the 12th inning. The loss left the A's six behind the Yanks in fourth place, with the Tigers and Senators also above them. Foxx had a scratch single in five attempts, an unfitting finish to a month which brought 13 round trippers. His 17 homers in 41 games had him knocking one out every 2.4 games, a pace which, if it had been maintained, would have left him with 64 homers by season's end.

Umpire George Moriarty was proficient at knocking 'em out as well. Described by sportswriter Stan Baumgartner in 1932 as "carrying a chip on his shoulder for many years, asking for someone to knock it off," Moriarty became annoyed with White Sox hurler Milt Gaston after the 6' 1" right-hander's objections to calls became too frequent and vociferous in Cleveland on May 30. Afterwards, the heavy-set umpire crashed through the Sox clubhouse doors and challenged Gaston to a fistfight. Gaston's mistake in accepting cost him a few moments of consciousness. Before he awakened, several of his teammates had assumed a prone position as well before the law of averages finally caught up with Moriarty, whose dare to take on the entire Chicago team one at a time ended with an effective right to his jaw. It was reported that several Sox hit and kicked the unpopular ump after he was down.

Moriarty, who suffered a broken hand and shattered nerves, was out of action for about a month after the tussle, but his attitude would change little upon his return. Before shelving mask and chest protector in 1940 and terminating a 22-year career, Moriarty had asserted his authority often enough that players generally acted wisely, refraining from inciting the ex–Yankee third baseman who in his playing days would attempt to steal home by crashing into opposing backstops and reportedly once got the better of a scuffle with the formidable Ty Cobb. (Moriarty wasn't the only intimidating umpire, however, and they didn't all limit their discipline to ballplayers and managers. In 1945, 6' 3" George Magerkurth became so incensed by a heckling fan that he approached the box seat and decked the culprit.)

June began in Philly with a doubleheader against the Yankees which was part of a crucial six-game showdown. Being six games from the lead, the A's could ill-afford anything less than a split. Two umpires would work the series at Shibe that day, a third going to Cleveland to replace the battered Moriarty. (By 1932 two-man and three-man crews were used intermittently. Mandatory use of a three-man crew began the next season. Following World War II, experimental four-man crews were used on occasion until they became the regulation units during the fifties.)

The A's began well in the opener and were within three outs of victory, but pitcher Ruffing, whose lifetime hitting stats included an impressive .269 average and 36 homers, batted for himself in the ninth and tied the score with a homer. Grove replaced Roy Mahaffey and retired the side, fanning Ruth in the process.

Ruffing pitched another two shutout innings before giving way to Jumbo Brown in the 12th, who added another pair of blanks before facing Foxx in the 15th. With one out, Jimmie nearly ended it with a deep fly to left, but Ruth snared it with his back against the wall, marking the second time in the game Foxx had flirted with a homer (he had tripled earlier). Brown then completed his fourth shutout inning.

When Grove took the mound in the 16th, he had seven scoreless frames in the bank but failed in his try for eight. A Coombs double and Ruth single brought home the go-ahead run, putting Lefty's eight-game winning streak in jeopardy. His dugout frown turned to a grin when Haas singled and Bishop hit a huge homer off Jumbo, giving Grove his ninth-straight and the A's the opener.

With momentum on their side, the confident Mackmen put four across in the first inning of the nightcap, two coming on a single by Foxx. The two clubs traded runs in the second, and after tallying in the third, the Yanks had a four-run inning of their own in the sixth. With one out in the seventh, Simmons walked, and Pipgras faced the potential go-ahead run at the plate. Foxx delivered with his 18th homer, which bounced off the left-field roof and onto Somerset Street. The game-winner gave the A's the sweep.

Gomez won 5–1 the next day, partly by passing Foxx three of the five times they faced, and Gehrig single-handedly evened the series on June 3 when he became the first player of the century to hit four homers in a game. He nearly had a fifth, but his drive to center in the ninth was corralled by Simmons. Foxx's 19th in the ninth was anticlimactic.

The series ended with a Saturday doubleheader split the next day. Foxx helped Grove win his ninth straight with his 4th homer of the week and 20th of the season, and Pennock crushed the hopes of the standing-room-only crowd of 35,000 with a complete-game win in the nightcap. In splitting the series, the A's lost no ground to the Yankees but lost another opportunity to gain.

Foxx made it four in five days with a homer in his final at bat against the Senators on June 5. He wouldn't connect again for another week, hindered in part by a hand injury suffered in a manner which must have tested the patience of the normally placid Mack. On the evening of June 8, Jimmie was playfully tossing a pen knife in his hotel room when he mistimed a catch and grabbed by the blade rather than handle. The resulting severe gash on his left thumb required mending by the A's trainer. Jimmie remained in the lineup, but his hampered grip resulted in 2 singles (one of the infield variety) in 14 at-bats in the next three games. Because he had been hot prior to the injury, the supposition can be made that Foxx would have added a homer or two to his total had he kept his knife in his bureau drawer.

On a sunny day at Navin Field on June 12, Foxx's 22d homer proved a harmless cloud for 18,000 Tiger supporters who watched a parade of

Bengal batters pour it on in the late innings en route to an 8–6 triumph. Foxx's homer the next day, which cleared the left-field scoreboard, landed on a rooftop across from the stadium parking lot and was immediately proclaimed in the press box as the longest ever at Navin Field. The feat was witnessed by 6,000 women guests of Tiger management, the Ladies' Day promotion having begun in Detroit two weeks earlier. The round tripper came in the ninth and was icing on a very sweet cake for Grove, who now had 11 victory candles in a row, his 10th having come five days earlier against the Indians. Lefty departed the field with some discomfort, as a comeback liner had drilled him in the left side of the hip, also causing him to sprain his left ankle. Heat treatments provided immediate relief for the sore hip, but the sprain would require a lengthy rest.

Jimmie finished his work in Detroit with two more tape-measure drives. A pair were aboard in the fifth when he bombarded the same house as the day before, and he exploded a rocket off a different dwelling in his next at bat. When the ball left the ballpark, it was "as high as a four-story building." Foxx's 25 homers officially started the countdown as it was reported he was now 16 days ahead of Ruth's 1927 pace. (When others would challenge the Babe in the future, the race would be reported in terms of games, not days.)

Foxx now had four homers in his last three games and nearly had another when his double in St. Louis hit a few feet from the top of the right-field screen. The A's lost to the Browns that day, punished their opponent the next two games, and then split a pair on getaway day. Foxx's 26th was the key blow in the nightcap, the three-run clout providing the margin of victory. It was another unprecedented homer for distance, reportedly the first time any ball traveled completely out of Sportsman's Park to the right of the scoreboard in left-center, clearing the bleacher wall by about ten feet.

The weather had been brutal in St. Louis, as record temperatures made for sleepless nights in suffocating hotel rooms; the A's were happy to leave for cooler Chicago on June 19. Not all were completely happy, however; Grove was grumbling over still being sidelined and was unable to convince the cautious Mack to let him pitch in the twin bill against the sixth place Browns. Connie hinted that Lefty would most likely remain out of action until the A's played the Yanks in a two-game set in New York at the end of the month.

It had been a productive road trip so far. Having left Philly on June 4 with a 26–21 record in fifth place, the A's won 9 of 14 in improving to 35–26 and second in the standings. Although Foxx remained their only consistent hitter, still leading in batting, homers, and RBIs, Simmons and Cochrane were among the league leaders in round trippers as well. The pitching was also sufficiently reliable to permit Mack to refrain from hurrying back his ace, a decision Cardinal manager Frankie Frisch might have made five years later when a still-hurting Dizzy Dean talked his way back to the mound following a broken toe. Dean's favoring the toe while he pitched led to a sore right shoulder which virtually ruined his career.

The confident A's had little to fear from the seventh place White Sox, who, except for those other Sox, had the worst record in baseball. Yet in the series opener this humble bunch got 18 hits and 11 runs off three A's hurlers. Fortunately for Philly, there was Doc Cramer's six-for-six performance (the first since Cobb's in 1925), and Foxx's 27th, another "longest ever" drive, to offset the ineffective pitching, as the A's prevailed 18–11. Jimmie's homer was reportedly his third hit out of Comiskey Park via left field, with no other player but Ruth having knocked one out of the 22-year-old stadium. (The Babe's cleared the right-field roof.) Whose went further? Grove would have bet on his teammate, saying after the game, "Foxx hits the longest homers of anybody, not even excluding Ruth." Home-plate umpire Harry Geisel might have agreed. "I think I got a bigger kick out of Foxx's drive than Jimmie himself," he said. "I stood transfixed."

It is interesting to note that while Foxx was by mid–June leading the world in round trippers, his closest competitor was none other than Ruth, and he wasn't far behind. Notwithstanding his four-homer game, Gehrig badly trailed his aging teammate, whose 21 homers by June 13 not only reigned supreme for the Yanks, but were only 2 behind Foxx. Jimmie did well to lengthen his lead to 6 with his 27th in Chicago, but the lead was not insurmountable. Foxx might have been chasing the record, but the record-holder was keeping him company.

A whistling drive into the Comiskey center-field seats gave Foxx his 28th on June 22, but the homer and his first-inning bunt single didn't prevent Chicago starter Vic Frasier from going the distance in a 9–4 win. It was the second straight defeat for the A's against a team they should have been mauling. The next day a puppy dog provided levity by scampering around the outfield in the first inning, preventing resumption of play until Foxx's diving two-handed catch, but the A's found no humor in their third straight loss to the White Sox, which dropped them eight behind New York prior to entering Yankee Stadium on June 25.

It was on that Saturday afternoon that Foxx hit the previously described tape-measure blast which allegedly shattered a seat and prompted Gomez' 20-minute walk to the spot in the left-field upper deck where the ball had landed. Rain nearly interfered with history, but the clouds held their moisture until shortly after the final out. (The weather did hold the crowd to under 20,000 instead of the 60,000 anticipated by Ruppert.) Jimmie's destructive drive came with two on in the fourth and put the A's back in the ballgame after the Yankees had tallied four times in the first two innings, with Gehrig's 19th homerun accounting for half the team's runs. The first baseman was playing in his 1104th straight game, which broke the record for most consecutive played with one club that was previously held by Joe Sewell, who played in 1103 in a row with Cleveland. The A's tied it in the 6th inning, but hurler Mahaffey was finished when he yielded a run in the seventh and then another pair in the eighth.

If Foxx's unprecedented blast haunted Gomez for decades to come, the Yankee ace might also have recalled beating the Phillies that afternoon for the fifth straight time, with a win that was his 11th straight, matching Grove's, and his 14th of the season with only one loss. His streak was snapped in his next outing, but Lefty still won 24 that year. Following retirement, the unpretentious Hall-of-Famer enjoyed joking about his failures on the diamond, but his self-deprecations belied a career which included winning 20 in a season 4 times and leading the league in wins and ERA twice and in strikeouts and shutouts three times. "Goofy" became known for his wit but had some serious seasons as a moundsman.

After contending with one future Cooperstown inductee, the A's faced another the next day. Ruffing limited the opposition to two runs on seven hits in a complete-game, 6–2 win in front of 33,000. Isaminger noted that a good portion of the crowd was Phillie fans, and he took a subtle stab at Pennsylvania conservatism by writing, "Denied Sunday baseball at home, there is no law to prevent them from leaving the city and spending money elsewhere to see their favorite sport."

The back-to-back setbacks against the Yanks spoiled what had been a successful road trip; the A's were glad to be back at Shibe on June 27 and were especially delighted to be hosting the Red Sox. The Phillies swept the series, Foxx assisting with four singles, a double, three RBIs, and five walks in the three games. Still looking for his 30th homer against the Senators on the first of July, Foxx came close with a double off the right-field wall in the sixth and excruciatingly closer with a triple which landed on top of the same wall, lingered momentarily, and then fell onto the field.

Number 30 remained elusive in a doubleheader with the Senators the next day, though Foxx again flirted with the fences, his deep drive to center good for an RBI double; he was walked once in each game. Pitchers threw tentatively when facing Jimmie in 1932. His 116 walks would be the highest single-season total of his career, save for the 1938 season, when he led the league in homers and RBIs while belting 50 homers. Although walks would be a key inhibiting factor in Foxx's attempt to hit 60, it was a problem

Babe had faced in 1927 as well. In fact, despite having Gehrig batting behind him throughout the season, Ruth's walk total that year (138) was higher than Foxx's in 1932, and his walk percentage was also higher, one every five plate appearances to Foxx's one every six.

Foxx's homerless streak stood at 10 games and 11 days when he faced Chicago's Sad Sam Jones in the second inning of the first of two played at Shibe on July 8. Jones was in his 19th season, his first as a White Sox hurler, having been traded along with Bump Hadley by Washington for outfielder Carl Reynolds at the end of the 1931 season. Jones' career, which ended with a broken finger three years later, included playing for six teams and can be characterized as mediocre. Still, the country-loving Buckeye had his share of memories. Twice a twenty-game winner, the six-foot righthander had been the first to throw a shutout in Yankee Stadium when he blanked the Senators 4–0 in 1923 (Ruth helped with a homer) in front of President Warren Harding, who was seeking escape from a simmering Teapot Dome scandal. (The tormented chief executive would die in office four months later.) That same year Jones became only the second Yankee in history to hurl a no-hitter when he defeated the Athletics 2–0, and he continues to hold the dubious distinction of being the only AL pitcher in history to do so without fanning a batter. He won his final game in 1935 at the age of 42, going the route in defeating Detroit 3–2 in 95-degree heat.

Jones' pleasant reminiscences couldn't have included that opener of the Sox-A's doubleheader of July 8, when he surrendered five runs in six innings, including Foxx's long-anticipated 30th, a routine upper-deck job. When Phillie starter Ed Rommel faltered in the ninth, Grove made his first appearance since June 13 and retired the final three batters, two on strike-outs, in notching the save.

Jones' problems would continue before he finished with a 10–15 mark and ERA over four, but neither would 1932 be particularly joyous for his counterpart in trade — Carl Reynolds. The righty-swinging outfielder caught a right punch from Bill Dickey after he crashed into the Yankee backstop while scoring on a squeeze play in the first of two on the Fourth of July. Reynold's broken jaw would keep him out of action for a month, but his absence was made somewhat less painful for Senators skipper Walter Johnson when he heard on July 9 of Dickey's $1,000 fine and month's suspension. Having recently handed out fines to Chicago's Charlie Berry, Milt Gaston, Frank Grube, and manager Lew Fonseca for roughing up ump Moriarty on Memorial Day, AL president Will Harridge's perspective regarding American holidays may have been somewhat altered by mid–July as he apprehensively awaited the Labor Day doubleheaders of September.

Dickey stoically accepted his punishment, saying, "I don't know what else I can do about it," but Grove was probably not as controlled emotionally following the snapping of his winning streak in the first of two against Chicago on the ninth. Lefty's lengthy mound absence waʳ evident as the Sox punished him with nine hits and six runs before he yielded to Ed Rommel, whose mop-up duty went unnoticed. Considering his work of the next day, however, Rommel's three-inning stint carried significance.

Although Grove pitched poorly, he may have complained about lack of hitting support as the A's were shut out for the first time that year (they would be blanked once more). Jimmie was collared in three at-bats, but had a pair of hits in the nightcap, including a double which fell short of the Shibe center-field wall. The A's gained a split with an 11–2 laugher before rushing to catch a train to Cleveland for a Sunday matinee. Knowing he would be back in Philly on Monday, frugal Mack ordered starter Lew Krausse and Rommel aboard but left behind the remainder of the pitching staff, saving the cost of train fare.

When Krausse was shelled from the box in the first, Rommel took over, knowing he would have to go the distance. Although he had thrown three innings the day before, hurling another eight wasn't too demanding a chore for a pitcher not yet pampered with 100-pitch counts. Throwing another 17 innings was another matter, but that's exactly what would be required of the righty reliever. The see-saw affair stood at 15-all after nine innings. Rommel had only himself to blame in the 16th when, after Foxx's homer provided a two-run lead, four Indian hits once again knotted the game. In the 18th, a Foxx single and Eric McNair's double again had the Phillies ahead, and Rommel finally ended his ordeal by retiring the Indians in the bottom half.

It was arguably, the most exciting game in history. The clubs exchanged the lead six times before entering overtime, at which point many outstanding defensive plays, particularly by A's center-fielder Mule Haas, kept the game going. Five players had five or more hits, with the Tribe's John Burnett leading all with a still-standing record nine. Loser Wes Ferrell wasn't quite the equal of workhorse Rommel, but his 11-plus innings in relief were noteworthy nonetheless. Perhaps most significant was the playing time, the 18-inning affair taking four hours, five minutes, the time it requires modern teams to conclude some nine-inning games.

With the possible exception of Burnett's work, Foxx's was the most outstanding that day as he played what was probably the greatest game of his career. Jimmie banged two singles, a double, and three homeruns into League Park's left-field bleachers, the first of two occasions in his career in which he would belt three in a game. (He would repeat the feat in 1933.) Foxx gathered eight RBIs, scored four runs, including the game-winner, and set a still-standing AL record of 16 total bases (shared by five others).

The Yankees lost two to the Browns that day (with Ruth managing only a single in nine trips), so the extra-effort victory pulled the second place A's to within six of the Bombers, but the momentum died the next day in Philly with a doubleheader drop to Cleveland. Moriarty, umpiring for the first time in a month, watched from the third base line as Earl Averill, a homer-hitter in the marathon the day before, hit for the circuit three more times in the twin bill, while Foxx connected for number 34 in the nightcap.

Grove pitched in the finale of July 12 and lost to Cleveland for the first time in two years. He carried a 6–5 lead into the final frame, when Ed Morgan, whose two-out error in the ninth made possible the 18-inning debacle two days before, made amends with a two-run homer. This homer became the game-winner after Joe Vosmik made an over-the-shoulder catch of Doc Cramer's drive in the A's half of the ninth, holding onto the ball as he recklessly crashed into the stands. The next day Grove suffered his second defeat in as many days when he relieved in the seventh and surrendered the tying tally in the eighth via a throwing miscue by Cochrane and the winning hit — a two-out, two-run single to the Tribe's Bill Cissell — in the tenth. It was his fourth straight setback after a 12–1 start and eleven straight wins, but Grove would right himself soon.

Foxx went hitless in five trips in the closer against Cleveland but rebounded with a pair of safeties against Detroit on July 14, one being his 35th circuit. Besides the Foxx homer, the 9–2 win by the A's was highlighted by the superb pitching of southpaw Tony Freitas, who scattered six hits in going the distance. The Portuguese hurler issued no walks, but his control wasn't quite perfect that afternoon. One of his third-inning flings found the noggin of the Tigers' star second baseman and future Hall-of-Famer Charlie Gehringer, who "dropped like a log" and remained on the ground for several minutes.

The beaning didn't prevent Gehringer from remaining in the game, but the lefty swinger's foot may have been in the bucket in his next two unsuccessful plate appearances. Interestingly, had the Mechanical Man reached Freitas for hits in his final tries, he would have finished the season over .300, rather than .298. Except for his first full season in 1926 and his final one in 1941, 1932 would be the only year Gehringer failed to hit .300 as a regular, and had he been successful it would have given him 14 consecutive .300 seasons, a meaningful near-miss accomplishment, considering only three junior-circuit hitters — Ty Cobb (23), Ted Williams (15), and Rod Carew (15) — have strung together more.

Although no specific rule yet existed allowing for the ejection of pitchers who threw beanballs, nor would one exist for another half-century,

American League umpires had been instructed in 1932 to take any means necessary to discourage intentional knockdowns, including expulsion. Yet it would be a rarely used disciplinary measure and did little to inhibit pitchers. Most beanballs weren't thrown with the intention of finding targets, though some inadvertently did — like Freitas' and Bump Hadley's five years later which ended Cochrane's career — but a batter's feet, legs, midsection, and even head were definitely considered fair game whenever batters appeared too cozy in the box. Only decades later, when anything close to the hitter would result in a possible ejection did the brushback become extinct, allowing hitters to dive fearlessly into what had previously been enemy territory, attacking pitches with confidence.

As a 19-year-old insurance clerk named Babe Didrikson was making a name for herself by winning the national amateur track and field championship (she would go on to greater glory on the golf course), baseball's Babe was having difficulty keeping pace with his rival. His 26th clout off Clint Brown on July 14 was countered by Foxx's 36th two days later, and the gap became a dozen when Jimmie connected twice against Detroit on July 17.

Although a strong wind in Philly worked in Ruth's favor the next day, as it held what appeared to be a sure Foxx homerun ball in the ballpark, Babe's hopes for defending his homer title (he had led in 1931 with 46) were dampened at Yankee Stadium when he fell while attempting to make a catch of a short fly ball in the seventh frame. Yankee trainer Earl Painter described the injury as a torn muscle in the right leg and predicted that Ruth would miss a month, but Babe returned as a pinch hitter a few days later and returned to the lineup on July 28 to belt a pair of homers in Cleveland, one of a record 72 times he would sock two in one game.

By July 28, when Ruth returned, Foxx had increased his season's total to 41. Number 39 had come in the second of two games on July 19 and despite it being Foxx's only inside-the-parker of the season, it was no less worthy a four bagger, the "savage drive" caroming off the top of the Shibe center-field wall. Foxx hit the forty mark for the first time in his career with a wallop in Washington on July 23, and nearly had another that day when his double missed "by inches" making the center-field bleachers. With Ruth watching from the bench on July 24, Foxx was held hitless by Gomez, who bested Grove in New York. In Philly the next day, Jimmie again drew the collar (along with four walks) as reliever Gomez suffered his first loss in seven decisions against the A's when, after a gimpy Ruth's pinch-single brought the tying and go-ahead runs home in the eighth, Haas won it in the ninth with a homer. After the game, Ruth's doctor was insisting to skeptical sportswriters that his patient was "good for another ten years," while offering a somewhat radical medical theory that "there is no such thing as bad legs."

Jimmie's 41st homer came in the first of two games played in Detroit on July 27. It would be his last of the month because he was held homerless in the following five games, including the Municipal Stadium opener of July 31. Hoping to be the first to properly inaugurate Cleveland's spacious ballpark, Foxx came close with a double, while teammate Cochrane's fifth-inning drive to right hooked foul by a few feet. No balls left the park that day, but Grove succeeded where others failed by becoming the first hurler to throw a shutout at Municipal. Cochrane's eighth-inning RBI single off Mel Harder decided the 1–0 affair in front of a major-league-record 81,000 spectators.

Foxx's dozen dingers in July gave him three straight months with 12 or more. When he connected for number 42 off Carl Fischer in St. Louis on August 5, Foxx was 23 days and games ahead of Ruth's 1927 pace. A feature article appeared in the *Philadelphia Inquirer* a few days later with the optimistic title, "Foxx Has Excellent Chance for Record." Even the record-chaser was feeling confident, saying, "I don't want to make any predictions, but I think I am equal to smashing 19 homers during the remaining days, providing I am not hurt."

Foxx's assessment displayed a disregard for superstition, and those more inclined to carry rabbits' feet and four-leaf clovers would claim that Jimmie jinxed himself that day. Later in the month while climbing a ladder to hang a curtain (perhaps he had walked under it first), Foxx fell, spraining his wrist and thumb. The injury wouldn't prevent his inclusion in the lineup but did affect his batting for a period of time that was extended several more days when a hard slide aggravated the sprain.

Other factors would hinder Jimmie's homer production in August. In the first week, strong winds worked to his disadvantage and reportedly robbed him of several homers in Detroit and Cleveland. His wife, Helen, became ill and by early August required hospitalization; her illness undoubtedly affected his on-the-job concentration. Foxx had a tooth pulled an hour before the start of a doubleheader in Boston on the thirteenth, which perhaps partly explains his failure that day to take advantage of Boston's hittable hurlers and reachable wall in left.

Jimmie's homer slump of August may have simply been a matter of the odds catching up with him. Still, he would hit another ten in the short baseball month of September (the season ended on the twenty-fifth). If one discounts August, when his 7 homers in 27 games equated to one every 3.86 games, Foxx's homer rate for 1932 was one every 2.49. It is not outrageous to conclude that had injuries, personal problems, and plain hard luck not interfered, Foxx would have again reached double figures in a month that was crucial to his chances for catching Ruth. Instead, the optimism of early August was replaced with a more realistic, even pessimistic, outlook by the thirty-first. A solar eclipse cast a shadow at Shibe for close to an hour that afternoon, helping to symbolize Foxx's gloomy hopes in the final month — his 49 homers necessitated his hitting a dozen in the last 22 games to eclipse the Babe.

Nevertheless, how many today would consider seven circuits in a month a slump, especially when they were accompanied by 19 RBIs and a .340 average for the same period? But those stats, too, were also inferior compared with Foxx's work the other months. His RBI rate for August was 0.70 per game compared with his pre- and post-August rate of 1.18. Excluding August, Foxx batted .369, nearly thirty points higher than his August mark. Since Foxx finished the year at .364, his August work decreased his average by five points and, along with his two-week September slump, was the key to his losing the crown.

At any rate, Foxx's deceleration was barely perceptible, and it was mostly through his stickwork that the team was able to improve from 61–43 at the beginning of the month to 80–51 by September 1 in going 19–8. Even his homers, though less frequent that month, usually were significant, with three of the seven providing the margin of victory. Just how vital was Jimmie's power to his team's success throughout the season is best shown by the club's 1932 record of 36–16 (.692) in games in which he hit at least one homer, compared with its 58–44 mark (.567) in games in which he was held homerless.

If August was Foxx's valley in terms of homer production in 1932, the pitching for the A's peaked that month. Walberg ran a winning streak to seven before finally losing late in the month. Freitas was even more superb, stretching a winning string to ten in going 4–0 in August with one shutout. Grove's first decision was a loss, but he won his next six that month, one of which was a whitewash.

Unfortunately, the success for the A's in August was countered by the Yankees being equally dominant. In fact, the A's actually lost ground and trailed by 11½ on September 1 after being behind by 8½ a month before. As always, Babe had had much to do with New York's winning, when given the chance. On the first of August, he was walked four times by Tiger hurlers, and he left the game early the next day after being hit with a pitch. By August 7, Ruth had his 31st homer, and he would connect another eight times before the month's end, when he trailed Foxx by ten.

With their team lagging behind the Yanks, A's fans began looking for scapegoats. Some found Simmons, whose two hits in his first 24 trips in

August even had Mack pointing an accusing finger. He pulled the sluggish slugger in the middle of an August 5 loss to the Browns for "acting so languidly at the plate. Simmons is not a good showman and when he is in a slump he suggests to the spectators that he is not trying. His failure to run out grounders puts him in a bad light." Even the press, which was more restrained then in criticizing ballplayers, began to agitate following a zero-for-nine performance which resulted in Al's leaving nine runners stranded in a doubleheader split in Chicago on the seventh. Reporters used such offending expressions as "old man of the sea," "delinquency," "fading star," and "severe handicap" to describe him.

In a mid–August game, Al appeared to be awakening after going five-for-five in the opener of a twin bill against Cleveland, but he was hitless in four trips in the nightcap, had one safety in five tries the next day, and was collared in six trips the next. Even a 9-for-14 spurt in the final three days which raised his August average to .315 and an RBI total of 26, an average of one a game, couldn't offset an August in which he hit but one homer. Mack was beginning to believe that the 30-year-old outfielder might be worth more on the marketplace than he was to a club destined to lose to the Yankees for years to come.

Both Foxx and Philly kept their seemingly hopeless quests alive in a doubleheader against Boston on September 2. The A's swept, and Foxx rifled his 49th homer into Shibe's left-field upper deck; one of nine homers that day, including a pair by Simmons and McNair. Foxx reached the fifty plateau the next day for the first of two times in his career. He gave his club an early two-run lead with a second-inning homer off Boston's Gordon Rhodes, but Grove yielded a run in the fourth, two more in the fifth, and appeared a loser as the A's took their last licks.

Rhodes was in his fourth major-league season, his first with the Red Sox. The six-foot righty had barely been used by the Yankees and had appeared in only 40 games in three-and-a-half years before he was traded to the Red Sox in May. The switch from pennant to basement contender robbed Rhodes of World Series shares for several seasons to come but also afforded him a spot on a starting staff, an opportunity with which "Dusty" accomplished little. From 1933 to 1935, he attained a 26–37 record and ERA near five. The Sox, whose fortunes were on the upswing by 1935, traded Rhodes to the A's, who by then were heading in the opposite direction. Rhodes ended his lackluster career by leading the league with 20 losses.

Only a small percentage of ballplayers are consistently outstanding, which explains the limited membership of the Hall of Fame (though some believe Cooperstown isn't sufficiently selective). Most players, however, occasionally perform brilliantly. For Rhodes, the game of September 3, when he limited the three-time defending league champions to four hits in eight innings and was besting the hurler destined to be the best of the decade, seemed to be one of those rare occasions.

Enter Jimmie Foxx as leadoff batter in the ninth. First pitch. Crack. Rhodes' lead vanishes, as does the ball, into familiar Foxx territory — Shibe's left-field upper deck. The disconsolate Dusty missed a chance at redemption when the next batter, McNair, matched Foxx with his third homer in two days. The box score indicates nothing which was unusual for any of its major contributors — Grove won, Rhodes lost, and Foxx hit a pair. As baseball history, or even a chapter on the 1932 season, Rhodes' effort that day is negligible. It should be noted, nonetheless, that this run-of-the-mill hurler pitched one hell of a game.

With 19 games remaining, Foxx's two homers off Rhodes left him with a slim but fighting chance at Ruth's 60, but he would be hard-pressed to find homers the next two weeks. Only once did he find the seats — when the Tigers' tall righty Buck Marrow served number 52 at Navin Field. With that exception, Foxx was contained from September 4 through the seventeenth. During nine homerless games, Foxx went to bat a total of 34 times and was stifled by such redoubtable starters as the Yanks' Lefty Gomez, the Tribe's Mel Harder, and the Tigers' Vic Sorrell and George Uhle. Jimmie was probably pressing during those two weeks, and that may be why he was also stopped by such ordinary pitchers as the Senators' Bud Thomas and Bill McAfee, the Indians' Clint Brown, the Browns' George Blaeholder, Lefty Stewart, and Bump Hadley, and Chicago's Ed Walsh (not to be confused with his father, Big Ed, a turn-of-the-century Hall-of-Famer who won 40 in 1908).

An injury may once again have been an inhibiting factor as well. On September 15, it was reported that in a game against Detroit five days earlier, Foxx had suffered a bruised shoulder when he collided with second baseman Max Bishop and that "it pains him to swing or throw." This statement was borne out by Foxx's 5 singles in 25 at-bats in the six games from the twelfth through the seventeenth (including an exhibition played in Grand Rapids on the thirteenth).

It would appear Foxx was pain-free on September 18 when he socked his 53d homer at Comiskey Park off Ted Lyons. The same could not be said for his homerun rival. On September 5, Ruth had walloped his 40th circuit in the first of a Labor-Day twin bill at Shibe Park. He was the starting right-fielder in the nightcap but was replaced late in the game by Sammy Byrd, who would spell the star frequently enough in his six years with the Yanks to earn the sobriquet "Babe Ruth's Legs." Babe would not return to the lineup until a September 21 game against the A's at Shibe Park.

Ruth had felt shooting pains in his side after the Labor Day twin bill, and when they persisted in Detroit the next day and were accompanied by a slight fever, he returned to New York for an examination. Dr. Edward King advised Claire Ruth, Babe's second wife (Helen had died in a fire three years earlier), that there was "something wrong with the Babe's appendix, but just how much isn't certain." Apparently not enough to require hospitalization or surgery but enough to keep him in bed for two weeks, with ice-pack treatments given so frequently that when Ruth once again took the field for a practice at Yankee Stadium, he complained of not having "thawed out yet."

As the A's took the field on September 21 knowing their opponents had already clinched the flag, Babe played with no hope of repeating as home-run champ for a then-unprecedented seventh straight time. (Babe's six straight remains the AL record, while Ralph Kiner's seven from 1946 to 1952 is the major-league mark.) Babe appeared "a little stiff" during the game and managed a bad-hop single in four at-bats, prompting some to wonder whether Ruth would be ready for the Series. Babe wasn't worried, claiming, "I'll be fine. I ought to get a few off those Cubs pitchers." Although Gehrig would be the primary force behind the four-game blitz of the Cubs, Ruth helped with a .333 average, six RBIs, and two homers, one being the alleged called-shot against Charlie Root. (Until his death in 1970, Root swore that Babe never pointed to the spot where he would hit it.)

Before season's end, Babe added a homer to his total with a smash off Boston lefty John Michaels, who was pitching in his first and only major-league season. Ruth's 41 homers came in 132 games as a starter (he was used once as a pinch hitter) and were more than any other player had hit except Foxx. His homer rate of 11.1 at-bats was only slightly inferior to Foxx's one every 10.1 at-bats. Had he been healthy all year, he would have had an additional 75–80 at-bats (based on his rate of 3.46 at-bats per game) and might have reached the 50 plateau for a fifth time. (No one else has had a season of at least 50 homers more than twice.) Considering his .341 average in 1932 (fifth-best in the league), .661 slugging (second), and 137 RBIs (fourth), it was a typically dominant year for Ruth, but also his last dominant one.

If a doffing of Ruth's cap toward his rival in the Phillies dugout was in order, it was to signify relinquishing of the homer crown, not his homer record. Foxx needed seven in the remaining five games to match the Sultan, and as Isaminger noted prior to the game of September 21, Foxx's "chances of performing this extraordinary feat are very remote." But Foxx would go out swinging. With Ruth watching in right, Foxx launched one over the left-field roof off Ruffing for his 54th. The bags were filled the next

Babe Ruth's final season was with the Braves in 1935. Here he poses with zany Boston teammate Rabbit Maranville, also in his swan-song season (National Baseball Library & Archive, Cooperstown, N.Y.).

day when he supplied Gomez with an additional anecdote by bouncing one across 20th Street and then victimized another hurler, Wilcy Moore, a few innings later with an even longer drive.

There remained a three-game set against Washington, with Foxx needing four to tie. Not easy, but neither was it impossible for the revitalized slugger. The series was meaningful for his teammates as well, with both teams fighting for a second place finish. The opener began in a steady drizzle, which by the fourth inning became heavy, causing a 48-minute suspension of play. Simmons was the first to bat when play resumed and, with Cochrane aboard, belted his 35th homer to put the A's in the lead 4–3. the Phillies prevailed 8–4 and with the win clinched second place, thus assuring the players a $1,000 per man cut of the World Series revenue.

Foxx was held to a single and double by Senators pitchers Dick Coffman and Lloyd Brown, which put him ahead of Alexander in the batting race, but no closer to Ruth's record. He swatted his 57th in the first inning the next day and came close with a pair of long fly-ball outs. In Sunday's season finale, played at the more spacious Griffith Stadium, Foxx had a pair of singles and a walk prior to his final at-bat, which was preceded by generous applause by 8,000 Senators fans. General Crowder was within two outs of a five-hit shutout, but Foxx whaled his second pitch into the left-field seats for number 58, an appropriate finish to his phenomenal season.

It was reported the next day that Foxx's three hits had "unofficially" assured him of the batting crown, since it left him with 213 hits in 583 at-bats for a .3653 mark, while Dale Alexander, who had a single and double in four trips in the Boston finale, finished with 143 hits in 392 at-bats, a .3647 average. A different story was written a few days later. Foxx was charged with an additional two at-bats, lowering his average to an even .364, whereas Alexander was credited with an additional hit, increasing his mark to .367. Thus was Foxx's unofficial Triple Crown transformed into an official close-call.

Foxx would succeed in his Triple quest the following season, but though he hit another 50 homers in 1938, he would never again seriously challenge Ruth's 60, which made his near-miss in 1932 more agonizing. Numerous factors entered into his failing in the end, some of which have already been mentioned, not the least important being minor injuries which, though not preventing his playing, inhibited his performance. Perhaps most significant is the number of times Foxx came within a yard or two of adding to his total.

Along with all nine triples, at least five of Foxx's 33 doubles in 1932 were near-homers. On June 15 his two bagger "missed by a yard" of going out. A Foxx drive on July 1 struck the top of Shibe's right-field wall, and another reached the center-field barrier on the fly the next day. He missed a homer "by inches" in Washington on July 23, and four weeks later he had a "booming double" off the left-field wall at Shibe. Based on *Philadelphia Inquirer* game summaries, only 4 of the remaining 18 doubles can be definitely ruled out as near-homers; not enough information is given to categorize the other 14.

It has been pointed out by writers and researchers that the ground-rule double, which allowed batters two bases for drives that bounced over fences or into seats and was in effect in 1932, worked to Foxx's disadvantage because the previous rule had rewarded hitters with homers. What isn't certain is how detrimental the edict was to Foxx's homer production. Some sources indicate that several of his doubles were of the ground-rule variety. Unfortunately, the *Inquirer* offers no evidence because none of the doubles are described in such a manner. It should also be remembered that Ruth wasn't helped by the ground rule in 1927, when all 60 of his homers cleared barriers on the fly.

It has also been pointed out that by 1932 a screen had been constructed atop the right-field wall of Sportsman's Park, and this extension hindered Foxx's homer output. Some of his drives would have cleared the shorter barriers which beckoned Ruth in 1927. How adversely Jimmie was affected is a matter of controversy; some offer the conservative figure of one homer lost, but others claim he lost five homers to the more containing dimensions. It would appear the conservatives have made the right call because Foxx had only two extra-base hits in 38 at-bats in St. Louis (one being a homer; the other, the previously described double of June 15), unless one or more of his nine singles caromed off the right-field wall as well.

There were numerous instances in 1932 in which Foxx's drives pushed outfielders to fences before they were caught. Scrutinization of game summaries indicates nine such occasions, and it is probable there were other long outs that went unreported. It has also been maintained by one Foxx biographer that he hit two homers in 1932 in games which were rained out, but nothing in the *Inquirer* accounts from that year offer proof of that assertion.

So close did Foxx come to matching Ruth that a comparison of their superb seasons is mandatory. Except for August, Foxx was consistently productive—13 homers in May, a dozen in June and July, another 10 in September, whereas most of Ruth's work came late, as he smashed a still-standing record 17 homers in September. The fact that both faced righty starters more frequently than they did left-handers should have given southpaw Babe a distinct advantage, yet, surprisingly, Foxx hit 45 homers off righties compared to Ruth's 41. Foxx fared better at homers than did Babe, 31 of Foxx's 58 homers coming at Shibe, while Babe hit only 28 of his 60 at Yankee Stadium, including his last eleven. Like Foxx, Ruth hit several off each AL team, socking it to his former club, Boston, 11 times, while Foxx smashed 13 off Detroit. In 1927, Ruth hit two homers in a game nine times. Foxx did it four times but also had one three-homer game.

Besides facing righties most of the time, Ruth's biggest edge over Foxx should have been his more favorable position in the lineup. Ruth hit third, while Foxx batted fifth, which might have afforded Babe a few more plate appearances in 1927 had he not missed 4 of the 155 games the Yankees played that year (one ended in a tie). In addition, Gehrig, who hit 47 homers in 1927, followed Ruth in the order, which should have provided some protection against pitchers purposely avoiding the Babe. Such formidable hitters as Cochrane and Simmons preceded Foxx in the order, and pitchers couldn't have been too intimidated by the likes of Mule Haas (six homers), Doc Cramer (3), Eric McNair (18), and Bing Miller (8), all of whom hit from the sixth slot during the course of the season. Still, the stats don't offer evidence of such an advantage. As mentioned previously, Ruth's 138 walks in 1927 led the league. Foxx's 116 were 14 fewer than Ruth's league-leading total in 1932, despite Babe's missing 21 games.

Foxx's inferior walk total is perhaps explained by a contention that pitchers actually wanted the likable A's slugger to break the Babe's mark. Some have even said that hurlers assisted by serving up fat pitches. Cramer told Richard Bak, author of *Cobb Would Have Caught It*, that in the closing days of 1932, "they laid the ball right down the middle for him. I know, because other pitchers have told me." Whether this actually happened is conjecture; pitchers have been known to tell tall tales. There is also the possibility that Cramer's recollection was faulty, considering he told the same author that Foxx "didn't hit any the last few games of the season," when in reality Foxx hit six in the final eight days.

If indeed Foxx saw some fat ones, it wasn't apparent in 1932 to *Sporting News* writer Bill Dooly, who in a September 15 column commented, "It should be brought to the readers' attention that the pitchers around the circuit have not been so kind to him *as they were to the big Bambino in 1927. In many cases, the hurlers tossed them down the slot just to see how far the Babe would drive them. But the same gentlemen have yet to throw down there to learn how far Foxx may slap it. Jimmie has had to earn every homerun that he hit this season* [italics added]." Did Babe benefit from pitcher generosity in 1927? His 138 walks that year make the concept less believable. Keep in mind, too, that local reporters (Dooly covered the A's and Phillies' season for the *Sporting News*) often showed a degree of bias which favored the club they were covering. Many modern ones still do.

Although it is obvious, one similarity between the Ruth-Foxx seasons should be pointed out. Descriptions of Ruth's long homeruns were frequent in 1927, but the same was true for Foxx's homers in 1932. In fact Isaminger described the extraordinary character of no fewer than 50 of his 58 homers. He used such flowery adjectives as "de luxe," "elephantine," "herculean," "cyclopean," "Leviathon," and "Brobdingnagian" (from

Jonathan Swift's region where giants dwarfed wandering hero Gulliver) interchangeably with more familiar adjectives such as "collosal," "mammoth," "robust," "savage," and "majestic." Based on newspaper accounts, it is difficult to judge which slugger belted 400-footers more frequently or whose tape-measure drives carried further. Foxx would have had Grove's vote, but Cramer commented that he "played with Foxx and Greenberg, but Ruth hit 'em further than both."

Cramer wasn't around the Tiger clubhouse in 1938 when Hank Greenberg became the second and last hitter to challenge Ruth's record until Maris succeeded in 1961. Like Foxx, Hammerin' Hank missed matching the Babe by two, but unlike Jimmie, he had an excellent chance of breaking the record going into the final week. A record 11 two-homer games helped him reach the 58 mark with five games remaining, but he was held homerless by the Browns' Howard Mills, who walked Hank four times. He managed a single in four tries against Bobo Newsom the next day. With the last three games in Cleveland, Greenberg was collared by Denny Galehouse, and, after a postponement, he needed two in a doubleheader at the spacious Municipal Stadium. Feller fired 18 strikeouts as Hank went hitless in the opener. In the nightcap, he came close with a 420-foot double but then was denied two more tries when the game was called because of darkness.

Greenberg's disappointment when he failed to sock sixty was probably keener than was Foxx's, but Jimmie's was compounded by his barely losing the batting title and Triple Crown as well. Disheartening, too, was the club's inability to capture its fourth consecutive flag, a failure that prompted Mack to resort to a familiar strategy of selling players at peak value. Simmons was the first superstar to be targeted; he was sent packing with Jimmy Dykes and Mule Haas to the White Sox for $100,000 three days after the end of the 1932 season. Mack retained Cochrane's services for another year before selling him to Detroit for another hundred grand. Connie held Freitas a year too long, as Tony followed his 12–5 season with two wins in 1933 and brought minimal cash in a deal with Cincinnati around Christmastime. Grove won 25 in 1932, but only 24 in 1933, so in December he was punished with banishment to Boston along with Walberg and Bishop for $125,000 and a couple of B players. Foxx remained in 1933 but played with a renewed contract that, amazingly, paid $300 less than the $16,666 of the previous year (Connie cried "depression"). Foxx happily accepted this offer because Mack's initial offer of $11,000 had been a 30 percent cut.

Although the A's had suffered from a similar Mack attack in 1914 which resulted in seven straight last place finishes, they rebounded nicely during the twenties. They would experience no such comeback after Mack's 1932 and 1933 selling frenzy. American League fans in Philly watched their team struggle for the remainder of its stay in the lovable city, finishing in the second division 19 of the 21 seasons from 1934 to 1954 and managing a fourth place showing in 1948 and again in 1952, two years after the once highly respected Mack had retired after half a century as the helmsman of the A's.

Probably Mack's most devastating deal was sending Foxx to Boston in December of 1935 for $150,000 despite his averaging 43 homers, 136 RBIs, and .345 from 1933 to 1935. Jimmie's production dropped in his six years with the Red Sox but not enough to prevent considerable sobbing on the part of A's fans from 1936 to 1941 when Double X averaged 36 homers, 129 RBIs, and .321. During his Boston stay came his second bat-

Like Jimmie Foxx, Hank Greenberg fell two short in his quest to catch the Babe (National Baseball Library & Archive, Cooperstown, N.Y.).

ting crown (1938), a fourth homer title (1939), his third RBI championship (1938), his last two of five slugging titles (1938 and 1939), and his second 50-homer season (1938, when Greenberg's 58 robbed Foxx of another Triple Crown).

Boston traded Foxx to Chicago in midseason of 1942; he had an uneventful year-and-a-half tenure with the club. In 1945 he was back in Philadelphia playing for the Phillies, where he socked his final 7 of 534 homers before retiring at the end of the season. Foxx had hoped to someday manage in the big leagues but, for reasons that are vague (perhaps his notoriety for imbibing), he was never given the chance.

As he dined with his brother on that hot summer evening in Miami in 1967, Jimmie suddenly began gasping. He lost consciousness before an ambulance arrived and rushed him to Baptist Hospital, where he was pronounced dead on arrival. Since Foxx had suffered a heart attack in 1959 and another in 1963, it was first believed that he had died from another, but an autopsy revealed the cause of death as "asphyxiation after choking on a piece of meat." With former A's teammate Walberg serving as one of the pall bearers, Foxx was buried at Miami's Flagler Memorial Cemetery beside his second wife, Dorothy, who had died of a heart attack the year before. Commenting on Foxx's death, biographer W. Harrison Daniel writes, "Jimmie's tragic death brought an end to more than twenty years of frustration and disappointment for one who felt discarded by a profession in which he excelled and to which he had devoted his life."

Foxx's postcareer life was characterized by an increase in poverty, alcohol intake, and job rejections. These problems were compounded by some snubbing on the part of hometown residents of Sudlersville, but Foxx was a keep-your-chin-up type of guy who griped little and faulted few, though he had reason to do both. Life was a struggle, yet Jimmie kept trying. He worked at numerous jobs, with a second heart attack not preventing his finding part-time work to supplement his meager social-security income. Critics enjoy pointing the accusing finger at Foxx, claiming reckless spending and drinking were the cause of his late-life turmoil. Foxx wasn't flawless, but that only makes him human.

In "Double X," poet Gene Carney writes:

> Include this gentle giant
> With Gehrig and Greenberg and Mize
> In any hot stove debate about
> Who's on First
> Forever.

As great a career as had Foxx, few remember him today. He is disregarded by a baseball elite who casually brush off the accomplishments of past athletes as being not worthy of comparison with those of "superior" modern ones. They forget that Jimmie and his contemporaries lacked today's advantages of streamlined bats, comfortable uniforms, air-conditioning, an easier schedule (few doubleheaders today), no knockdowns, smaller ballparks, lawyers, agents, and financial security which makes it possible to work only six months a year.

If Foxx and other past superstars are ignored, there is one whose fame lives on. Ruth was the first to belt homers with regularity, and his vivacious personality only enhanced his renown. Mention the name Foxx to one of today's sports-loving youngsters and you'll inspire a quizzical expression. Say the name Babe Ruth to derive a different reaction.

Foxx was one of many to play in what author Brent Kelley labels "the shadow of the Babe." Yet that shadow would have been significantly diminished had Foxx succeeded in belting 61 in 1932. The failure of such a worthy adversary only served to exalt Ruth further, as did Greenberg's later unsuccessful bid. By 1961, when the "undeserving" Maris tagged Tracy Stallard for his 61st on the last day of the season at Yankee Stadium, Ruth was revered to the point that supporters sought excuses and asterisks for his fallen record.

Rather than complaining about his failure in 1932, Jimmie might have commented, "Well, I gave it my best shot."

Jimmie Foxx's 58 Homers in 1932

No.	Date	Opponent	Opp. Pitcher (lefty/righty)	Ballpark	Score
1	4/12	Yankees	L. Gomez (L)	Shibe Pk.	12–6 (NY)
2	4/15	Yankees	R. Ruffing (R)	Shibe Pk.	9–8 (Phi)
3	4/17	Senators	F. Marberry (R)	Griffith Sta.	11–3 (Phi)
4	4/18	Senators	C. Fischer (L)	Shibe Pk.	15–7 (Was)
5	5/2	R. Sox	W. Moore (R)	Fenway Pk.	3–2 (Phi)
6	5/5	Indians	W. Ferrell (R)	Shibe Pk.	15–3 (Phi)
7	5/7	Indians	W. Hudlin (R)	Shibe Pk.	10–7 (Cle)
8	5/14	Browns	B. Hadley (R)	Shibe Pk.	3–0 (Phi)
9	5/15	Tigers	T. Bridges (R)	Navin Fld. (Tiger Sta.)	7–2 (Det)
10	5/18	Tigers	G. Uhle (R)	Shibe Pk.	8–2 (Phi)
11	5/19	R. Sox	B. Kline (R)	Shibe Pk.	4–2 (Phi)
12	5/21	R. Sox	D. MacFayden (R)	Shibe Pk.	18–6 (Phi)
13	5/21	R. Sox	H. Lisenbee (R)	Shibe Pk.	6–3 (Phi)
14	5/22	Yankees	H. Johnson (R)	Yankee Sta.	4–2 (Phi)
15	5/26	R. Sox	E. Durham (R)	Fenway Pk.	7–1 (Phi)
16	5/29	R. Sox	B. Weiland (L)	Braves Fld.	6–4 (Phi)
17	5/30	Senators	G. Crowder (R)	Shibe Pk.	8–6 (Phi)
18	6/1	Yankees	G. Pipgras (R)	Shibe Pk.	7–6 (Phi)
19	6/3	Yankees	L. Gomez (L)	Shibe Pk.	20–13 (NY)
20	6/4	Yankees	J. Allen (R)	Shibe Pk.	10–7 (Phi)
21	6/5	Senators	F. Marberry (R)	Griffith Sta.	11–7 (Phi)
22	6/12	Tigers	E. Whitehill (L)	Navin Fld.	8–6 (Det)
23	6/13	Tigers	T. Bridges (R)	Navin Fld.	8–1 (Phi)
24	6/14	Tigers	V. Sorrell (R)	Navin Fld.	10–5 (Phi)
25	6/14	Tigers	R. Sewell (R)	Navin Fld.	10–5 (Phi)
26	6/19	Browns	L. Stewart (L)	Sportsman's Pk.	6–3 (Phi)
27	6/20	W. Sox	P. Caraway (L)	Comiskey Pk.	18–11 (Phi)
28	6/22	W. Sox	V. Frasier (R)	Comiskey Pk.	9–4 (Chi)
29	6/25	Yankees	L. Gomez (L)	Yankee Sta.	7–4 (NY)

30	7/8	W. Sox	S. Jones (R)	Shibe Pk.	6–4 (Phi)
31	7/10	Indians	C. Brown (R)	League Pk.	18–17 (Phi)
32	7/10	Indians	W. Ferrell (R)	League Pk.	18–17 (Phi)
33	7/10	Indians	W. Ferrell (R)	League Pk.	18–17 (Phi)
34	7/11	Indians	M. Harder (R)	Shibe Pk.	12–7 (Cle)
35	7/14	Tigers	T. Bridges (R)	Shibe Pk.	9–2 (Phi)
36	7/16	Tigers	I. Goldstein (R)	Shibe Pk.	14–3 (Phi)
37	7/17	Tigers	W. Wyatt (R)	Navin Fld.	6–3 (Phi)
38	7/17	Tigers	W. Wyatt (R)	Navin Fld.	6–3 (Phi)
39	7/19	Browns	W. Hebert (L)	Shibe Pk.	16–6 (Phi)
40	7/23	Senators	D. Coffman (R)	Griffith Sta.	6–5 (Was)
41	7/27	Tigers	E. Whitehill (L)	Navin Fld.	13–8 (Phi)
42	8/5	Browns	C. Fischer (L)	Sportsman's Pk.	9–8 (StL)
43	8/14	R. Sox	G. Rhodes (R)	Fenway Pk.	6–1 (Phi)
44	8/20	W. Sox	S. Jones (R)	Shibe Pk.	6–4 (Chi)
45	8/24	Browns	L. Stewart (L)	Shibe Pk.	5–3 (StL)
46	8/25	Browns	B. Hadley (R)	Shibe Pk.	15–5 (Phi)
47	8/26	Browns	G. Blaeholder (R)	Shibe Pk.	5–4 (Phi)
48	8/30	Tigers	W. Wyatt (R)	Shibe Pk.	6–4 (Phi)
49	9/2	R. Sox	B. Kline (R)	Shibe Pk.	15–0 (Phi)
50	9/3	R. Sox	G. Rhodes (R)	Shibe Pk.	4–3 (Phi)
51	9/3	R. Sox	G. Rhodes (R)	Shibe Pk.	4–3 (Phi)
52	9/11	Tigers	B. Marrow (R)	Navin Fld.	5–4 (Phi)
53	9/18	W. Sox	T. Lyons (R)	Comiskey Pk.	4–3 (Phi)
54	9/21	Yankees	R. Ruffing (R)	Shibe Pk.	8–4 (Phi)
55	9/22	Yankees	L. Gomez (L)	Shibe Pk.	8–7 (NY)
56	9/22	Yankees	W. Moore (R)	Shibe Pk.	8–7 (NY)
57	9/24	Senators	B. McAfee (R)	Shibe Pk.	8–7 (Was)
58	9/25	Senators	G. Crowder (R)	Griffith Sta.	2–1 (Was)

Foxx's Monthly Totals

April	May	June	July	August	September
4	13	12	12	7	10

Ballpark Breakdown of Foxx's Homers

Shibe Pk.	Navin Fld.	Griffith Sta.	Comiskey Pk.
31	9	4	3

Fenway Pk.	League Pk.	Sportsman's Pk.	Yankee Sta.
3	3	2	2

Braves Fld.	Municipal Sta.
1	0

Team Breakdown of Foxx's Homers

Tigers	R. Sox	Yankees	Browns	Senators	Indians	W. Sox
13	10	10	7	7	6	5

Pitcher Breakdown of Foxx's Homers

Gomez	4	Kline	2	Caraway	1	Lisenbee	1
Bridges	3	Marberry	2	Coffman	1	Lyons	1
Ferrell	3	Moore	2	Durham	1	MacFayden	1
Rhodes	3	Ruffing	2	Frasier	1	Marrow	1
Wyatt	3	Stewart	2	Goldstein	1	McAfee	1
Crowder	2	Whitehill	2	Harder	1	Pipgras	1
Fischer	2	Allen	1	Hebert	1	Sewell	1
Hadley	2	Blaeholder	1	Hudlin	1	Sorrell	1
Jones	2	Brown	1	Johnson	1	Uhle	1
						Weiland	1

Right-handers 45   Left-handers 13

Three

Whipped by a Wormburner

On June 22, 1947, young Joyce Mergard was watching the Cincinnati Reds battle visiting Brooklyn from her box seat near the dugout in the home half of the sixth inning when Babe Young scorched a vicious foul that caromed off the left side of her face, knocking her out of her seat. Joyce was taken to a hospital, where stitches around her eye were required.

It is possible that despite the seriousness of the injury and profuse bleeding, Mergard departed Crosley Field somewhat reluctantly, for no Dodger batter had yet reached base on a hit, a fact made more noteworthy by the Cincy hurler stopping them, Ewell Blackwell. In his previous outing, Blackwell had thrown a no-hitter against the Braves. Could the sidearming fireballer match teammate Johnny Vander Meer's incredible 1938 feat of back-to-back no-hitters, a record regarded by many experts today as the most difficult to break?

No doubt many of the 31,000 in attendance thought it a possibility, including Blackwell. Interviewed on radio following his no-hitter against Boston, the sidearmer had predicted he would throw another one in his next start. He was now within nine outs of fulfilling that prophecy against a team that would take the pennant that year and boasted a lineup containing such imposing batsmen as rookie Jackie Robinson, recently acquired Al Gionfriddo, Carl Furillo, Dixie Walker, Pee Wee Reese, and Gil Hodges.

Another factor that aided Blackwell in his quest for immortality was confidence. His record was 2–2 after the first month, but Philly skipper Ben Chapman wasn't fooled by Ewell's slow start and predicted in April, "Blackwell is going to have a fine year. He'll make those hitters moan." Moan indeed, as Blacky became the hottest pitcher in the big leagues, winning ten of his next twelve decisions, including nine straight. He had three shutouts, including the no-hitter, and was atop the NL leaderboard in strikeouts.

In contrast, the Dodgers couldn't have felt too bold hitting against the pitcher nicknamed "The Whip." Their lineup included several righties ready to "step into the bucket" or "bail out" whenever the 6' 5" lanky hurler, who to sportswriter Red Smith "looked like a fly rod with ears," unleashed bullets and benders with a terrorizing crossfire motion. The Dodgers' Walker described trying to hit against the hurler who seemed all arms and legs by saying, "He looked like a man falling out of a tree."

Blackwell's effectiveness against righties became so renowned that even as a seldom-used pitcher with the Yankees near the close of his career he could intimidate. In mid–May of 1953, White Sox skipper Paul Richards pinch-hit for longtime righty slugger Vern Stephens with the bags jammed and his team down by two, preferring southpaw-swinging pitcher Tommy Byrne, who won the game with a grand slam.

Yet even against the Dodgers' southpaw swingers, Blackwell's reputation for going after batters gave him a psychological advantage that day in 1947. "M-E-A-N," spelled Pirate Hall-of-Famer Ralph Kiner in assessing Blackwell's pitching character while waiting out a rain delay during a Mets broadcast in 1995. "He would floor you in a second. Bob Feller is the pitcher who had the best stuff that I ever saw, but Ewell Blackwell is the toughest pitcher I ever faced."

Batters found it still more unnerving that Blackwell was dangerous even without trying; his propensity for wildness is indicated by a lifetime rate of one base-on-balls every 2.35 innings and the fact that he once walked ten in a ballgame. Given these tendencies and Blackwell's unusual pitching motion, it's no wonder lefties and righties alike took tentative footholds and timid cuts, helping Ewell attain a superb career average of 5.7 strikeouts per game. At the same time, as he once acknowledged in describing his pitching strategy, he was "content to let them hit the ball. Often they couldn't." As noted in *The Biographical History of Baseball*, "Blackwell generated more dread among National League batters than any other right-hander in the late 1940s."

For a hurler who was the talk of baseball in 1947, Blackwell hadn't had a particularly impressive rookie season the year before, when he won only 9 of 22 decisions. Nevertheless, his league-leading six shutouts were just one shy of the NL record for rookies (this record was surpassed by Fernando Valenzuela's eight in 1981). Blackwell's six shutouts and his admirable ERA of 2.45 were enough to convince manager Bill McKechnie to include him in the starting rotation in 1947.

As with many that preceded him, Blackwell's rise to the big leagues had been gradual. Born in Fresno, California, in 1922, Ewell was four years old when his family moved 240 miles south to the small town of San Dimas, located about 40 miles from Los Angeles, and it was there that he later played

All arms and legs — that's how Ewell Blackwell appeared to opposing batters (National Baseball Library & Archive, Cooperstown, N.Y.).

high school and sandlot ball. Ewell's coach at Bonita High put him at first base, but when the 5' 5" sophomore suddenly transformed to a 6' 3" junior with an ability to whip the ball around the infield with exceptional velocity, he was used as a pitcher as well.

The young phenom won a scholarship to a teachers college but quit after half a year to concentrate on a semipro career. Reds scout Pat Patterson spotted Blackwell in 1941 and approached him with a contract to play for the Class C club in Ogden, Utah. Ogden being his mom's hometown made the deal more alluring, but though Ewell signed, he never pitched there. The Reds brought him up immediately in 1942, with Blacky appearing twice in relief before being sent to Syracuse of the International League. His winning 15 with a 2.02 ERA with the Triple A club virtually assured his making the Cincy roster the following season.

Uncle Sam's team interfered with that plan in December of 1942, almost precisely a year following the notorious Pearl Harbor attack. Blackwell went overseas and fought with the 71st Division of George Patton's Third Army infantry, pitched ball for the Third Army club between action, and was honorably discharged in March of 1946.

Two weeks following his army release, Blackwell was at the Cincy spring training camp at Tampa. When the team headed north at the end of the month, he was left behind to work with the Syracuse club at Plant City. The additional work required was made more difficult by the batters' disinclination to step into the box against him during batting practice. Recalled Blackwell decades later, "I guess I was so glad to be back in baseball, I bore down a little too much." A week later Blackwell joined the Reds.

Deprived of three years of major-league action, Blackwell quickly made the most of his retarded career. Merely exhibiting potential in 1946, he erupted in May of 1947 and by June 1 had already won six games. His seventh was a superb 5–0, six-hit whipping of the Phils on June 5, and he had another whitewash in the works five days later against Brooklyn until the Dodgers plated one in the ninth. The first place Giants became the runner-up team in the league following Blacky's seventh straight victory on June 14. As the Braves entered Queen City on the nineteenth, the stage was set for Blackwell's contribution to no-hit history.

It was a night game, only a slight novelty by then, with a dozen years separating it from the first one in major-league history, when Franklin Roosevelt threw the switch to light up Crosley Field on May 24, 1935. If the 18,000 fans at Crosley were accustomed to baseball under the stars, it may have seemed somewhat strange to the sizzling Cincy hurler, whose previous 1947 outings had been day games. No doubt Brave batters were considerably more uncomfortable hitting against the fireballer with the unorthodox delivery under the lights.

The Braves hadn't won a pennant since their "miracle" year of 1914, when the ballclub led by George Stallings came from the bottom of the pack in midseason to take the flag. After a second place showing in 1915 and third the following year, Boston hadn't again contended, finishing in the first division (among the top four teams) only 4 times in the 31 seasons from 1916 to 1946 and finishing as close as nine games behind only in 1933.

Yet many were taking McKechnie's former club seriously in 1947. (He had skippered Boston from 1930 to 1937.) Billy Southworth, in his second season at the helm, couldn't have been too nervous whenever sophomore starter Warren Spahn toed the slab. Next to Blackwell, the high-kicking southpaw was the league's foremost hurler; his nine wins matched Blackwell's for tops in baseball. Nor was Southworth jittery while righty Johnny Sain worked, who in his first year as a starter in 1946 won twenty games, led the league in complete games (24), was second in ERA (2.21), and was third in strikeouts (129). Except for power-hitting Bob Elliott, acquired from the Pirates during the winter, and veteran Tommy Holmes, the Braves lineup didn't appear especially formidable on paper, but it was sufficiently productive to be leading the league in hitting and to be second in runs. Strong pitching mixed with timely hitting is a potent combination and resulted in the Braves holding the top spot as they faced Blackwell in Cincinnati on June 18. With the defending champion Red Sox in the running in the American League, hopes were high in Beantown for an unprecedented all–Boston Series.

As the Braves took their pregame batting swings in a steady rain that threatened the game's commencement, Blackwell stared motionless in the corner of the Reds dugout, thinking about the early-season confrontation when he was knocked from the box. As he told *Boston Herald* reporter Arthur Sampson, "I couldn't get the ball where I wanted it that day. You have to have good control to make those sidearm pitches effective." With that in mind, he decided to use mostly fastballs, hoping the lights would make it more difficult for Braves batters to "catch up" with them. Another problem may have crossed his mind. Should the game be postponed, Spahn would be his adversary the next day, rather than the unimposing Ed Wright, the scheduled Boston starter that night.

Southworth's strategy of "Spahn and Sain, and pray for rain" might have been useful a year later, but if he appealed for help with the weather that night in Cincinnati, heaven wasn't heeding. The rain let up, but after walking Holmes to open the game, Blackwell didn't. He disposed of Johnny Hopp and then induced a double-play ball off the bat of Bama Rowell (yes, from Alabama). It wasn't until Hopp was walked in the seventh that another Brave reached safely. By then, the Reds led 3–0.

Rowell followed Hopp's walk with a drive to right that appeared destined to spoil both no-hitter and shutout. The heavy air impeded the ball's flight, however, enabling outfielder Frankie Baumholtz to race back and make a last-second leaping snare of the ball. It marked the third close call for Blackwell. Earlier, third sacker Grady Hatton had twice robbed Holmes by making nifty pickups of blistering grounders before making in-the-nick-of-time tosses.

After a shaky eighth which saw Blackwell walk a pair and the inning end with a scorching liner into Hatton's mitt, it was apparent the pressure was getting to Blackie. As "The Whip" admitted afterwards, "When that ninth inning came up and the goose eggs were still there, I began to feel a little tight." Despite the jitters, Blackwell retired the side in order in the ninth, including a swinging strikeout of Rowell to end the 6–0 contest. As 18,000 spectators screamed, some while leaping onto the field, Reds backstop Ray Lamanno raced to the mound to embrace his battery mate before being joined by ecstatic teammates and fans.

The Boston setback, which knocked the Braves into second place, was the second no-hitter against them in as many years, with Brooklyn's Ed Head hurling one in 1946. Blackie's was the first no-no of the year, though the Indians Don Black and A's Bill McCahan would each throw one before season's end. By then, Southworth and Company were forced to settle for third place, a disappointing showing considering midseason aspirations, but encouraging as well considering Boston's efforts for the past three decades. The next year the long drought would end as the Braves, behind a Herculean September by Sain and Spahn (and, as legend would have it, a cooperative weatherman), won their second and final pennant for Boston (they would move to Milwaukee in 1953), though they would lose in six to the Cleveland Indians, in the 1948 Series.

On June 15, 1938, Brooklyn offered customers baseball under the stars, one of two historical firsts that night, the other coming when Vander Meer hurled his second straight no-hitter. As with Blackwell, Johnny's first had come against the Braves four days earlier. Now, by further coincidence, Blackwell needed to no-hit Brooklyn if he hoped to match the Dutch Master's mark. That dream moved tantalizingly closer to reality after Blackwell easily retired the Dodgers in the seventh and eighth innings and disposed of leadoff batter Gene Hermanski on a fly ball in the ninth. Shouts of encouragement filled Crosley Field as Blackwell awaited his next victim, the pesky, pugnacious, unpopular Eddie Stanky.

Few players ever suited the role of spoiler better than Stanky, once described by Dodgers manager Leo Durocher as a player who "can't hit, can't run, can't field, but comes to kill you." Phil Rizzuto never forgave his infield rival of the 1951 Series for kicking the ball out of his glove on an attempted steal that led to a Dodgers victory in Game Three, but National League opponents were used to the Brat's dirty tactics by then. Stanky would bait umpires by kicking dirt on home plate, insult pitchers and catchers while batting, tamper with balls in play, and incite arguments or fights with aggravating antics on the field. These antics included waving and flapping his arms as a means of distracting hitters and making taunt-

ing comments off the field, like the time he yelled to former Brooklyn teammate Jackie Robinson in the opposing clubhouse to shove a bat up a delicate part of his anatomy. Regarded by many as the dirtiest player in baseball, Stanky continued to be irritating while he was a manager. As helmsman
for the White Sox in 1967, he once infuriated Boston star Carl Yastrzemski
by labeling him "an All-Star from the neck down" and would similarly affront
his own players, fans, and employers.

So if Blackwell was known for being mean on the mound, Stanky was
his counterpart at the plate. The righty-swinging "Mugsy" was already in
the middle of his fifth big-league season. His highest average had been an
unremarkable .273 in 1944, and his current mark of .235, tenth from the
league bottom, confirmed Durocher's assessment of his limited hitting
skills. On paper, there were few in the Brooklyn lineup Blackwell could
have preferred facing. Nevertheless, Stanky's competitive nature made him
a challenging final barrier to a no-hitter, as did his proficiency in accumulating walks. The 5' 8" Philly native had led the league in 1945 and 1946
and was again among the league leaders in 1947.

With lefty Al Gionfriddo waiting on deck, Blackwell went right at
Stanky. While teammate Vander Meer watched near the dugout steps, wanting to "be the first one out there to shake his hand," Blackwell fired a one-
strike fastball which Eddie converted into a ground-hugging comebacker
to the mound. The anxious hurler misjudged the speed of the medium-
paced grounder and lifted his glove too soon. Blackwell felt the ball brush
against his right leg and then watched helplessly as it skidded through the
infield into center field while 31,000 groaned in unison, realizing that history wouldn't be repeating itself that afternoon.

Blackwell surrendered an opposite-field hit to Jackie Robinson later that
inning, which might have made Stanky's single less meaningful had Gionfriddo not first skied to right for the second out, or what would have been
the third had Blackwell hooked the wormburner. Two hours and twelve
minutes after his first pitch, Blackwell retired Furillo to end the game.

If Stanky's safety was heartbreaking, the California crackerjack wasn't
crying following his second straight shutout and fourth of the season. Nor
was Blackwell moaning two weeks later when, as the NL starter in the All-
Star Game, he hurled three shutout frames which included strikeouts of
Ted Williams, George Kell, Lou Boudreau, and Joe Gordon. His feat was
noteworthy, if not as astounding as Carl Hubbell's consecutive whiffs of five
future Hall-of-Famers in the July classic of 1934.

It is not an exaggeration to rate Blackwell's 1947 season as one of the
greatest by any right-hander in history. His league-leading 22 wins, 23 complete games, and 193 K's, along with runner-up stats in ERA (2.47 to Spahn's

2.33) and shutouts (six to Spahn's seven) are enough to impress the severest evaluator but were merely his minor accomplishments that year. The no-hitter and near no-hitter stretched a consecutive hitless string to nineteen innings, two shy of Vander Meer's still-standing NL mark. Blacky's season also included a stretch of 16 straight victories, a feat matched or surpassed by only seven other hurlers in history. He was within two outs of number 17 on July 30 when the Giants' Willard Marshall homered to tie it in the ninth before Buddy Kerr's two-out single made Blackwell a loser the next inning.

Unfortunately, health problems caused Blackwell's pitching to degenerate. A shoulder injury resulting from pitching a complete-game exhibition on a cold, rainy day in the spring of 1948 would plague him the rest of his career, and a kidney operation in 1949 resulted in a combined 12 wins in 26 decisions during those years. Blackwell rebounded with 17 and 16 wins in 1950 and 1951 respectively, and though he pitched poorly in 1952 with the Reds, he won a key September start shortly after his trade to the Yankees — a shutout against the Red Sox which followed teammate Tom Gorman's blank of Boston in the opener of the twin bill. As the Game Five starter in the Series against Brooklyn that year, Blackwell left the game with a 5–4 lead after five frames but lost his chance for a win when Johnny Sain yielded a tally in the sixth before losing in the eleventh. (Johnny had only recently come to New York — August 30, 1951, to be precise.) Blackwell was sold along with Gorman to Kansas City in the spring of 1955 for $50,000 and was used twice in relief that season before retiring. He succumbed to cancer at age 74 on October 29, 1996.

With the abundant attention given to no-hitters, two remain the most memorable. Don Larsen's strikeout of pinch-hitter Dale Mitchell in Game Five of the 1956 Series ended the only no-hitter and perfect game in the history of the fall classic. And of the more than 200 no-hit hurlers in history and the 25 who have thrown two or more, only one moundsman was able to pitch a second consecutive no-hitter. Nearly sixty years later, Johnny Vander Meer is still remembered for his record performance.

In contrast, how many of today's fans are aware of Blackwell's stab at immortality in 1947? The record books duly note his no-hitter, while ignoring his nearness to another. Baseball books often laud Vander Meer's achievement while ignoring Blackwell's, Ken Burns' *Baseball* being a notable example. Yet how much greater was Vander Meer's effort than Blackwell's when all that separated the two was an inch between glove and ball?

Such is our nature — remembering those who succeed and forgetting those who merely give a good try.

Ewell Blackwell's No-Hitter and Near No-Hitter, 1949

Date	Opponent	Ballpark	Score	Hits	BB	SO
6/18	Braves	Crosley Field	6–0	0	4	3
6/22	Dodgers	Crosley Field	4–0	2	2	6

Four

Ted's Try for a Third Triple Crown

Achieving the Triple Crown in baseball may be the most elusive single-season feat for a batter. The fact that only 11 ballplayers have been able to lead their respective leagues in batting average, homers, and RBIs attests to its difficulty. Of the 11 players, 2 were able to win the Crown twice. Rogers Hornsby led the National League in the Triple categories in 1922 and repeated in 1925. Ted Williams won it in 1942 and again in 1947.

In 1949, Williams came within a fraction of a percentage point of taking an unprecedented third Triple Crown. The Splendid Splinter won the homer and RBI titles (he actually tied Vern Stephens for most ribbies) but fell short of the batting championship. The Tigers' George Kell edged him out on the last day of the season, becoming the first third baseman in American League history to win it. Had Williams hung on, his three Triples would have been, arguably, the greatest achievement in baseball history.

Williams headed into the final month of the 1949 season with a comfortable advantage over his closest pursuer, Kell, and appeared on his way to a third consecutive batting championship. A homer on the last day of August against Detroit had upped Ted's average to .356, a dozen points higher than the average held by Kell, who had managed one hit in three at-bats in the same game. Both competitors poked a hit apiece in a 7–0 whitewash by Detroit the next day. With the loss, the Red Sox fell three games behind front-running New York.

The Bombers couldn't have felt too comfortable with that advantage, however. In August, Boston had made up 5½ games on New York with a 24–8 spurt. To solidify their offense, the Yankees picked up veteran slugger Johnny Mize in a trade with the New York Giants. Mize told reporters soon afterwards how he knew it was coming. "Horace Stoneham [the

Giants' owner] only a month ago said to me, 'Johnny, just so long as I have anything to do with this ball club, you will remain with it.' My wife heard this and whispered, 'John, better start packing.'" It didn't take long for the Big Cat to make the Yanks start purring; he homered in his second game as a starter for the Bombers on August 25.

The remaining schedule in September seemed to favor the Yanks because 17 of their last 25 games were at home, while the Red Sox had only 14 games of 26 to be played in the friendly confines of Fenway Park and its short left-field wall. Nevertheless, the two rivals would be meeting head-on another seven times before the season ended. New York's superstar slugger, Joe DiMaggio, was back in the lineup after missing much of the season with foot problems but Joltin' Joe was still hurting.

The Red Sox, on the other hand, were prepared to spoil the Yanks' quest for a 16th pennant as the Cleveland Indians had done the year before. Joe McCarthy, in his second season as Boston manager after 15 years at the helm for the Yankees, could boast of two hot starters in his rotation. Mel Parnell was 20–6 going into September, and Ellis Kinder was only slightly cooler at 17–5 and had won his last seven decisions. Besides Williams, cleanup hitter Vern Stephens was punishing the ball consistently in battling Ted for the homer and RBI crowns. The Yankees, still as proud (some claimed arrogant) as always under new skipper Casey Stengel, were worried.

When Kinder won his eighth straight on September 3, he had help from teammate Ted, who banged out a single and his 37th round tripper in raising his average to .353. Afterwards, Williams noted that his outstanding offensive stats were being accumulated at the peak of pitching prowess. "During my days in the majors," said the Kid, "there never has been better all around pitching in the American League than I've looked at this year."

While Ted was homering in Boston, Kell kept pace in Detroit by poking two hits, putting him at .344. The next day Kell was collared while Ted managed a hit at Fenway as the Red Sox defeated the Philadelphia A's 4–2 and were within 1½ games of the Yanks, who lost to the lowly Senators.

The New York lead remained at 1½ when the Red Sox visited Yankee Stadium on September 7. The House That Ruth Built, which seated over 65,000, was already sold out for the three-game set before the first contest began. Fans on the East Side, West Side, and all around town were buzzing about the confrontation, wondering whether their proud team would be able to put away their closest pursuer once and for all. Nightclubs posted banners reading, "Beat the Red Sox." People everywhere were scurrying about looking for extra tickets. As *Boston Herald* sportswriter Arthur Sampson put it, "It isn't often that Pa and Ma Knickerbocker go slap-happy over an ordinary baseball game. But even staid, sophisticated Manhattanites could be heard mumbling in their beards tonight when the Red Sox arrived."

The Yankees opened the series with their hard-throwing righthander Allie Reynolds, who boasted a 14–4 record. The Big Chief had early control problems, however, and walked the first three batters to face him, Williams being the third. Reynolds blew three quick ones past Vern Stephens, who had a golden opportunity to increase his RBI lead over Williams. Bobby Doerr made Allie pay for his wildness by drilling a single to score the first two runs of the game.

If the Red Sox felt confident after picking up the early runs, the work of their moundsman must have added to their hopes for winning the series' opener. Jack Kramer, who had an unimpressive 4–7 mark prior to the game, pitched effectively for the first six frames, yielding only one unearned run in the fourth. Unfortunately, the Beantown bats fell asleep after Doerr's drive, and Kramer buckled in the seventh in his attempt to cling to the 2–1 lead.

As with Reynolds, Kramer's sole trouble of the game began with his own wildness. Facing Charlie Keller, Jack ran the count even at 2–2. He then tried to fool Keller with a curve, as he had done in fanning him the previous at bat, but the ball just missed. On the next 3–2 delivery, Kramer again tried a curve. King Kong Keller either had nerves of steel in laying off the pitch or was so completely fooled that he froze. Fortunately for Keller and the Yanks, umpire Art Passarella refrained from raising his right arm, granting Charlie a base-on-balls instead. Catcher Birdie Tebbetts and Kramer became visibly upset. Kramer's disgust at not being awarded a strike call on at least one of the two tosses may have led to his losing concentration on the next hitter.

The Red Sox hurler faced Bill Johnson, clearly not the Bombers' biggest threat in the lineup. Yet Kramer again ran the count full, prompting Casey Stengel to employ some strategy. The Old Professor substituted baserunner Keller for fleeter-of-foot George Stirnweiss. As was often the case throughout Casey's career with the Yanks, it was a perfectly timed move.

Johnson drilled the next pitch down the left-field line, and the ball headed for the stands. Williams, adept at playing balls off the towering wall at Fenway, at times had problems judging balls in visiting ballparks. He made the decision to try to catch the ball, just missing the one-handed attempt. The ball struck the fence and bounced away from Ted toward center field. By the time the ball was retrieved and thrown to the infield, Stirnweiss had touched home plate.

More problems followed. Shortstop Stephens tried to catch Johnson, who was stretching his hit to a triple, and the toss hit the runner, deflecting into the dugout. Amid wild screaming throughout the stadium, Johnson shook the dust from his uniform and waltzed home with the go-ahead run.

Although the Bombers added two more runs in the eighth, the game was decided the inning before. Wildness by its pitcher, a controversial call by the ump, a misjudged fly ball, and an errant throw had sealed Boston's fate. Reynolds won his 15th game, while the Sox, facing the prospect of falling 3½ behind the next day with only 18 games remaining thereafter, looked like losers — also-rans for yet another season.

But after rain washed out the second game, the Sox bounced back on September 9, led by their red-hot hurler Kinder. Ellis diffused the Bombers on four hits and a single run, while the Red Sox attack returned, punishing Yank starter Eddie Lopat. Williams stroked a pair of hits and RBIs, accounting for two of Boston's seven runs. The 36-year-old Kinder maintained his unbeaten record for the past two months in winning his 9th straight and 19th of the season. Hopes in Beantown remained alive.

With his three-for-seven performance in New York, Williams' average stood at .354, still comfortably ahead of Kell's .337. Ted drilled two hits when the Red Sox defeated the A's in Philadelphia on September 10, maintaining his average, while Kell kept pace with a pair in Chicago. The win by Boston had brought the club to within one of New York, but the A's crushed the Sox in a doubleheader the next day, winning 6–4 and 4–0. The twin killing, coupled with the Yanks' doubleheader sweep against the Senators, must have brought a complete turnabout of emotions within 24 hours among baseball fans in Boston, who saw their team so close one day, so far away the next.

Williams managed only a scratch single in seven at-bats in the doubledip, lowering his average three points while Kell was maintaining his .339 mark with one hit in three tries. When the third place Tigers entered Fenway on the thirteenth, Williams and Kell had a chance to duel head to head. The Tiger third baseman bested the Splendid Splinter in the first game, singling twice in four chances, while Ted went one-for-five. What would become more significant to the batting race was Kell's suffering a broken thumb late in the game, resulting in his missing the next seven contests.

With Kell out of the lineup, the pitching task was that much easier for Ellis Kinder the next day in his try for ten in a row. Wet weather held the attendance to only 13,000, but by game's end, few of those who showed up were second-guessing their decision to attend, despite having to wait out a half-hour rain delay. As Arthur Sampson wrote the next day: "This one had all the elements of the blistering contests played during the deadball era. The game was studded with seven double plays. It produced several fielding gems, at least three of them saving runs. And it contributed a brand of pitching which made you wonder why it's necessary to sit through some of those three-hour donnybrooks which wear out everybody at the park except the concessionaires." It's a safe guess Sampson wouldn't have enjoyed today's brand of ball, where a game rarely finishes under three hours.

The Bengals' Hal Newhouser matched blanks with Kinder until the Red Sox half of the sixth. Williams stepped to the plate for his third crack at Newhouser, having been retired twice before. Teddy Ballgame added credence to the nickname, going with a fastball away and sending it sailing over the left-field wall. It was his 38th four sacker, matching his career-high of 1946, and according to Sampson, it was his sixth opposite-field blast that year, an unusually high total for a hitter so notorious for pulling the ball that an infield shift had been invented, a strategy still used by modern managers seeking to discourage power-hitting pull-hitters.

For Kinder, the one run was all he would need and would get. Newhouser sewed up the Sox the rest of the way, finishing with a four-hitter in taking a tough 1–0 loss. Kinder had his 20th victory, tenth in a row, and his third whitewash of the season against the Bengals.

The victory kept Boston within three of the Yanks. The Bombers then took equal advantage of Kell's absence in the Tigers lineup, beating them in the next two games, while the Red Sox were grabbing two from the seventh place St. Louis Browns. Williams went one for six in the series, with teammate Stephens getting two homers and three ribbies as he vaulted over Ted to the top of the league in both categories.

Stephen's lead didn't last long. The White Sox entered Fenway on September 18, and didn't fare any better in the lion's den. The Boston batters feasted on Chicago hurlers in stroking a dozen hits, leading to eleven runs. Stephens accounted for one of them with his 150th ribby, but most of the muscle provided for pitcher Kinder came off Williams's bat. The Thin Thunderbolt (another nickname given Ted, who may have had more than any other player save Babe Ruth) went ahead on the count in his first at-bat against starter Randy Gumpert. Gumpert, like many other pitchers, was wary of throwing fastballs to Williams, even when behind in the count. His attempt to fool Ted with a changeup didn't work. The ball landed ten rows deep into the right-field grandstands. Not to be outdone, Stephens followed his rival's circuit with one of his own.

Ted's next try came in the next inning. With the bags jammed and the infield daring him to pull the ball, he poked a single through the vacated left side for 2 more RBIs. His 4 in the game raised his total to 151, one more than Stephens, but Williams wasn't finished.

In the fourth, Ted came to bat for the third time. On a 2–1 pitch, he lined a screamer that struck the rightfield screen. His 40th homer gave Ted the league-lead once again and scored Johnny Pesky ahead of him, giving Williams 6 ribbies in the game and 153 for the season. The next inning, Stephens came to the plate with the bases loaded but failed to drive a run home. When at season's end Vern had to settle for a share of the RBI crown with Williams, he may have remembered that slugfest at Fenway when he failed to cash in on another ribby opportunity.

Williams was batting .351 following the game against Chicago, still a safe ten points ahead of Kell, whose average remained unchanged because of his injury. Williams lost a point the next day, going 0–2 and walking once against the Tribe's Bob Lemon. Lemon, in fact, had been frustrating the entire Boston lineup, blanking them on no hits through the first five innings. With his team ahead 1–0, Lemon took the mound in the sixth, but before he could throw another pitch, McCarthy came out of the dugout and approached home plate umpire Cal Hubbard. "All I did was ask the umpire to look at the cap," said Mac in explaining his actions later.

Look at the cap Hubbard did and he was sufficiently suspicious to demand that the Indians hurler replace it with another. Lemon reluctantly agreed, at which point his pitching became suddenly quite agreeable to Red Sox batters, who battered him for five runs in the inning en route to a 5–2 victory, delighting the 22,000 fans at Fenway. The Cleveland loss eliminated the defending world champions from the pennant picture.

The next day Lemon had the last laugh, striding in from the bullpen before the start of the game wearing a felt hat. His comedy wasn't enough, however, to help his team overcome the streaking Sox. Trailing 4–1 in the fifth, Boston went to work on Cleveland's Mike Garcia. With one out, they loaded the bases on two hits and a walk. When Garcia went to 3–0 on Pesky, Tribe skipper Lou Boudreau pulled out all the stops and called on his staff ace, Bob Feller, to quench the rally. His first pitch was ball four, making the score 4–2. With the bases still full, Williams connected on a Feller fastball but hit it to the wrong part of the park. The ball was caught in front of the fence in deep right-center. The fly ball scored the Sox's third run and, more importantly, advanced the other runners one base. When Stephens followed with a hit, the lead was Boston's.

The game was deadlocked at six apiece when Williams batted in the seventh. Ted proved he could deliver under pressure. (After the game he shouted, "Can't hit in the clutch!" at *Herald* sportswriter Bill Cunningham, who had earlier in the year criticized him for not hitting when it counted.) Ted rocketed his 41st round tripper into the rightfield bullpen, putting the Red Sox in the lead for good. With the Yankees having blown an 8–1 lead in New York, Boston trailed the pinstripers by only two games.

If there was one day in 1949 which could be considered most significant to America, it may have been September 23. On that day Americans became alarmed at a pronouncement by President Truman that the Russians had ended the U.S. atomic bomb monopoly. This announcement precipitated a nuclear arms race that would last four decades. In baseball, George Kell returned to the Tiger lineup, precipitating a batting race between him and Williams which would not be decided until each of their last at-bats of the season. And the Red Sox prepared to do battle with the Yanks in three games — two in Boston and the third at Yankee Stadium — hoping to sweep the Bombers out of their first place position. As it turned out, the pennant race would not be decided until the last day of the season, when the two ballclubs met for the final time.

A crowd of nearly 35,000 withstood the chilly autumn winds at Fenway on September 24. With his victory string now at a dozen and his season total at 22, Ellis Kinder was McCarthy's preferred choice as the opening pitcher and it was his turn in the rotation anyway. If the Yanks thought the righthander would fold under the pressure, Kinder proved otherwise. He mastered the mighty Yanks, limiting them to no runs and a mere six hits, collaring such stars as Tommy Henrich, Yogi Berra, and Hank Bauer. New York, unquestionably handicapped by the absence from the lineup of their reinjured star Joe DiMaggio, played uninspired baseball for a game with so much meaning, displaying little of the confident superiority for which they were known. The Red Sox, on the other hand, gave an all-around effort. The offense complemented Kinder's effectiveness, banging out twelve hits, with Stephens the only batter not to get one. Williams had the big blow of the game with his 42d four bagger, a 425-foot blast.

Willliams socked another the next day, helping Mel Parnell win his 25th. While the Yankee lineup *sans* DiMaggio was only one run more productive than the day before, Ted supplied two of the four Boston runs with his homer. The blast came in the seventh and broke up the pitching duel between Parnell and Allie Reynolds. With the victory, Boston and New York were tied for the lead. The Sox could take the top spot for the first time by beating the Bombers the next day, but they would have to do it at Yankee Stadium.

In the locker room after the game at Fenway, the Red Sox players were sounding confident. Said Parnell, "This was the game that we just had to win." After reading a letter from a friend, he then complained, "Now, I suppose he'll be after me for World Series tickets." Dom DiMaggio echoed, "Well, I guess this means the World Series." Williams didn't offer much to reporters, other than to acknowledge that his homer came off a fastball and to bark at a photographer, "Just one shot."

If Ted read Bill Cunningham's column the next day, his wrath towards reporters may have been appeased. Wrote the *Herald* columnist: "I said Mr. Williams didn't hit in the clutch. The implication was plain that he wouldn't or couldn't, come through under fire, and that he probably wouldn't in the future. Mr. Williams has now driven that right back down my throat."

In an article in *Sporting News* on September 21, Steve O'Leary agreed that it was unfair to classify Williams as a poor clutch hitter. "Your great hitter is a great hitter regardless of the fact that now and then he may miss out," claimed O'Leary. "Williams has failed in that respect just as the Hornsbys, the Ruths, the Gehrigs, and Speakers, and any other great hitter you want to mention have missed the boat." As proof, O'Leary pointed to Williams' average of .400 in the 17 games played against the Yankees, adding, "Is that choking?"

Over 60,000 fans packed Yankee Stadium to watch the two best clubs in the league battle for first place. The Red (hot) Sox, having won ten straight ballgames, jumped to an early lead with three in the opening inning, but the proud pinstripers fought back with four in the fourth. Stengel, realizing the psychological as well as positional importance of winning the game, called on relief specialist Joe Page to put out a rally by Boston in the fifth. Page was successful and unhittable for the next two frames, while the Yanks padded their lead with single runs in the sixth and seventh.

But Stengel's strategy in using Page early backfired in the eighth. By then, the fatigued fireman's fastballs weren't as blurry to Bosox batters' eyes, and he was ambushed for three runs to tie the game. With runners on the corners and only one gone, Boston was primed to regain the lead.

Bobby Doerr was the next Sox hitter, but he became a bunter instead. When first baseman Henrich rushed in and fired to the plate, it appeared the suicide squeeze had failed. What failed was Yank catcher Ralph Houk's attempt to block the plate, and Pesky's leg snuck under the backstop's tag. The "safe" call by home-plate ump Bill Grieve touched off an explosive protest by Houk, Stengel, and several Yankees, who rushed onto the field to attack Grieve verbally. At one point, outfielder Cliff Mapes allegedly yelled to the beleaguered arbitrator, "How much did you bet on the game?" Grieve, however, adamantly denied having made a bad decision, saying afterwards: "I called it right. Houk did not have the plate blocked and Pesky was safe, without a question."

The Bombers were retired in the last of the eighth but still had their last licks in the ninth. McCarthy also wanted this one badly, and he called on Kinder to finish off New York. Bobby Brown was retired, bringing Henrich to the dish. Old Reliable then whistled a liner that appeared destined for the seats in right, but Boston's Al Zarilla timed his leap perfectly and robbed Tommy of the game-tying blast. One out later the Red Sox were leaving the field atop the standings for the first time that year. For once, it was the Yankees who looked like losers. When Joe McCarthy had said "we can still win the pennant" on July 4, with his team a sizable distance from the lead, it had seemed like wishful thinking, but few were doubting the Irishman's prediction after his club's sweep of the Yanks.

There were many heroes in the game. Besides his game-saving catch in the ninth, Zarilla had robbed Johnny Lindell of a three-run homer in the second with a similar circus catch. Stephens' three ribbies boosted his total to 155, three fewer than Williams'. Ted had one hit in three at-bats, but it was a timely one that extended the crucial eighth-inning rally. His average stood at .348, six points better than Kell's.

Williams and Stephens had an RBI apiece the next day when the Red Sox dismissed the last place Senators in Washington. The Boston streak was snapped at eleven on September 29, as the Nats rallied for a pair of runs in the ninth, the winning score coming on a wild pitch by reliever Parnell. With a Yankee victory over the A's in the Bronx, the pennant picture was again a deadlock.

Williams was collared in the loss to the Senators, and his average sunk to .346. He was stopped again on the last day of the month, though two of his five trips to the plate resulted in walks. Kell also faltered and trailed the Kid .340 to .344 going into the season's final two games.

For Williams, the last games were crucial for more important reasons. Having beaten the Senators in the finale of the three-game set in Washington while the Yankees were losing to the fifth place A's at home, the Sox had regained the league lead. One more victory by Boston would ignite a pennant celebration in Beantown for only the second time in over 30 years. The schedule maker couldn't have arranged a more perfect climax to the season if he had been psychic. The Red Sox would have to beat the Bombers in their own backyard to take the flag. And as Cunningham warned in his column written from New York on October 1, "The Red Sox better come in here prepared to shoot their all. From what the local scribes tell me, the Yanks are really sore."

As if enough drama had not already been staged, there was yet another reason for fans to flock to the Bronx. It was Joe DiMaggio Day at Yankee Stadium, and the crowd totaling nearly 70,000 watched as their hero accepted expensive gifts and then hobbled toward center field as a last-minute starter. With the season in the balance, Joltin' Joe had forced Stengel to pencil his name in the lineup. If the Yanks were going down, it wouldn't happen without their leader's efforts to prevent it.

The Sox pounced on Yank starter Reynolds to take a 1–0 lead in the first, with Williams' single setting up the tally. It would be his last hit of the game, and of the season. When Boston rallied for three more runs in the third, the outlook was bleak for even the most optimistic Yankee rooter. But the Bombers edged closer with two runs in the fourth off Parnell and tied the score with another pair in the fifth. The game then became a pitching duel between Joe Page and Red Sox reliever Joe Dobson; it ended with a game-winning, ninth-inning homer by Johnny Lindell that gave the Yanks the win.

In the Yankee locker room, DiMaggio, who stroked two key hits in the game, admitted having played in pain. "I was just playing from inning to inning," Joe said. "I'm darned glad it didn't go more than nine innings because for the last few outs my shin bones were getting cramped." Stengel chimed in, "That DiMaggio is a wonder. How about him playing the whole game?"

In contrast to the boisterous, exuberant bunch across the hall, Red Sox players were predictably subdued in their clubhouse, realizing they had blown one chance and that the pennant hung in the balance in the next game. The quiet was broken when Williams asked, "Who's pitching for them tomorrow?" The remark indicated the worried mood of the team.

Although he probably wasn't thinking about it, Ted had other reasons to worry. His one-for-three performance had kept his average at .344, while Kell, in going one-for-two against the Indians' Mike Garcia, had moved a point closer at .341. The batting championship was still within reach of the Tiger third baseman, despite the incorrect announcement in the *Sporting News* on October 5 that Williams "led both leagues in hitting, winning his fifth batting title." Although Williams had a comfortable cushion in homers, his margin over Stephens in RBIs had been erased when Vern drove home a run with a sac fly in the Boston first. The rival teammates would have to settle the issue of the ribby crown the next day.

In *Summer of '49*, author David Halberstam writes, "Certain games are classics, seized on by baseball aficionados and remembered long after they are over. Such was the [Vic] Raschi-Kinder finale." Before that final game began on October 2, American League president Will Harridge announced it would have to be finished in the daylight, saying he wouldn't overlook the league rule of barring night play on Sundays simply because of the game's importance. Whether or not this was additional motivation for the Bombers to take the lead early, that's exactly what happened. Williams' difficulty in fielding a Phil Rizzuto liner in the first inning turned a double into a triple. The Scooter scored on a Henrich groundout for a 1–0 advantage.

Starter Kinder didn't allow the quick score to interfere with his concentration. For the next six innings, he yielded no more runs and only two hits. Unfortunately, the Boston batters were feeling the pressure and were doing nothing against the speedy deliveries from Raschi. When Kinder took his turn at bat in the eighth, McCarthy, his team still trailing 1–0, had no choice but to pinch-hit for his stalwart starter. Mel Parnell replaced Kinder in the bottom of the inning, and the Yanks scored four runs, highlighted by a Henrich homer, that negated a three-run rally by the Sox in the ninth. Kinder lost as a starter for the first time since June 9. That this loss came in the most crucial game for his team that year was unfortunate.

It was not unfortunate for the Yanks, who won their 16th pennant. "I want to thank all these ball players for giving me this," said an elated Stengel after the game. "This is the greatest thing in my life." Rumors had it that the rookie skipper would be quitting after the World Series, but Casey went on to become the most successful manager in baseball history, winning ten pennants and seven world championships, including an unmatched five consecutive ones from 1949 to 1953.

The normally regal Yankees were a particularly joyous and excited bunch after winning again. Announced DiMaggio, who had taken himself out of the game in the ninth for a defensive replacement, "I've been on a lot of winners before, but honestly, this one is the greatest thrill of my baseball career." Rizzuto, shrugging off announcer Mel Allen's suggestion that he be named MVP of the American League, stated: "No single player should get it. They should give it to the whole team."

For the Red Sox, and McCarthy, it was a case of coming close but failing for the second year in a row. When reporters asked McCarthy if he would return as manager the next year, Joe snapped, "If you want me back, print it." Mac did return but was replaced by Stephen O'Neill before the 1950 season ended.

Williams had gone oh-for-two in the game, and though he had taken the homerun championship with 43 and tied Stephens for the RBI crown with 159, his cherished batting title was being challenged in Detroit. George Kell faced a difficult mound opponent in Bob Lemon, but in his first at-bat, he lined a double to center. Kell singled to left in the third and then worked a base-on-balls in the sixth. He was retired on a fly ball by another Indians hurler in the seventh — the formidable Feller. With his two for three, Kell's average stood at .3429. The game having already ended in New York, Williams's mark was a shade less at .3428. Kell had replaced Williams as batting leader for the first time that year.

There was still the chance that Kell would be retired in the ninth because his club was trailing and would have to take their last turns at bat.

Ted Williams lost more than the batting title on the last day of the 1949 season (National Baseball Library & Archive, Cooperstown, N.Y.).

The Tiger third baseman was due to hit fourth, and if he made an out, his average would fall below Williams'. Feller retired the first Detroit hitter but yielded a single to pinch-hitter Dick Wakefield. Those at Briggs Stadium may have then wondered whether manager Red Rolfe would let Kell put his lead in jeopardy by allowing him to hit in his next turn. According to a *Sporting News* article from October 19, rookie Joe Ginsberg grabbed a bat and waited at the top of the Detroit dugout steps while Eddie Lake was hitting. Kell waited in the on-deck circle, not knowing he would be sitting out his last at-bat.

As fate would have it, Ginsberg's one chance for fame, as the man who helped Kell win the batting championship, never materialized. Lake grounded into a double play to end the game, and protecting Kell's batting title became unnecessary.

Kell spoke with me in early 1994 and recalled his relief after watching the twin-killing. "Williams was a great competitor. It's an old story of how he could have sat out the final two games of the '41 season to ensure his batting .400 that year. But Williams didn't want to do it sitting on the bench. I suppose he would have expected the same from me. I'm just glad I didn't have to make that decision."

In his autobiography *My Turn at Bat*, Williams recalls how he felt getting off the train at Boston following the loss of the pennant and batting title. "There was a welcome-home crowd waiting," he recalled, "but all I wanted to do was get out of there, get packing and go someplace out in the sticks where I could fish. Fishing has always been a great refuge for me."

Williams could agonize over not only his losing the batting crown on the last day of the season, and by a fraction of a percentage point, but that the forfeiture of the title also prevented his becoming a Triple-Crown winner for the third time. Some argued that Kell's missing 20 games and accumulating 44 fewer at-bats than Ted worked to the Bengal hitter's advantage. They also pointed to the pressure of the pennant race which Williams had to endure the final month. And despite having a solid hitter in Stephens batting behind him, Williams had the handicap of seeing fewer good pitches to hit than Kell. Ted's 162 walks that year were the most in American League history except for Ruth's 170 in 1923.

Still, all the arguing in the world couldn't change the fact that Kell won, and deserved, the batting crown. And as Kell explains, Williams was rarely distracted while hitting. "I don't think the pennant race of 1949 either helped or hurt Williams in the batting race. I knew him well enough as a hitter to know that every time he walked to the plate, he was thinking base hit. He had such great pride in his ability that whether the score was 10–0 in favor or against his team, he would bear down and try to get a hit. Pitchers were probably trying to pitch around him, especially in the final game when Ted went 0–2 with two walks. But generally, Williams wasn't bothered by pennant races. They didn't affect his hitting."

Williams could have changed his style of hitting by being less selective. That almost certainly would have increased his homer and RBI production each year and possibly his average as well. Mr. Ballgame explained once why he refused to give in to pitchers by swinging at balls out of the strike zone. "I dislike a base on balls," Ted said. "But if they help produce runs and win games for my team, I believe it is better to accept them than to go after bad pitches."

As competitive as Williams was, he was generally courteous with both teammates and opponents. Recalls Kell: "The next year at spring training, we were in Sarasota playing an exhibition game against the Red Sox. A writer asked me if I would go with him to pose for a picture with Williams. When I told him I would, he went over to the Sox dugout to ask Ted. He came back with Williams. I told Ted, 'I was coming to you.' He said, 'No. You won the batting title, so I should come pose with you.' He's that kind of a guy. Williams and I became very close friends."

Kell also helps destroy Williams' public image of being a recalcitrant by relating Ted's activities at Cooperstown. "I wrote Ted a letter a couple of years ago after seeing him at the Hall-of-Fame induction ceremonies. He shows up almost every year to sign autographs, participate in activities, and just be a major part of the scene. Everyone knows he hates doing that kind of stuff. I wrote, 'You're a credit to baseball, and even though you have every reason in the world to hide from people, you show up at the Hall-of-Fame to help out. A lot of so-called superstars won't appear because they know they're going to be harassed by people. You are a real gentleman.'"

Despite his team's winning the flag in 1949, Rizzuto would have to wait one more year before he could boast of being the MVP. Williams won by almost 100 votes more than runner-up Scooter. It was his second and last MVP award; he had also won it in 1946.

Few claimed that Ted didn't deserve the MVP by year's end. Williams was one of the best hitters in baseball history, but 1949 was his most dominant season. The Thumper led the league in every important offensive category, including doubles (39), homers (43), RBIs (159), walks (162), total bases (368), slugging average (.650), on-base-percentage (.490), and runs (150). Every major category but one.

Joe Carrieri was the Yankee batboy in 1949. In his book *Searching for Heroes*, Carrieri recalls speaking with Williams after he helped the Sox win an August game with a double and homer. "In order to succeed in baseball, you have to love the game," Ted lectured. "But loving the game is not enough. You have to be willing to work hard at it and practice constantly." Williams might have added that even with exceptional diligence, luck can sometimes work against you.

It is ironic that Ted Williams' greatest year ended with two haunting failures — his team's losing the pennant and his losing the batting title and the Triple Crown with it. Only three players have accomplished the most difficult of offensive feats since Williams nearly repeated in 1949. Mickey Mantle (1956), Frank Robinson (1966), and Carl Yastrzemski (1967) each took the Triple once. None of them came close to repeating. In winning it twice, Williams and Hornsby share a record that is as unapproachable as any in baseball. Yet claims that Williams was the greatest hitter in history would have been more difficult to dispute had he won his third Triple Crown — an accomplishment that might have been realized had a third baseman from the Motor City been forced to go to bat just one more time.

1949 Batting Race Between Ted Williams and George Kell
(September–October Stats)

	Williams					Kell			
Date	Opponent (Home/Away)	AB	H	Avg	Date	Opponent (Home/Away)	AB	H	Avg
9/1	Tigers	4	1	.355	9/1	R. Sox (H)	3	1	.344
9/2	A's (H)	4	0	.352	9/2	W. Sox (H)	5	1	.342
9/3	A's (H)	4	2	.353	9/3	W. Sox (H)	3	2	.344
9/4	A's (H)	5	1	.352	9/4	W. Sox (H)	2	0	.343
9/5	Senators (H)	3	1	.352	9/5	Browns (H)	4	1	.342

9/5	Senators (H)	3	2	.353	9/5	Browns (H)	4	1	.342
9/7	Yanks (A)	2	1	.354		No Game			.341
	No Game			.354	9/8	Indians (H)	5	1	.340
	No Game			.354	9/8	Indians (H)	4	0	.337
9/9	Yanks (A)	5	2	.354		No Game			.337
9/10	A's (A)	5	2	.355	9/10	W. Sox (A)	3	2	.339
9/11	A's (A)	4	1	.354	9/11	W. Sox (A)	3	1	.339
9/11	A's (A)	3	0	.352					
9/13	Tigers (H)	5	1	.351	9/13	R. Sox (A)	4	2	.341
9/14	Tigers (H)	4	1	.350	9/14	R. Sox (A)		inj	.341
9/16	Browns (H)	4	1	.349	9/16	Yanks (A)		inj	.341
9/17	Browns (H)	2	0	.348	9/17	Yanks (A)		inj	.341
9/18	W. Sox (H)	4	3	.351	9/18	Senators (A)		inj	.341
					9/18	Senators (A)		inj	.341
9/20	Indians (H)	2	0	.349	9/20	A's (A)		inj	.341
9/21	Indians (H)	5	1	.348	9/21	A's (A)		inj	.341
	No Game				9/23	Indians (A)	3	2	.342
9/24	Yanks (H)	2	1	.349	9/24	Indians (A)		inj	.342
9/25	Yanks (H)	3	1	.349	9/25	Indians (A)		inj	.342
9/26	Yanks (A)	3	1	.348		No Game			.342
9/27	Senators (A)	4	1	.348		No Game			.342
9/28	Senators (A)	3	0	.346		No Game			.342
9/30	Senators (A)	3	0	.344	9/30	Indians (H)	3	0	.340
10/1	Yanks (A)	3	1	.344	10/1	Indians (H)	2	1	.341
10/2	Yanks (A)	2	0	.3428	10/2	Indians (H)	3	2	.3429

Final Month's Totals

	Games	At-Bats	Hits	Average
Williams	26	91	25	.275
Kell	15	51	17	.333

Five

Failing in the Long Run

"Bloomington isn't as warm as Tampa, but at least it's closer to home," thought Cincinnati head groundskeeper Lenny Schwab as he worked on the Indiana University baseball field in March of 1945. The campus had been selected as the Reds' spring training camp (traditionally the team trained in Tampa) in compliance with baseball commissioner Kenesaw Landis' wartime edict that major-league clubs choose northeastern rather than Florida sites in order to conserve transportation costs. Sent to Bloomington a few weeks ahead of the ballplayers, Schwab hired several Hoosier freshmen to help get the field in shape. Among them was Ted Kluszewski who, when not working, liked to take a few cuts in the batting cage. Schwab liked to watch.

Ted was one of six children born to John and Josephine Kluszewski in the small town of Argo, Illinois; his birth weight of 14 pounds was an indication of bigger things to come. By the time Schwab spotted his 400-foot drives to the outfield, Big Klu had grown to over six feet and weighed more than 200 pounds. Most of the physical transformation occurred after his first year at Argo High, yet despite a 5' 5", 125-pound frame as a freshman, Kluszewski became a three-sport athlete. More muscles were added after graduation, when the death of his parents and his eagerness to marry high-school sweetheart Eleanor Guckel (described by future Reds teammate Art Fowler as "an itty-bitty girl") led Ted to a job lugging 145-pound sacks at the Corn Products Refining Factory, maker of Argo Starch. Klu quit this job when a football scholarship sent him to Bloomington. (Being of draft age, he might have been bound for the Pacific had a childhood back operation not resulted in a 4F classification.)

Schwab was sufficiently impressed with Klu's clouts that he mentioned him to Bill McKechnie when the Reds manager arrived from Cincinnati. Equally astounded by the lefty-swinger's power, McKechnie urged general manager Warren Giles to offer Kluszewski a contract. Having replaced the innovative Larry MacPhail nine years earlier, Giles was a veteran at swapping and signing by 1945, but despite being a wily negotiator, he had sufficient scruples to refrain from tampering with the young athlete before speaking with Klu's collegiate coach, Bo McMillin. Bo also recognized talent when he saw it. The head Hoosier thanked Giles for his courtesy and then requested a hands-off policy while he asked his star end to continue carrying the pigskin for at least another year.

Kluszeweski's outstanding play in 1945 helped Indiana to an unbeaten season and the Big Ten championship. Even as a football player, Ted's strength and size were considered extraordinary, though he would hardly be noticed among today's giants of the gridiron. Known for his impressive runs and sure-handed catches, Klu must also have been an effective blocker. Pete Hihos, who caught a touchdown pass thrown by Klu in a 6–0 defeat of Northwestern that year and would enjoy a successful pro career with the Philadelphia Eagles, once exaggerated, "If you ran around him you were out of bounds."

As exciting as was the championship season for Kluszewski, the prospect of another one in 1946 was outweighed by a lucrative contract offer by Giles. Klu would receive a tax-free $15,000 bonus and an annual salary of $7,000 for two seasons. In fact, other clubs had heard about the power-hitting prospect by then and had tempted Ted with bigger bucks. Kluszewski chose Cincy, realizing the conditions of the contract which guaranteed a two-year salary whether he played in the majors or minors might motivate the Reds to hasten his major-league debut. As for opting to obtain a degree at Indiana, he never seriously considered it. His poor academic performance, eagerness to get married, and a rumor that a $6,000 bonus limit would be placed on future signings of prospects did little to encourage him to spend another four semesters at his alma mater.

Kluszewski spent the obligatory year of minor-league ball playing for Columbia in the Class-A South Atlantic League, and his 1946 league-leading average of .352 helped earn the early chance he hoped for. In 1947 he was placed on the Reds' roster, but sloppy fielding necessitated his being sent back to the minors. When he led the Southern Association with a .377 mark playing for Memphis, it was decided his shortcomings with the leather could be overlooked. Klu's days as a bush leaguer were over.

Not that the 23-year-old first baseman was a regular in 1948. Starting against righty hurlers, the still-unsteady gloveman sat against southpaws, with outfielder Hank Sauer shifting to first. Nevertheless, Kluszewski accumulated 379 at-bats that year while batting a respectable .274 and blossomed as a full-timer in 1949 with a .309 average, though his power stats of eight homers and 68 RBIs reflected an inability to pull fastballs, a hitting deficiency caused in part by big wrists and massive shoulders which were hampering his effort to turn on the inside pitch. He socked 25 round trippers in 1950, but that total was halved the next season despite his accumulating nearly seventy additional at-bats, while his average of .259 was two points below the league norm.

The prospect that Kluszewski would develop into a dud had Reds management edgy. That nervousness was manifested in harsh criticism of him for not being amenable to extra batting practice during the 1951 season and for excessive do-it-yourself renovations on his new split-level California ranch which the Reds believed were sapping his strength and endurance. Klu recalled a few years later how front-office pressure in 1951 affected both Eleanor and him emotionally, saying: "It was rough while it lasted. Whenever my wife and I look back on anything, we always put it in terms of before or after the bad year."

If his hitting was disappointing, Ted's fielding was improving. Red skipper Luke Sewell had coach Tony Cuccinello hit grounders to Kluszewski each morning until he became sufficiently satisfied to remark in midseason of 1951 that Ted might "become the best first baseman in the league," even likening Kluszewski's persistence to that of Lou Gehrig. (Sewell became manager when he replaced Bucky Walters, who had replaced John Neun, who had replaced McKechnie. Sewell didn't last much longer than his predecessors. He was fired in 1952, and his replacement, Rogers Hornsby, was canned the following year, making it six skippers in the eight years from 1946 to 1953. Reds owner Powell Crosley, Jr., might be considered the George Steinbrenner of his day if Giles hadn't been the main man behind some of the moves.)

Klu's persistence paid off as he became one of the finest glovemen at his position, leading the league in fielding average in 1951 and the next four years as well. Criticized both during and after his career for an inability to get to fieldable grounders (*The Biographical History of Baseball* belittles Ted for having "modest range that kept him away from errors of ambition"), Kluszewski nevertheless covered as much ground as could be expected, considering gravity's effect on 225 pounds in motion. Catcher Andy Seminick might have been biased when he once commented about his former teammate, "He didn't get much credit for it, but he was a good first baseman, with good hands," but Kluszewski's fielding ability was probably underrated.

With his strength and talent, it was only a matter of time before Ted's hitting shortcomings would be conquered as well. He rebounded with a .320 batting mark in 1952, third best in the league, though his homer output of 16 remained relatively low. Help from Hornsby, who worked on adjustments such as leveling Klu's uppercut swing, may have been one factor leading to his emergence as a superstar in 1953, though the shortening of the distance to right field (366 feet to 342) probably helped. Kluszewski maintained a high average (.316) while clouting 40 homers and gathering 108 RBIs. Pitchers like Bob Buhl, a rookie in 1953, grew to respect Kluszewski's ability to hit for average and power. Following his 15-year career, Buhl would rate Kluszewski "the toughest hitter in the league for me," a significant acknowledgment, considering the numerous Hall-of-Fame, senior-circuit sluggers who terrorized moundsmen in the fifties and sixties. Jamming Ted with fastballs became a decreasingly effective strategy and an increasingly dangerous one, as catcher Rube Walker recalled in 1994 in *We Played the Game,* "You could bust him inside and he'd still muscle the ball out of the park." While Kluszewski's power stats increased, his improved knowledge of the strike zone made him a difficult strikeout victim for hurlers. His 40 homers in 1953 were accompanied by only 34 whiffs, an impressive ratio which would characterize his entire career.

Ted Kluszewski became equally respected for his good-natured demeanor. Although he was known for his Samsonian strength, he gained a clubhouse reputation for gentleness and amiability, withstanding seemingly endless teasing from teammates. Pitcher Art Fowler would kid Klu to the point of instigating a friendly headlock, but that would be the extent of violence shown by Kluszewski who, according to Fowler, "wouldn't fight because he was afraid he'd hurt someone." Once roommate Johnny Temple, whom Ted outweighed by fifty pounds, began shouting at him for what he thought was sloppy and lackadaisical play. The outburst might have caused another player to let one go in the direction of Temple's chin, but Kluszewski just laughed.

Ted's nonviolent attitude carried onto the field as well. He rarely participated in bench-clearing brawls, but would often "suggest" to one of the opposing players that he stand near the sidelines as a spectator. It was an intimidating request rarely declined, especially after eyeing Ted's bulging biceps distinctly exposed through purposely shortened sleeves.

Ted's extraordinary power, which caused umpire Larry Goetz to fear that his line drives would one day kill someone, made him a frequent target of knockdown pitches, which Klu would normally take in stride. An exception came when Milwaukee's Ernie Johnson threw behind his head, prompting Kluszewski to lay a bunt down the first base line on the next pitch, a hitting strategy opposing hurlers may have wished he would always choose. If Johnson was pleased initially, his attitude changed after he fielded the ball, stepped on the bag, and was leveled by a vicious slide. Klu lingered nearby, waiting for the retaliation that never came.

Kluszewski continued crushing the horsehide in 1954, and by July was the fans' selection as starting first baseman in the All-Star game. Ted belted a two-run homer in the National League 11–9 loss and then stayed in the groove with 6 blasts in the next 14 games, raising his total to 28 by the beginning of August. Although he committed three errors in 100 games, his fielding remained remarkably reliable until a pair of miscues in an August 7 contest revived memories of a four-error performance in the minors.

As baseball's dog days dragged on, Ted began slumping. He went homerless for ten straight games while falling seven behind league-leader Willie Mays. Klu then exploded for a pair of four baggers off Cub righty Warren Hacker on August 11, and he hit one out in each of his next four games, the last being a ninth-inning, 420-foot blast into the Crosley Field bleachers on August 15, the second of three consecutive homers by the Reds. (Or Redlegs, as they were being called then. The much publicized trial of Soviet spy Alger Hiss in the late forties and Senator Joseph McCarthy's subsequent campaign to root out un–American Americans were mainly responsible for a "Red scare" in the early fifties that prompted owner Crosley to adopt the more politically correct nickname for his club.)

The August 15 game had been characterized by stifling heat and humidity, which forced home-plate umpire Bill Stewart to leave the game in the sixth inning, to the delight of the 12,000 jeering fans in attendance. Stewart had been involved in a controversial call at Crosley a few days earlier that resulted in a Redleg loss and rookie skipper Birdie Tebbetts' loss of temper. When the former Indian labeled Stewart a lousy umpire, citing his 1948 Series call of "safe" on a Bob Feller pickoff attempt as an example of ineptness, and suggested the arbiter call it a career, it was bye-bye Birdie. Stewart filed a report to the National League president the next day. If Tebbetts expected sympathy from former Cincy exec Warren Giles, who had replaced Ford Frick as senior-circuit boss in 1951, it came in the form of a fifty-dollar fine.

By August 25, as Cincy hosted Jackie Robinson and the Dodgers, Kluszewski had pulled within one of Mays' league-leading 37 homers, was among the top ten in batting at .320, and was among the top four in RBIs with 101. Ted's slugging wasn't helping the Redlegs, who were a remote 20 games behind the first place Giants. Despite the absence from the lineup of Robinson, who was suffering from an upset stomach, and All-Star catcher Roy Campanella, whom Dodger skipper Walter Alston thought "hadn't looked good lately," along with the collaring of Duke Snider in six at-bats, Brooklyn nonetheless shellacked Cincinnati 13–2. During the rout, a mysterious smoky pall settled over the infield, a viewing obstacle many of the

Like Jimmie Foxx before him, Ted Kluszewski cut short his shirt sleeves to expose his menacing biceps (National Baseball Library & Archive, Cooperstown, N.Y.).

10,000 disgusted spectators may have welcomed despite its obscuring Klu's fourth-inning RBI double, one of only three hits surrendered by Billy Loes. Ted was stranded at second, an event hardly worth mentioning considering the game's outcome, but worthy of note in regards to Ted's subsequent stab at Red Rolfe's still-standing, major-league record 18 consecutive games scoring at least one run, an attempt which would fall short by one.

Ted's try had its origins the next day against Pittsburgh. After assisting in the league's only triple play of the year — a sixth-inning Bobby Adams to Temple to Kluszewski around-the-horn conversion of a one-hopper, Klu connected in the ninth off Max Surkont for his 37th homer. By touching home plate, he simultaneously ended the game and began his run-scoring streak.

Ted scored another crucial run against the Bucs the next day. With his team trailing by one in the sixth, Kluszewski doubled home Gus Bell and then came around on successive fly balls to the outfield. Undoubtedly, the heavy-footed hulk took some riding in the dugout after scoring the go-ahead run by twice tagging and advancing a base. Ted's "speed" proved decisive, as his tally was the difference in the Redlegs' 2–1 victory.

Kluszewski lengthened to four his run-scoring string by homering in both ends of a twin bill against the Phils on August 29. In the opener, his first-inning blast off a Robin Roberts fastball gave the Reds an early 2–0 lead. Roberts lost 3–2, but still won 23 that year, the fifth of what would be six straight seasons with 20 or more victories.

On August 30, Ted singled off the Phils' Curt Simmons to open the second and then scored in his fifth straight game on hits by Jim Greengrass and Temple and a walk to Seminick. Ted finished his month's work the next day as effectively as Commie-hunter McCarthy's career was being finished on the floor of the Senate. (A special committee was debating whether to censure the overzealous patriot for "unbecoming conduct." McCarthy was censured, and before the year ended, he would be officially condemned by the entire Senate.)

Klu slugged a pair of homers, giving him 41 for the season (breaking the club record of 40 he set the year before), 13 coming in August and 12 in the last 23 games. No notice was made of his modest six-game scoring streak, but praise for Kluszewski was hardly lacking. *Sporting News* writer Tom Swope labeled him "the most feared hitter in the league," and Tebbetts called him "our anchor all season," while lobbying for Ted's selection as the league's most valuable player.

After watching a pregame stunt involving Redlegs catchers' attempts to catch balls dropped out of a helicopter (two were successful), a crowd of 17,000 fans was treated to a 9–7 defeat of the pennant-bound Giants, rhubarbs with umpires involving Leo "The Lip" Durocher and future World Series hero Dusty Rhodes, and a four-hit performance by Kluszewski, one of which resulted in his scoring a run, extending his string to seven. But the entertainment of September 1 was mediocre compared with the next day's excitement. Following Kluszewski's two-run homer in the eighth, a bench-clearing free-for-all was initiated in the inning when baserunner Greengrass construed as overly aggressive a tag by Milwaukee Braves shortstop Johnny Logan and came up swinging. Although Klu remained passive during the brawl, the field featured various fistfights until calm was finally restored after 15 minutes. Both instigators were ejected, but the game continued with perceptible tension until Jack Dittmer's 12th-inning poke off Frank Smith won it for Milwaukee 3–2.

Bad feelings continued the next day. Bench-jockeying emanated from both dugouts, to an excessive degree from the Braves' side as umpire Stewart sent manager Charlie Grimm, Lew Burdette, and Catfish Metkovich to early showers. Milwaukee again won in extra innings when Del Crandall, whose round tripper had tied the game in the ninth the night before, hit his second of the game in the 11th, but not before Kluszewski had run his run-streak to nine games by singling in the seventh and then scoring when Bob Buhl surrendered a walk to Temple and a hit to Lloyd Merriman.

As Ted Mack's national renown for televised talent searches increased in 1954, the National League's talented Ted continued enhancing his reputation as the game's latest slugging king. On September 5, he stretched his run-scoring streak by hitting a homer in both ends of a twin bill, thereby increasing to 44 and 118 his respective league-leading totals in homeruns and RBIs (34 of his taters coming at home, which remains a Cincy club record today). His hitting helped the Redlegs little, as pesky Dittmer's homer in the opener and a seven-run seventh inning in the nightcap led Milwaukee to a sweep.

Within one game of the Giants, the Braves had reason to rejoice afterwards, but concern may have pervaded the clubhouse. In the eighth inning of the nightcap, their prize rookie, Hank Aaron, had been injured sliding into third on a triple, his fourth hit in as many at-bats. Aaron was rushed to Cincinnati's Christ Hospital, where team physician Charles Lucks diagnosed the injury as a fractured leg. Hank sat for the remainder of the season, his homer total of 13 that year his lowest until he returned to Milwaukee and hit a dozen for the American League Brewers in 1975, one year after breaking Ruth's record for career homers.

Hank's trade from Atlanta to Milwaukee in 1975 was a sentimental gesture, as was Willie Mays' return to New York in 1973 to play for the Mets following 21 years with the New York-turned-San Francisco Giants, but the deals prevented both players from becoming one of a select twentieth-century group who ended a career of 20 or more seasons all with the same club. The lucky 13 include Brooks Robinson, 23 years with the Orioles; Carl Yasztremski, 23 years with the Red Sox; Mel Ott, 22 years with the Giants; Stan Musial, 22 years with Cardinals; Al Kaline, 22 years with the Tigers; Walter Johnson, 21 years with the Senators; Ted Lyons, 21 years with the White Sox; Willie Stargell, 21 years with the Pirates; George Brett, 21 years with the Royals; Red Faber, 20 years with the White Sox; Luke Appling, 20 years with the White Sox; Mel Harder, 20 years with the Indians; and Robin Yount, 20 years with the Brewers. Some near misses were Gabby Hartnett, 19 seasons with the Cubs before ending his career with the Giants in 1941; Joe Judge, 19 years with the Senators before finishing with the Red Sox in 1934; Sam Rice, 19 years with the Senators before finishing with Cleveland in 1934; Warren Spahn, 20 years with the Braves before finishing with the Mets and Giants in 1965; Harmon Killebrew, 21 seasons with the Washington Senators turned Minnesota Twins before finishing with the Royals in 1975; and Dwight Evans, 19 years with the Red Sox before finishing with the Orioles in 1991.

Aaron wasn't the only slugger to be injured during the doubleheader of September 5. In the third inning of the nightcap, Kluszewski singled and then slid hard into second trying to break up a double play. Ted limped off the field, and although the twisted ankle wasn't severe enough to necessitate his removal from the game or prevent a sixth-inning clout off Spahn, by the next morning it was too swollen and painful to allow his inclusion in the Labor Day lineup against the Cardinals, who handily defeated the Klu-less Redlegs 8–1.

On September 8, Kluszewski crushed his 44th circuit over the right-field wall off hurler Murry Dickson in the sixth to break a 3–3 deadlock. While extending his run-scoring streak to a dozen, Ted also stretched a hitting string to 19 with this homer, but it was snapped in New York on September 10. (The hitting streak would be the longest of Klu's career.) Ironically, Cincinnati thoroughly pummeled Giant pitchers that day en route to an 8–1 laugher, while birthday-boy Klu was being collared in three official at-bats. Kluszewski's less-recognized streak was lengthened, however, when he drew a walk in the fourth and scored in his 13th straight game.

Heavy rain threatened to postpone the Redlegs-Giants game the next day, but the Polo Grounds grounds-crew manned pumps for seven hours so that by game time, which was delayed by four hours, the field was soggy but playable. A sparse crowd of 3,500 watched manager Durocher shouting encouragement from the third-base box as the Giants took a come-from-behind, 7–5 decision, despite a 400-foot drive to right field by Kluszewski off Ruben Gomez in the sixth.

Cincy traveled to Pittsburgh on September 12 for a Sunday doubleheader (how common they were then) in which Kluszewski had what was probably the greatest offensive performance of his career. He drove in six runs in the opener with a single and a pair of homers off Paul LaPalme and Bob Friend and then added another three RBIs in the nightcap on a trio of singles, while lengthening his run-scoring streak to 16 with three tallies. His nine ribbies set a still-standing club record for a double header and were only one shy of Enos Slaughter's record for a twin bill, which was later surpassed by Nate Colbert and Mark Whiten, whose major-league marks of 13 RBIs were set in 1972 and 1993 respectively.

The last place Pirates again played host to the Redlegs on Monday in front of 1,148 fans, the smallest night audience in the history of Forbes Field. Perhaps it is appropriate more than ironic that such a sparse crowd would witness Kluszewski's extending his run-streak one last time, since few, if any, were aware of the streak anyway. For the past couple of weeks, no mention of it had been made in local papers or major baseball publications. It is doubtful whether even Kluszewski realized he was setting a new National League record when he singled off Dick Littlefield and scored in his 17th consecutive game.

Kluszewski could have matched Red Rolfe's major-league mark set in 1939 by scoring in the next game against Brooklyn on September 14. Unfortunately, he couldn't have chosen a more formidable mound opponent to stop him. Sophomore southpaw Johnny Podres had earned a complete-game win in his previous start, indicating that the off-again, on-again hurler, who would never win more than 18 in one season during his career but would be at his best in World Series competition, was back in the groove. He stayed that way, overpowering Redleg righties with fastballs while stymying lefties with slow breaking balls, en route to a three-hit, 4–0 whitewash.

Although Klu was held hitless and scoreless in three plate appearances, he had come close in his last try. Leading off the seventh, Ted timed a Podres curve and belted it towards the center-field wall. Duke Snider raced to the barrier, reached high, and snared the sphere with his gloved hand. The ball would not have cleared the wall, but Kluszewski was robbed of at least a double. With no one out at the time, Ted would probably have tallied from second and secured a tie of the run-scoring record had his drive eluded the Duke. In the ninth, Klu watched from the on-deck circle as Podres retired Gus Bell, probably oblivious to the full significance of the final out.

Although he failed to match the major-league record, Klu's NL mark was remarkable nonetheless. Besides scoring 24 runs in the 17 games, he had a dozen homers (a rate of one every six at-bats), 32 RBIs (nearly two per game), and 31 hits in 72 at-bats for a .431 average. (By way of comparison, Joe DiMaggio hit .408 during his much longer and more prestigious 56-game hitting streak, averaging one homer every 15 at-bats and one RBI per game.) Ted reached base safely in each of the 17 games, failed to get a ribby in only 3 games, and homered in 10. The Reds, who finished the season 6 games below .500, benefited from Klu's streak by winning 10 of the 17 games.

Appropriately, 1954 would be Klu's greatest season. His league-leading 49 homers, the fifth highest in NL history at the time, set a club mark not surpassed until George Foster's 52 in 1977, and Klu's mark remains the Reds record for left-handers. His .642 slugging average is also a still-standing team mark. Ted led the league in RBIs with 141 but failed in his attempt for the Triple Crown when his .326 batting average was bettered by four others.

Kluszewski continued his mauling of hurlers the next two seasons. He led the league in hits in 1955 while connecting for 47 round trippers, and he belted another 35 the following year. Then, according to one source, a clubhouse scrap with a teammate in 1957 resulted in his reinjuring his back, and "the man who in mid-decade had seemed most likely to be the next threat to Ruth's home run record had his career all but ruined." The 32-year-old appeared in only 69 games that year and was traded to the Pirates in 1958, where he was platooned at first base with the less sure-handed Dick Stuart (or Dr. Strangeglove as he was later called). Ted managed only four homers that year, but his strength still made him dangerous; he nearly proved correct umpire Goetz' direful prognostication by drilling a Philadelphia pitcher in the chest with a line drive. The incident made such an impression on teammate Frank Thomas that he recalled decades later, "I thought it killed him, that it went right through his chest."

Kluszewski was sent to the White Sox in 1959, where he was also used sparingly. The old Kluszewski resurfaced briefly, but at a most opportune time for the Pale Hose that year. Ted hit .391 in the Series, had an .826 slugging percentage, socked three homers, and drove in ten runs against otherwise effective Dodger pitching. His efforts were to no avail, however, as the Sox lost in six.

Ted hit but five homers in 1960, but he should have had six. A late-season, pinch hit, three-run blast off Oriole righty Milt Pappas, an apparent game-winner, was forfeited when the umpire ruled that time had been called prior to the homer. Klu was traded to the expansion Los Angeles Angels in 1961, where he ended his career on a positive note with 15 homers in 253 at-bats.

Although he has thus far been snubbed by the Hall of Fame, Kluszewski nevertheless is considered by experts to be one of the greatest sluggers of all time and is placed seventh among all first basemen in major-league history (behind Gehrig, Terry, Foxx, Sisler, Johnny Mize, and Jim Bottomley) in *Ranking Baseball's Elite*. Klu connected for 279 homers in 15 seasons, playing many of the latter years in pain as a part-timer. His .298 batting average matches Mickey Mantle's career mark, and like the Mick, he would have finished at .300 had he retired one year earlier.

More obviously outstanding are Ted's seasonal accomplishments. He hit 40 or more homers in three straight years, had five seasons with 100 RBIs, four of them coming consecutively, and batted over .300 in seven seasons, five consecutively. Kluszewski is one of only five players in history to hit 40 homers in a season while striking out fewer than 40 times (DiMaggio,

Gehrig, Mize, and Ott being the others), and he is the only one to do it three times. Klu is one of only seven players in history to bat .300, hit forty homers, and accumulate 100 RBIs in a season three times, and he is one of only four to do it in consecutive seasons (Ruth, Foxx, Snider being the others). The most significant stat, however, may be that only 16 players have ever reached the .300, 30-homer, and 100-RBI plateau in one season four times and Kluszewski is the only one of the 16 not to have been elected to the Hall of Fame.

If Ted's effectiveness as a batsman waned in later years, his personality didn't suffer. He remained popular with teammates, who would often take advantage of his pacifist nature. Brawny Buc slugger Frank Thomas liked to kid Klu about his exposed biceps, calling them "chicken wings." Lanky Jim Landis would stand alongside Kluszewski flexing barely perceptible muscles until provoking the inevitable laughter from his Sox teammate.

Following his retirement in 1961, Ted became a coach for Cincinnati, where he was admired and respected by most players. During the notorious brawl between Met shortstop Bud Harrelson and scrappy Pete Rose in the 1973 National League championships, it was the consummate peacemaker who, in the words of author Roger Kahn, "threw those mighty Polish arms around Rose and dragged him away."

It is a fact of baseball life, though an unfair one, that the propelling of pitches out of parks receives an inordinate degree of attention, whereas proficiency in scoring runs is virtually ignored. Few of baseball's greatest run-scorers are remembered for that skill. In a discussion between fans involving the achievements of Ruth or Mays or Musial or Gehrig or Aaron or Frank Robinson, the fact that all are among the top ten run-scorers in history isn't likely to be mentioned. Even such less proficient homer-hitters as Ty Cobb, all-time runs leader, and Pete Rose, fourth on the run-scoring list, are remembered for amassing an amazing amount of hits as well as an aggressive attitude, not for surpassing the 2,000-runs plateau.

So it is not surprising that Ted Kluszewski's National League record run-scoring streak of 17 consecutive games is one of baseball's best-kept secrets. But if you took the advice of an old professor and looked it up, you would find it — right below Red Rolfe's major-league mark.

Ted Kluszewski's 1954 17-Game Run-Scoring Streak

Date	Opponent	Opposing Starter	Outcome		R	H	HR	RBI
8/27	Pirates (H)	Surkont	3–2	Reds	1	2	1	1
8/28	Pirates (H)	LaPalme	2–1	Reds	1	1	0	1

Date	Opponent	Opposing Starter	Outcome		R	H	HR	RBI
8/29	Phils (H)	Roberts	3–2	Reds	1	2	1	2
8/29	Phils (H)	Mrozinski	8–4	Reds	2	2	1	1
8/30	Phils (H)	Simmons	5–1	Reds	2	1	0	0
8/31	Phils (H)	Wehmeier	9–3	Phils	2	2	2	2
9/1	Giants (H)	Hearn	9–7	Reds	1	4	0	3
9/3	Braves (H)	Burdette	3–2	Braves	1	1	1	2
9/4	Braves (H)	Conley	5–4	Braves	1	3	0	1
9/5	Braves (H)	Spahn	11–8	Braves	1	1	1	2
9/5	Braves (H)	Wilson	9–7	Braves	1	2	1	4
9/8	Phils (A)	Dickson	9–3	Reds	1	1	1	3
9/10	Giants (A)	Liddle	8–1	Reds	2	0	0	0
9/11	Giants (A)	Gomez	7–5	Giants	1	1	1	1
9/12	Pirates (A)	LaPalme	11–5	Reds	2	3	2	6
9/12	Pirates (A)	Thies	13–2	Reds	3	3	0	3
9/13	Pirates (A)	Littlef'id	6–5	Pirates	1	2	0	0
Totals			10W	7L	24	31	12	32

Six

Losing Face

On May 7, 1959, the Cards' Stan Musial led off the ninth with his 400th career homer off Cub righty Don Elston to break a 5–5 deadlock and send 7,000 satisfied spectators to the Sportsman's Park exits. The Man would crack another 75 homers before retiring, and his 475 mark is a still-standing Cardinal record. Musial's twelve homers in his final year of 1963 marked his 21st consecutive season with double-digit homer totals, a feat matched or bettered by only one other major-leaguer — Henry Aaron, who had 23 seasons with ten or more.

In Pittsburgh, about an hour after Musial's game-ending poke, Ted Kluszewski led off the bottom of the tenth, his team deadlocked with the Phils at Forbes Field. Right-handed starter Jim Owens was still straddling the mound, having allowed but six hits to that point, two by Ted. Those remaining from the 10,000 fans who had pushed through the turnstiles 2½ hours earlier cheered for Klu to connect for his first of the season. He would oblige.

Ted had suffered back pain throughout the 1958 season but expressed optimism the following spring that the spasms would not return. After cracking a homer against his former Red teammates in an exhibition game at Fort Myers, Klu commented, "This is the best I've felt in a long time." His playing in nearly every game that spring caused no recurrence of the back problem and led Kluszewski to predict that he would play in 100 to 125 games in 1959.

It was not to be. Although he played pain-free most of the year, Ted had a different obstacle with which to contend — competition. Pirate skipper Danny Murtaugh had another first baseman capable of providing long-distance service. Power-hitting Dick Stuart had been impressive as a rookie in 1958, belting 16 homers after the All-Star break. The choice between a promising 26 year old and a 34 year old with possible physical problems was no choice at all. Despite Stuart's obvious shortcomings with the leather,

Murtaugh's mind was made up before the 1959 season began, and he fore-warned sparse use of Kluszewski when he stated in Florida, "I'm going to give Stuart every possible chance of shooting for the fences. If he falters, I can fall back on Klu."

Ted entered the May 7 affair against the Phils having accumulated only 26 at-bats playing in half of the Pirates 20 games, several as a pinch hitter. Given a starting opportunity, Kluszewski took advantage of it by stroking a single off Owens and scoring one of four Pirate runs in the fourth, then adding another single the following inning. Having another chance in the tenth to open wide Murtaugh's eyes, Ted tomahawked an Owens fast-ball and whistled a drive into the lower right-field seats, giving the second place club of the previous year only their 10th win in 21 games.

Klu's homer would be one of two he would hit for the Pirates in 1959. Stuart continued belting four baggers frequently, so Kluszewski had started in only 20 games by August 25. The little-used overweight slugger was then shipped to Chicago for Harry "Suitcase" Simpson, whose third trade of the season made suitable his sobriquet. Ted promised to shed pounds and shell moundsmen if given the chance. Starting in 29 games for the Sox, he accu-mulated unremarkable but respectable stats, batting close to .300 with a pair of homers and ten RBIs before becoming the star of the Series.

The beneficiary of Klu's tenth-inning decider against Owens might have been Vernon Law, who had pitched the first nine, but Murtaugh had replaced the nine-year Buc veteran with pinch-hitter Rocky Nelson in the ninth. When the Phils took their cuts in the tenth, they faced ElRoy Face, who retired the side and picked up the win.

Face was somewhat of a novelty in baseball in 1959 — a relief special-ist. Few if any bullpen residents were valuable commodities then. A team's best pitchers were its starters who were accustomed to going the distance. Occasionally, a prominent reliever would surface — Detroit's Elden Auker in the thirties, the Yankees' Joe Page in the forties — but most were brought in only when a manager became convinced that his starter was finished.

By 1959, Face was in his sixth season with the Pirates, was making about $25,000, and was striving to accomplish two goals. Page was paid $45,000 by the Yankees in 1950, then the record for relievers, which in retrospect seems comical considering many of today's firemen earn an equal amount for one game. Face hoped to someday surpass Page's salary. He also planned to save enough money to invest in a restaurant and bar, where his name and flair for country music would provide an added attraction for cus-tomers.

The 5' 8" guitar strummer hadn't initially intended to play second fid-dle in his baseball career. In the minors, he was used almost exclusively as a starter, accumulating a 69–28 record in the four years from 1949 to 1952, including a no-hitter in his final year at Fort Worth. Face explained the pitching transition in a 1977 interview for *Baseball Quarterly*. Playing for Bobby Bragan in 1952, he was occasionally used in relief. By the time Bragan became skipper of the Pirates in 1956, Face was in his third year as a spot starter and reliever with the club. "He (Bragan) put me in the bullpen because he needed somebody who could throw every day," Face recalled. "When he was fired in '57 and Murtaugh took over I never started another game again."

In 1959, ElRoy Face's forkball helped him approach Rube Marquard's 1912 record of 19 consecutive wins (National Baseball Library & Archive, Cooperstown, N.Y.).

"The Baron of the Bullpen" found fame largely because of a trick pitch he had learned while in the minors. "I threw the ball overhand or three-quarters most of the time," ElRoy told this author in an interview in December of 1993. "My best pitch was the fork ball, the kind Rube Marquard and Joe Page used to throw. People ask me about the difference between the fork ball I threw and the split-finger they throw today. I tell them, 'About three million dollars.'"

ElRoy Face learned from the master himself when, after a brief appearance with the Pirates as a rookie in 1953, he was shipped to New Orleans of the Southern Association by general manager Branch Rickey, who felt Face needed to add to an arsenal which included a good fastball, a slow curve, and impeccable control. Meeting Page down yonder, Face was taught the fork ball and showed a penchant for using it during the 1954 season. By the following spring, the moundsman had mastered the pitch sufficiently to make the Pirate roster.

Face saved six in 1956, another ten in 1957, and easily led the league with 20 in 1958, while winning his last five decisions that year. He was having another strong season in 1959, the May 7 victory being his fourth of the year without a loss. ElRoy was no longer learning but was teaching others. In a game in Pittsburgh, he showed lanky Lindy McDaniel how to throw the fork ball. By the end of the season, he may have wished he hadn't. The Redbird righty with the exaggerated overhand delivery led the league with 15 saves, and would join Face as one of the league's top relievers in forthcoming seasons.

ElRoy's first four wins of 1959 weren't significant at the time, but the victory streak would be stretched to 17 before being snapped late in the year. It left him two shy of the major-league mark set by Marquard in 1912. Combined with the five he had notched at the end of the 1958 season, Face's winning streak was actually 22, which was also two short of the big-league mark, with Carl Hubbell having strung together 24 during the 1936 and 1937 seasons.

The game that broke the streak was the opener of a twin bill, and Face today still recalls how reporters surrounded his locker between games and asked how he felt. His reply, "Well, I'll just have to start another streak," didn't reveal the disappointment Face felt, but it was appropriate for one who not only was a success in his profession but was lucky to be alive.

ElRoy was born to Joe and Bessie Face on February 20, 1928, in the small rural community of Stephentown located in northeastern New York. Joe was a jack-of-all-trades, working intermittently as woodcutter, carpenter, farmer, and millhand, so the family moved frequently. Of the four children, ElRoy seemed the least likely to be destined for an athletic career. He developed rickets, and one night when he was racked with fever he nearly died. His recovery was both slow and unsteady. ElRoy staved off pneumonia five times in his youth, his last bout necessitating a heavy dose of antibiotics which saved his life but weakened his heart.

Warned to refrain from physical activities, ElRoy taught himself to play the guitar, but on occasion he would practice pitching by tossing stones at a target on the side of his house when his dad wasn't around. Sometimes he was and delivered a somewhat restrained whipping. Another example of ElRoy's practicing at an inopportune time occurred when he was caught throwing erasers in school one afternoon. The second grader was confined to the corner of the room the following morning, a punishment which probably didn't faze the withdrawn youngster who felt comfortable in solitude.

ElRoy's love of the game was too intense to allow poor health to interfere permanently with ballplaying, and upon entering Averill Park High

School, he was sufficiently recovered to make the team. In 1945 he led the club to its first championship, tossing a shutout in the final game, but he dropped out of school to join the army in 1946, where he served a year-and-a-half stint.

Honorably discharged in 1947, Face earned a modest salary as a gas station attendant, but he lost the job when he skipped work one day for an unsuccessful tryout with a Class-C ballclub in Pittsfield, Massachusetts. An auto mechanic opening drew Face to Lebanon, New York, where on week nights and Saturdays he played semipro ball; the big-league dreams of the 20 year old had been virtually abandoned by that point. After several impressive outings, however, Face attracted the attention of Phillies scout Fred Mathews, who traveled to Lebanon with a minor-league contract. After two seasons in the PONY League, Face was drafted by the Dodgers in the winter of 1950, and he pitched in the Western League for two years. He was grabbed by the Pirates in December of 1952, and after pitching briefly the following season, he was sent by Rickey to New Orleans for an education.

Face's first big year was 1956, when he led the National League in appearances with 68, though his dozen losses in relief were also a league high. He appeared in 59 games in 1957, and though he dropped his first two decisions in 1958 with May losses to the Giants and Braves, he finished the season with a 2.89 ERA and a league-leading 20 saves. He had won his last five games. The Pirates were getting used to winning with Face. "When he comes out of the bullpen, the whole team seems to get a lift," Murtaugh told *Sporting News* columnist Les Beiderman. "He struts to the mound and has that look about him that seems to say, 'Okay, boys. I'll take charge from now on.'"

The day after seven astronauts were selected by NASA to participate in the Mercury program, America's first concerted effort at manned-space flight, the 1959 baseball season began on April 10, with Murtaugh and his Buccaneers hoping to improve by one their previous year's second place finish. Besides Law, the Pittsburgh staff included Bob Friend, in his ninth year with the club. Bob's first successful season came in 1955 when he topped the senior circuit with a 2.83 ERA. Coming off his best year, "The Warrior" led the league in complete games (38) and wins (22) in 1958. Friend hoped to do it again in 1959 but would instead take high "honors" in defeats with 19, a feat he duplicated in 1961.

The Pirate offense appeared potent if their .264 team average in 1958, the third best in baseball (behind the Yankees and Braves), was an indication. Roberto Clemente hadn't yet blossomed into superstardom — his four batting crowns and 13 of 14 seasons hitting over .300 were accomplishments he would attain in the next two decades — but he had displayed enough skill with the lumber and leather in the previous four years to warrant his being considered Pittsburgh's most valuable commodity. When he was on the field, the green Stuart frightened Murtaugh, but his raw power frightened opposing hurlers even more. Second baseman Bill Mazeroski was a solid but not spectacular hitter, sure-handed in the infield, and the same was true of shortstop Dick Groat. Left-fielder Bob Skinner's .321 average was fifth best in the league in 1958, and center-fielder Bill Virdon, though no Mickey Mantle, was adequate. Steel City fans had reason to be optimistic.

Pessimism prevailed, however, in the first month. By May 1, Pittsburgh had lost 8 of 14 games and held next-to-last place in the standings. Face claimed two of their victories. On the 22, after Americans participated in a ten-minute shelter drill, with traffic halted and citizens seeking safety in designated areas in a simulated Red nuclear bomb attack, the Cincinnati Reds bombed Friend in Pittsburgh that night with six runs in the third, and another in the fifth. Buc batters treated 16,000 fans to a seven-run seventh but trailed again after Gus Bell put one in the seats against former teammate Face in the eighth. ElRoy then retired the side in order, did the same in the ninth, but remained pitcher-of-record on the losing side. The Pirates made him a winner with a pair in the bottom of the ninth.

Two days later ElRoy had number two. He entered with one out in the seventh and retired the side, but the Phils reached him for two runs in the eighth. Again as the prospective losing pitcher in the final inning, Face was saved when the Bucs ambushed Philly for four, highlighted by a Smokey Burgess two-run double. ElRoy retired the side in the bottom half to win it.

With some luck, Face might have won more. In the team's second game on April 11, he pitched perfect ball the final two frames in the Pirates 4–3 loss to the Braves' Lew Burdette. Snowed out the next day, Pittsburgh took to the road for the first time in 1959; they lost their third straight game on April 13 to Cincy and dropped a 3–2 decision the next day, with Face relieving in the final frame. The Bucs still hadn't won when they visited the Braves on April 17 and remained winless when rain halted the 2–2 tie after nine innings, with Face hurling scoreless ball the final three. The Pirates dropped another one-run decision on May 1, despite a 500-foot Stuart homer that was described as "the longest ever hit in Pittsburgh" and Face's blanking the Redbirds in the ninth.

On May 3 the last place Cardinals, led by feisty player-manager Solly Hemus, lost a 4–3 fight in the first of two at Forbes Field, and were literally outfought in a bench-clearing brawl in the nightcap. After Face pitched perfect ball the last three innings of the ten-inning opener to win his third game of the year, with Mazeroski's RBI triple providing the winning margin, the second game began precariously when Hemus was hit on the leg by a pitch thrown by right-hander Bennie Daniels. The angry batsman shouted at Daniels while walking towards first and then made a move toward the mound. Stuart stepped in front of Hemus as both benches emptied, but calm was quickly restored.

Murtaugh claimed afterwards that Hemus had intentionally tried to get nailed by sticking his foot out, an accusation made more credible by Hemus's vexatious personality. Hemus was in his first year as skipper, his last of 11 years as an active player. Never more than a mediocre infielder and hitter, his only noteworthy achievements were to lead the league in runs-scored in 1952 and in brawling throughout the decade. His temperament changed little once he was at the helm, and he was ejected eight times by umpires in 1959. If he possessed leadership abilities, they weren't made evident to St. Loo pitcher Jim Brosnan, who threw for the Cards in 1959 and stated 35 years later that "Hemus had no idea how to manage." Brosnan's assessment was made plausible by the Cards next-to-last place finish in 1959 and Hemus' brazen announcement of plans to bench Musial in 1960, which caused a near riot in the Gateway to the West.

The Pirates were trailing 2–1 when Daniels again faced Hemus in the sixth. The first pitch was a fastball that tailed towards Hemus' head. Ducking just in time, the rattled Hemus stepped out of the box briefly before resuming his stance, swung at the next pitch, and let the bat fly in the direction of Daniels. If Hemus' aim was off, his message registered, and the rookie hurler charged toward home plate. Players meant business this time as they filled the field, with several scraps resulting in minor cuts and injuries, mostly to Redbird belligerents. Slugger Bill White and hurler Howie Nunn needed repairs in the clubhouse, while Hemus was cut on the chin by Pirates coach Lenny Levy and was assisted by trainer Bob Bauman before returning to the batter's box amidst jeers from the 26,000 onlookers.

Mercifully, Pennsylvania's Sunday law, which prohibited play after six o'clock (it was abolished later that year), went into effect 15 minutes after the altercation, eliminating any chance for further hostilities. The suspended game would be replayed later in the season. The possibility that Hemus' bat-tossing had been accidental was discounted by the manager's facetious comment to reporters, "The bat slipped out of my hand. I guess the ball slipped out of Daniels' hand when he conked me."

After Kluszewski helped Face win his fourth game, the forkballer was leading baseball in victories and ERA (1.69) on May 10. ElRoy threw a combined three scoreless innings in his next two no-decision outings before notching game number five in Los Angeles on May 13. Entering in the seventh with the Bucs down by one, Face benefited from a Dick Stuart two-run blast in the eighth. He held the Dodgers scoreless to win it, but not without anxious moments. Wally Moon and Ron Fairly led off the eighth with singles but were stranded when Face retired the next three, two on strikeouts. In the ninth, ElRoy was uncharacteristically wild in walking the first two hitters, but he set aside the next two and, after yielding a long foul fly, whiffed Moon to end it.

Face and Stuart each made it six for the season in defeating the Dodgers the next night. As would be the case with several of his 17 victories in 1959, ElRoy won ugly. With two outs in the eighth and Pittsburgh ahead 6–4, he replaced Friend and promptly yielded a two-run single to Moon. It was Stu to the rescue again, however, as he crushed his sixth homer off veteran righty Clem Labine in the ninth. Face fanned two in the bottom of the inning in retiring the side in order.

Face's next appearance came on May 17 in Chicago. He relieved Law in the ninth with runners on the corners and no outs, the Pirates ahead 5–3. He walked the next batter to load the bases and then induced a double-play grounder before another groundout gave him his second save of the year.

It would be ElRoy's last outing for a while. Three days later he broke a glass in the bathroom sink of his hotel room, severely cutting three fingers on his pitching hand. Face wouldn't be available until the end of the month. At the same time, Clemente was placed on the 30-day disabled list as a result of a strained right elbow. Rumors circulated that the two Buc stars had sustained the injuries after quarreling and fighting in their hotel. In truth, Roberto had been hurting for a week after an attempted diving catch in Los Angeles on May 14 caused his elbow to swell. He was removed from a game on the nineteenth in St. Louis, the day before Face's injury.

The loss of Face and Clemente didn't seem quite as painful to Murtaugh after the Pirates won five in a row. The streak raised them to third in the standings a game behind second place San Francisco, with the chance to trim the four-and-a-half game bulge enjoyed by the front-running and defending-champion Braves in a game in Milwaukee on May 26. They would face a difficult opponent. Burdette had won seven of his first nine decisions.

Hurler Harvey Haddix hadn't been as fortunate in struggling to take three of five. His two setbacks were by scores of 3–0 and 3–2, the latter a tough-luck loss to the Cubs on May 16. Entering the ninth having retired the last 15 batters, he threw a third strike past Al Dark that eluded catcher Hank Foiles, allowing Dark to reach first. Ernie Banks failed to sacrifice, then singled. Walt Moryn followed with a bunt that straddled the first-base line before stopping on it for a hit. Bobby Thomson, known for his pennant-clinching poke off Ralph Branca in 1951, ended Haddix's nerve-racking ordeal with a game-winning single off Don Hoak's glove.

The 33-year-old lefty with pinpoint control had appeared destined for greatness early in his career. The Buckeye won 20 in his sophomore season of 1952 and another 18 the next season, but "the Kitten" wasn't purring following several mediocre seasons with the Cards, Phillies, and Cincinnati. He was traded to the Pirates at the end of the 1958 season, but despite a 2.67 ERA which placed him fifth among league starters, he was finding it difficult to win for a club that was next-to-last in runs-scored. Although the team had been winning lately, Haddix took the mound knowing he would have to pitch near-perfect ball to beat Burdette.

After nine frames, Haddix had bettered his goal. Not one Braves batter had reached safely, as Haddix became the fifth major-leaguer of the century, the first since 1922, to hurl nine perfect innings in regular-season play. (Don Larsen had done it four years earlier in the Series.) Only once did Milwaukee come close to a hit. With one out in the third, Johnny Logan whistled a liner toward left-center, but shortstop Dick Schofield interrupted its flight with a leaping one-hand catch. Haddix retired Burdette on strikes for the 27th out, assuring his place in the record books.

Unfortunately, Haddix hadn't assured himself of a win. Although not as perfect as his counterpart, Burdette had nevertheless been equally stingy in allowing no runs after regulation. The Pirates did have chances. They stroked three hits in the third inning, but a baserunning blunder prevented their tallying. In the ninth, Skinner hit a screamer with runners on the corners, but first baseman Joe Adcock snared it.

Haddix set the side down in order in the 10th, had a bit of a scare in the 11th when, after Adcock was retired, Wes Covington and Del Crandall both pushed Virdon to the fence with long drives, and then threw another hitless inning in the 12th. Burdette breezed through extra innings as well and finished his 13th shutout inning having yielded but a dozen hits and, like Haddix, no walks. Haddix's masterpiece, arguably the most famous of baseball pitching feats, has obscured the fact that Burdette pitched a dandy that night as well.

Second baseman Johnny O'Brien had started for the Braves but was removed for pinch-hitter Del Rice in the tenth. In leading off the bottom of the 13th, substitute second sacker Felix Mantilla would be Milwaukee's 37th opportunity to break through against Haddix. On a two-strike curve (Haddix thought he had caught Felix looking on the previous pitch, but home plate umpire Vinnie Smith ruled a ball), Mantilla dribbled a grounder to Hoak at third, who took time to count the seams on the ball before throwing a one-hopper to first that Rocky Nelson couldn't field, bringing groans from the 19,000 County Stadium spectators. (Murtaugh chose Nelson to start that night, and though it is doubtful Stuart would have handled Hoak's errant toss, it is interesting to speculate whether Kluszewski might have.)

The disappointed Haddix still had a no-hitter, shutout, and possible win with which to concern himself. Slugger Eddie Mathews, asked to sacrifice by skipper Fred Haney, succeeded, causing the next batter, Aaron, to be intentionally passed. If Haddix could get the slow-footed Adcock to hit a grounder, the inning would be over. Instead, the tall, righty batsman, who once hit four homers in a game, connected on a Haddix outside slider, the ball barely clearing the right-center-field fence.

Confusion prevailed following the homer. Baserunner Aaron had failed to touch third prior to scoring ahead of Adcock. An umpire's meeting resulted in Aaron and Mantilla being told to recircle the basepaths. In the clubhouse, umpire Frank Dascoli ruled Adcock's blow a double and the final score 2–0. The next day National League president Warren Giles overruled him, claiming the game ended 1–0 with Mantilla's tally.

Two-to-nothing or 1–0. Either way, it meant not only another tough-luck defeat for Haddix, but the toughest in baseball history. It didn't matter that the official box score and other mementos from the game were headed to Cooperstown, that Pennsylvania legislators would consider honoring him with a commendation, that the league would present him with a silver tray along with twelve silver cups, each inscribed with an account of one of his dozen perfect innings. As a disgusted Virdon noted in the clubhouse afterwards, "A pitcher does this once in a lifetime — once in baseball history — and we can't win it for him." In recalling the heartbreaker fifteen years later, Haddix admitted to author Joseph Reichler, "It still hurts."

Face was no longer hurting when he ended a two-week layoff by picking up his third save on May 30. Entering the game with one out and one on in the eighth, he retired the Reds' Johnny Temple on a foul popup, whiffed Vada Pinson to end the inning, and pitched a perfect ninth. The appearance dropped his league-leading ERA below 1.40, while his 6–0 record was the best in the league, with knuckleball reliever Hoyt Wilhelm's 7–0 the only one better in baseball.

Face remedied that discrepancy with a win in the second of two played in Cincy the next day. After Law's complete-game eight-hitter in the opener, the Pirates and Reds combined to sock 6 homers, chase 10 pitchers, and put 25 runs on the board before 17,000 spectators rose for the seventh-inning stretch. By the time they were reseated, Face was on the mound. He protected the 14–11 lead provided by pinch-hitter Smokey Burgess' homer in the top of the seventh by allowing a harmless single, while fanning five of ten in the closing frames.

Some would say that number seven was indeed lucky for Face because he was credited with a win despite not being the pitcher of record, having entered the game with the Pirates already enjoying a three-run cushion. Critics would point to the rule issued in 1951 and still in use which declared that "no pitcher can be credited with a victory unless he is the pitcher of record when his team assumes the lead and maintains the lead to the finish of the game." The rule allows, however, for an exception: "Do not credit a game won to a relief pitcher who pitches briefly *and ineffectively* and is the pitcher of record when his team assumes a lead which it maintains over a period of innings to the finish of the game. *If a succeeding relief pitcher pitches effectively in helping to maintain his team in the lead credit such relief pitcher with the victory* [italics added]."

The pitcher of record prior to Face's appearance was Bob Smith, who entered an 8–8 tie in the fifth and promptly surrendered three runs in the inning. Pittsburgh's scoring six in the next two frames in jumping to a 14–11 lead was hardly a result of anything their lefty fireman had accomplished. Official scorers logically credited the win to the one pitcher in eleven in the slugfest who hadn't been scored upon (except for Don Williams and Orlando Pena, each of whom threw to one batter). Face was deserving of number seven as much as any of his 17 straight wins. And with it, as the *Sporting News* noted, "counting the three saves, he has been responsible for ten of the Broncos 24 triumphs."

The Pirates returned home to face the Cardinals in a June 2 doubleheader, as a jubilant crowd of 30,000 (somewhat less joyful following a 3–1 loss in the opener) cheered Haddix in between-game ceremonies. Harvey thanked teammates and fans and even acknowledged the opponent in recalling that he "was a skinny 136-pound pitcher-left-handed shortstop in high school, but they (Cardinals) signed me." Any notions of another perfecto were quickly eradicated when, following Haddix's taking the mound to the accompaniment of a standing ovation, he surrendered a single to leadoff batter Don Blasingame. (Said Haddix in the clubhouse afterwards, "No it didn't upset me. After all, the last man I faced got a hit off me.") In no other way did Haddix disappoint that night as he went the distance in shutting out the Redbirds on eight hits and even contributed an RBI single.

Face wasn't used in the twin bill but notched another save the next night by throwing an inning of perfect ball after the Bucs had come from behind with four in the eighth. The outing lowered his ERA to a meager 1.20 and kept the Pirates in third place 4½ behind the Braves.

ElRoy sat while the Pirates lost two of three to the Cubs, which included a tape-measure homer off a sinking fastball by Stuart which sailed over the 457-foot sign in straightaway center. It reportedly marked the first time anyone had cleared the barrier, helping to explain Stu's joyous leap prior to his homerun trot. (Longtime Pirate Pie Traynor claimed he had never witnessed such a feat, and the *New York Times* and *Sporting News* each attested to its uniqueness.)

Face saw action in both games of the doubleheader finale against the Cubs on June 7. Another 30,000 fans packed Forbes Field in anticipation of another Haddix pitching gem, but despite hurling effectively, the lefty departed in the eighth with his club trailing 4–2, one of the Cub runs being unearned. Face struck out two in pitching a scoreless ninth, but Haddix had an even record once again when Pittsburgh was shut down in the bottom of the inning.

A sidelined Willie Mays didn't prevent the Giants from scoring nine runs against Pittsburgh on June 8, but Forbes Field spectators erupted after their heroes exploded for five in the eighth to tie it, two runs scoring on another Stuart blast. With the game deadlocked, Murtaugh called on ElRoy, who continued to add credence to the still-popular theory that good pitching stops good hitting. The previously potent Giants were held to three hits and no runs the next three frames, and Face had his eighth win when Harry Bright pinch-hit a three-run homer in the 11th.

Another shutout inning against Frisco on June 10 gave Face an ERA below 1.00 and a scoreless inning string of 13. The latter number should have been an omen. The following afternoon he replaced Friend in the eighth with his club hanging to a 7–5 edge in a sloppy affair involving a dozen miscues. One of Face's streaks ended when Mays, who had delivered a clutch pinch hit in the eighth inning of the series opener, lashed a pinch three-run homer to give the Giants the lead. But ElRoy's luck wasn't changing just yet. The Pirates pushed five across in the bottom of the inning, and, with Face removed for a pinch hitter, Law mopped up in the ninth.

Some might argue that Face, like Smith in his end-of-May outing, didn't deserve credit for the victory. However, only one of the three runs resulting from Willie's wallop was charged to ElRoy, who entered the game with two runners aboard and easily retired the side after the Mays homer. Moreover, unlike ElRoy, who had looked good in three innings work in the May 31 game, Law wasn't impressive in surrendering a run prior to setting down the Giants in the ninth.

On June 12, Face threw another hitless ninth in the Dodgers 9–6 defeat of Haddix, who received a pen-and-pencil set from Giles for being named Player-of-the-Month in pregame ceremonies. ElRoy won his tenth two days later. He entered in the eighth in a 3–3 tie, retired the side, watched his mates push three across in the bottom half, and then disposed of the Dodgers in the ninth. Although he yielded a pair of hits, four of the six outs came on strikeouts. The Pirates took the second of the doubleheader behind Law's eight-hit pitching and Stuart's two homers. The twin wins gave the Bucs a 32–29 record and pulled them to within three of the Braves, who fell to the Cubs and Ernie Banks' 200th career homer that afternoon.

By mid–June, Face seemed both unbeatable and indestructible. Aside from his perfect 10–0 mark and 15 straight wins, he had appeared in 25 of his club's 61 games, was responsible for nearly half their victories, and had an ERA near 1.00. Was it merely a matter of time before the slender hurler would begin to wear down? After all, Face was no Superman.

Nor was television's George Reeves, which he would tragically prove on the morning of June 17. Born in Woolstock, Iowa, in 1914, Reeves was a teenager when he headed to California to study acting in the late 1920s. Although he worked bit parts in such memorable flicks as *Gone with the Wind* and *From Here to Eternity*, the Hawkeye didn't achieve prominence until 1951, when he landed the role of Superman. The show aired throughout the decade and made Reeves both rich and the idol of millions of American children. By 1959, however, the sulking superhero had become frustrated with a stereotypical image which was preventing his landing more challenging television and film roles. By the evening of June 17, the 45 year old had become so distraught that Lenore Lemmon, his fiancée whom he would be marrying in two days, predicted to friends at his home that Reeves would attempt suicide. At 2:30 A.M. on June 18, he made good her prognostication, firing a .30 caliber bullet through his temple. A crippled career, not Kryptonite, had destroyed Superman.

Face showed no signs of mortality on June 18 in Chicago as he hurled five frames of shutout ball in taking his 11th, allowing only four hits while fanning four. He entered in the ninth after Stuart had connected for a pinch-homer to give the Pirates a 2–1 lead in the seventh and the Cubs' Jim Marshall had knotted it in the eighth with a pinch-homer off Kline. Face won on a Skinner RBI single in the 13th. The five innings work was ElRoy's longest stint in two years, and his appearance was his 8th in the Pirates last 11 games.

Another outing, another shutout inning, though Face received merely a save in cleaning up the Cards on June 21. The 10–8 win offset the Pirates loss to St. Louis in the twin bill opener, which featured a pair of doubles by Musial. Stan finished his career with 725 two baggers, which places him third on the all-time list behind the AL's Tris Speaker and NL's Pete Rose.

Face remained hot in hurling a pair of scoreless frames against Frisco on June 24. He was removed for pinch-hitter Kluszewski in the top of the ninth, and the Bucs lost in the bottom half on a dropped fly ball by Virdon following a pair of walks by Daniels. The defeat dropped the Bucs to fourth behind the Braves, Giants, and surging Dodgers.

The Pirates won a thriller the next day, with ElRoy the beneficiary. The Giants' slow-ball specialist, Stu Miller, held a precarious lead until Stuart's sac fly in the seventh squared the score at one apiece. It remained tied after Face, replacing unlucky Haddix in the tenth, retired the side in order and then surrendered a harmless walk in the eleventh. Knuckleballer Eddie Fisher took the mound in the 12th, yielded a single to Mazeroski and then a 400-foot, left-field homer to Cuban-born Roman Mejias.

Face pitched shakily in closing the contest. Willie Kirkland led off the Giants' 12th with a single and one out later, he was sent to second on a Jackie Brandt hit. ElRoy retired Jim Davenport but walked pinch-hitter Felipe Alou to fill the bases. With the tying run on second and the winning run on first, Face induced a comebacker off the bat of Eddie Bressoud and tossed to first for his 12th win, his 17th straight.

Sweden's Ingemar Johansson was the talk of the sports world on June 27 following his upset victory over world heavyweight champ Floyd Patterson (they only had one then) in front of 30,000 shocked spectators at Yankee Stadium the previous night. The southpaw Johansson pummeled the likable black boxer with right hooks that sent Floyd reeling to the canvas no fewer than seven times in the third round until ref Ruby Goldstein decided enough was enough, making Johansson the first non–American to hold the title since the hulking Primo Carnera stripped Jack Sharkey of the prize in 1933. Said Patterson manager Cus D'Amato afterwards: "Of course, we'll exercise our return-fight privileges. Where and when, well, we'll have to see about that." It would be a year later that Patterson's revenge was realized, his fifth-round knockout of Ingemar making him the first heavyweight in history to regain the belt.

There seemed no losing in Face's future as he continued his mound mastery with another save at the end of June. Haddix started in Philly that day and allowed two early runs on four hits, but he yielded nothing from the fifth until the ninth, when a one-out single prompted the nervous Murtaugh to call on ElRoy. The Bucs' Groat had provided the 4–3 lead in the top of the inning with an RBI hit off Robin Roberts, which became the game-winner when Face whiffed pinch-hitter Harry Anderson and retired Ed Bouchee on a foul popup.

Face became the second Pirate in two months to win Player-of-the-Month honors when he received 30 of a possible 40 votes from baseball writers and broadcasters. As noted by the *Sporting News*, the Pirate pitcher became the recipient of the two-year-old award on the basis of 14 June relief appearances in which he won 5, saved 4, had an ERA of 0.37 in 23 innings, and struck out 18 while walking only 3. Face's closest competition came from teammate Stuart, who busted out in June by smacking 10 homers, including the record tape-measure at Forbes Field, and gathering 22 RBIs in 26 games.

July began typically for Face and the fourth place Pirates — ElRoy hurling an inning of shutout ball and the Pirates struggling, with Ron Kline the unfortunate 1–0 loser in Philadelphia. Pittsburgh was now only a game above the .500 mark, was four games behind the third place Dodgers, and was only a half-game away from slipping into the second division.

By July 5, unseeded Australian Rod Laver's dream of a Wimbledon tennis title had ended in a straight-sets loss to Peruvian Alex Olmedo (Laver would net four Wimbledons before retiring), America had officially raised its new 49-star flag (Alaska had been admitted in January), and Face had saved Haddix by throwing a perfect ninth against the Reds in Pittsburgh that night in his final appearance before the All-Star game at Forbes Field on the seventh.

The fireman had been one of three Pirates selected to the NL squad (Mazeroski and Groat being the others), and he entered the midseason classic in a 1–1 tie in the seventh. ElRoy delighted the partisan crowd by retiring the side, but he struggled in the eighth after the National League reached the Tigers' Jim Bunning for a pair. Disposing of the first two hitters, Face gave up a single to Nellie Fox, a walk to Harvey Kuenn, another single to Vic Power, another walk to Ted Williams, and a double to Gus Triandos. NL skipper Fred Haney then pulled Face, who stood to be the losing pitcher (a defeat in the exhibition game would not, however, have broken ElRoy's winning streak), but the Nationals came back with a pair in the bottom of the eighth and won 5–4.

There would be nothing unlucky about Face's 13th win and 18th straight from his standpoint. After an off day, the regular season resumed on July 9, with the Pirates hosting fifth place Chicago. Vernon Law was masterful in breezing through the first eight innings and appeared assured of his tenth win after retiring two in the ninth. When Sammy Taylor prolonged the game with his fourth hit in as many tries, however, Cub skipper Bob Scheffing sent veteran southpaw-swinger Irv Noren to the plate as a pinch hitter. The Deacon was pulled and Face brought in.

Noren, who gathered 98 RBIs as a rookie with Washington in 1950, sent a Face forkball to deep center, the triple sending Taylor home. With the tying tally 90 feet away, Tony Taylor lashed a single off Face, who then retired George Altman to end the inning. The Bucs were retired in the bottom of the ninth, as were the Cubs in the top of the tenth. Clemente, making his first appearance since leaving the disabled list, led off the Pirates' half with his second single. Murtaugh removed Face for pinch-bunter Mejias, who successfully sacrificed Roberto to second. With lefty Bill Henry on the mound, Virdon gave way to righty batter Bright who came through with a game-winning single.

If the victory hadn't been pretty, ElRoy was satisfied nonetheless. He became the ninth pitcher in history to win 13 straight games in a season, and he matched the club mark set in 1910 by another Pirate Deacon, Charles "Deacon" Phillippe. Following his inning-and-a-third stint, Face led the majors in ERA (0.80) and wins, while remaining the only undefeated hurler (Wilhelm had four losses by then).

Face's 14th win on July 12 was again accomplished at the expense of a fellow hurler, but bad luck was nothing new for Haddix. He stood to be the winning pitcher after Face replaced him and retired the final batter in the eighth. The visiting Cards trailed 5–4 when Don Blasingame opened the ninth with a single, was pushed to second on a Gino Cimoli sacrifice, and scored the game-knotter on Bill White's hit. The tally ended a string of 12 straight scoreless appearances by Face, covering 19⅓ innings. His more significant streak appeared in serious jeopardy when the next batter, Ken Boyer, reached safely, but the righty wriggled out by inducing a double-play grounder off Joe Cunningham's bat.

The game became a battle of forkballers. Lindy McDaniel threw his second straight shutout inning, and Face matched him in the tenth, with the help of another twin-killing. It was then left to Roy's alleged antagonist, Clemente, to again help win it. With the bases loaded and one out, Roberto singled off the right-field wall, making a loser of McDaniel and giving Face a club-record 14 straight for the year. Now within a reachable five of Marquard's and Hubbell's streaks, Face also set sights on the club record for most relief wins in a season, which was held by Mace Brown's 15 in 1938, and the major-league mark of 16 set by Philly fireman Jim Konstanty of the 1950 Whiz Kids.

Face made another appearance that afternoon in the nightcap of the doubleheader at Forbes Field. Don Gross had pitched two scoreless innings but wavered in the ninth, surrendering a Cimoli homer and Musial single before Face was called in. ElRoy fanned pinch-hitter George Crowe, but as another pinch-swinger, Wally Shannon, strode to the dish, the curfew took effect, robbing the reliever of a save opportunity.

By July 15 the Dodgers held third place and were hoping to surpass the second place Braves with a win over the Bucs in Pittsburgh. Face took the mound in the ninth and routinely put a zero on the scoreboard, but Buc batters had not scored against Don Drysdale through the first eight frames and fared as poorly in the ninth. The shutout gave Drysdale his 11th win, the Dodgers second place, and Face a wasted outing. Two days later against the league-leading Giants, Murtaugh again called on his ace reliever with the club trailing late in the game. This time Face yielded a pair of runs, though a Stuart miscue contributed to both, and the Giants prevailed 4–1. His next appearance came on July 21 in the resumption of a suspended May game. Kluszewski was the first batter up that night and rifled his second and last homer of the year for the Pirates into the lower right-field seats. The blast lengthened Haddix's lead to three, but the hurler had some anxious moments in the dugout as Face struggled in the ninth, surrendering a two-run triple to Harry Anderson before retiring the Phillies' Dave Philley and Richie Ashburn to close the contest.

As the fight for first in the National League continued, some verbal sparring was taking place in Moscow on July 25. Russian leader Nikita Khrushchev and American vice president Richard Nixon, two shrewd if not lovable statesmen, were engaged in their famed "Kitchen Debate" at the American National Exhibition in Moscow, which displayed America's modern conveniences, or "gadgetry" as Khrushchev called it while viewing washing machines, color televisions, and electric stoves. (Pointing to the television, Nikita quipped, "This is probably always out of order.") Referring to the competition in arms and industry between the rival nations, Nixon remarked that though Russia might be ahead in rocketry, America had superior commercial technology. When Khrushchev refused to admit as much, Nixon exclaimed, "You see. You never concede anything." Countered Khrushchev, "No. I do not give up."

The conversation was a memorable moment in a dangerously delicate cold war period between the two superpowers. Relations deteriorated less than a year later when Gary Francis Powers, a U-2 pilot, was captured by the Russian military and exposed as an American spy. The two superpowers were pushed to the brink of nuclear war during the early sixties by such notorious incidents as the construction of the Berlin Wall, the Bay of Pigs Invasion, and the Cuban Missile Crisis. Those who lived through the Sword of Damocles situations of the sixties are probably more aware today than they were then of the potential for catastrophe that existed during this period.

On July 27, Face again took the mound, but his two shutout innings went for naught in a nightcap 2–1 loss to the Braves, both tallies coming on a Joe Adcock homer. With the Pirates having fallen to Spahn in the opener also, the double-drop stretched a losing string to six, which was elongated to nine before the Pirates played the first place Dodgers, whose precarious lead on July 30 was a half-game over the Braves and Giants. Face blew a save opportunity that night when, after relieving for Friend in the seventh, he yielded the tying tally in the next inning. It took twelve frames before the Pirates prevailed, ending their losing streak and the Dodgers' hold of the top spot.

The tradition of two major leagues was threatened at the close of July, when the formation of the Continental League was announced by its chairman, William Shea, following a meeting at the Biltmore Hotel in New York. The league would consist of eight cities, which would include New York, Houston, Toronto, Denver, and Minneapolis-St. Paul, with three others to be determined at a later date. Play was scheduled to begin in 1961. The league, with Branch Rickey as president, never materialized as its prospective birth forced big-league owners to grudgingly accept expansion, which began in 1961 with the inclusion of the Los Angeles Angels and the Washington Senators in the American League in 1961 (the old Washington Senators moving to Minnesota) and the Houston Colt .45s and the New York Mets in the National League in 1962. If the Continental League's folding before it started irked Shea, at least he would have the Mets' new stadium of 1964 named in his honor.

Face had an uncharacteristically ineffective outing in a tense afternoon affair against the Giants on the first of August in front of a Seals Stadium crowd of over 21,000. A free-for-all occurred in the second inning after Buc third-sacker Don Hoak was injured on an aggressive slide by baserunner Daryl Spencer. Hoak rushed at Spencer and the inevitable bench emptying ensued, but no damaging blows were landed.

The Pirates had a 5–4 lead in the seventh when the Giants put their first two batters aboard. Enter ElRoy, Murtaugh's fourth choice of the day. A Willie Kirkland liner nearly struck Face in the face as it whistled by him on its way to center, sending rookie Willie McCovey home with the tying run. (McCovey was in his third major-league game, having smashed two singles and two triples in debuting two days earlier.) One run seemed all the Giants would produce as Face easily retired the next two hitters. Murtaugh then ordered slugger Leon Wagner intentionally walked, as Frisco skipper Bill Rigney countered by using Dusty Rhodes as a pinch hitter.

If Rhodes' career was forgettable, his play during the 1954 Series remains memorable. In Game One, following Willie Mays' famed game-saving, over-the-shoulder basket grab of Vic Wertz' long fly to center, Rhodes won it in the tenth with a pinch three-run homer. As a starter the next day, he drove in two of his club's runs in the Giants' 3–1 win. Dusty finished as the Series' top hitter with a .667 average, two homers, and seven ribbies.

Stepping to the plate with a .192 average in what would be his final season, Rhodes still proved reliable in a pinch when he cleared the bases with a double that fell just inside the left-field foul line. The Giants added another before the five-run explosion ended, three being charged to Face. Rhodes' clutch hit carried significance in the tight pennant race, but not as much as it might have if the Giants had won the flag at season's end. Dusty's double also gave Face his second blown save opportunity in as many days, not his first loss of the season.

The Giants roughed up ElRoy again the next day. After McCovey had pulled his team to within one with his first big-league belt — a two-run blast off Kline into Seals Stadium's right-center bleachers — and Willie Mays doubled home the go-ahead run in the seventh, Face pitched the eighth, hoping to keep it a one-run game so that his mates could win it for him in the ninth. Instead, he gave up three hits and another run, as faltering Pittsburgh fell 5–3 and 9½ games from the lead.

"What's going on here?" That question must have crossed Harvey Haddix's mind while he was hurling a complete-game win on the night of August 6. His team scored three in the first, four in the eighth, and ten in the ninth in coasting to an 18–2 laugher in St. Louis. Haddix was not accustomed to such support from his mates. (Nor good fortune. The game had appeared destined for postponement prior to its start, with a heavy downpour causing a long delay.) But the Bucs paid for their three-hour pounding of the Cards. They were scheduled to play the Cubs the following afternoon and didn't arrive at their Chicago hotel until 4 A.M. Moe Drabowsky took advantage of their fatigue by winning his first game in nearly a month, a 4–0 whitewash. Pirate Dick Groat blamed the feast-to-famine offense on the scheduling, complaining after the game, "This isn't fair. We aren't supposed to play night games on getaway days. We don't get our proper rest."

After a good night's sleep, the Pirates tried again at Wrigley Field. The Cubs grabbed an early lead in the first, but the Bucs fought back with a tying tally in the seventh and then took the lead with two in the eighth. The Cubs were threatening in the bottom half when Face was brought in. He yielded a sac fly to Tony Taylor and a single to Jim Marshall and then yielded to the green Freddie Green, who faced Lee Walls, who was pinch-swinging for another rookie, future Hall-of-Famer Billy Williams. Green fanned Walls, and reliever Bob Porterfield finished the eighth by disposing of Art "Dutch" Schult. Chicago tied it in the ninth, but Pittsburgh won it in the 14th. For Face, it was yet another blown save, and he hadn't won a game in nearly a month.

The Cubs and Bucs closed the series at Wrigley on August 9 with a Sunday afternoon game in front of a paid crowd of close to 20,000. Law pitched well through seven innings but was trailing 2–1 when he was removed for a pinch hitter in the eighth. Face was reached for a run in the bottom half, but the Pirates knotted it with two in the ninth. ElRoy threw a blank in the Cubs' ninth, watched his mates score two in the tenth, and then closed out the Cubs in the bottom half for his 15th win and the first since July 12, while the Pirates improved their extra-inning record for the year to 15–1, their only loss being Kuenn's 13-inning, near-perfect heart-breaker.

Although he now owned a share of the club record for relief victories in a season, was within one of the major-league mark, and was within four of Marquard's and Hubbell's record win streaks, Face couldn't have been pleased with stats that showed his allowing 13 hits and 9 runs in his previous 9 innings. Nor could he have been overjoyed with another no-decision effort in Philly on August 10 in which he was reached for three hits and two runs in working a pair of innings in a 6–4 Pirate defeat. And he might have been more than a little concerned after surrendering a walk, four hits, and three runs to the Braves in an inning-and-a-third in his next appearance on August 15, though he again escaped with a no-decision. ElRoy's ERA stood at 1.82, and though it was still the best in baseball, it had risen one run in one month's time. He no longer led the majors in wins, as the Giants' two-time, twenty-game winner Johnny Antonelli had 16.

Having returned from his negotiations with the Red chief in Moscow, Nixon offered advice to baseball negotiators in mid–August. The vice president dampened hopes of a third league when he concurred with Commissioner Ford Frick that expansion was the preferable choice for baseball. To the chagrin of the Continental's Shea, Nixon claimed it would be "more practical to expand the present two (leagues) to ten teams each."

A few days later Face ended a string of ineffective outings with a pair of shutout innings against the Braves at Forbes Field. He stumbled again, however, in his next appearance, allowing four hits and two earned runs to the Cards in the ninth. His luck was still holding as the loss went to his predecessor, reliever Don Gross.

On August 21, after a day of celebration commemorating the Union's latest official member, Hawaii, the Dodgers were celebrating in the clubhouse following a come-from-behind win in Pittsburgh. Trailing 3–1 in the seventh, they had pushed four across to take the lead and had added an insurance run in the ninth which proved vital when the Bucs tallied once before reliever Sandy Koufax notched a save by retiring Burgess to end it. Face had closed out the top half by retiring the last two Dodger batters.

Despite the win, Los Angeles lost ground when the first place Giants swept in Philadelphia, and fell a full game further the next day when San

Fran crushed the Phils while the Pirates were winning 2–0 in a game marred by a disputed call which precipitated a barrage of towels, helmets, and ice-filled buckets from the Dodger dugout. Haddix gave Pittsburgh the lead in the four-game series with a complete-game win in the first of two on August 23. The nightcap, a key game for the Dodgers, who would fall to third with a loss, became a pitcher's duel between Law and rookie righty Larry Sherry. The 1–1 deadlock was snapped on a two-run double by Duke Snider in the eighth. Sherry was reached for a hit in the bottom half, and Johnny Podres and Don Drysdale finished the inning, but not before the Bucs had plated one. Face, who prior to the twin bill received a trophy and clock from the Elks in recognition of his being "the greatest relief pitcher in baseball," took the mound and retired the Dodgers in the ninth, one out coming on a pick-off at second of the gifted base-stealer Maury Wills.

Drysdale returned to the hill and walked leadoff batter Skinner. Groat was successful in sacrificing, and Stuart, who for a month hadn't been "hitting a lick," came off the bench to drill an RBI single that tied the score. Face dismissed the Dodgers in the tenth, but not easily. Wally Moon reached on a bunt hit and advanced to second on a sacrifice. (How proficient players seemed then in "laying one down.") Snider was intentionally passed, and after Fairly popped out, Roseboro walked. Face then threw a forkball to pinch-hitter Carl Furillo, who lined a rope that Skinner caught in left, stranding the three Dodger runners.

Drysdale began the bottom half shakily by surrendering a single, but he appeared out of trouble when pitcher Face bunted into a double play. (Well, they weren't always successful at sacrificing.) Virdon kept the inning alive with a single and went to third on a Burgess hit. Drysdale then walked the dangerous Skinner intentionally, preferring to pitch to captain Groat, who answered the insult by drilling Drysdale's first pitch to left for the ball game.

As 25,000 fans rejoiced at Forbes Field, Face received congrats from his mates for the victory which lengthened a win string to 16 for the season, 21 overall. He had matched Konstanty's mark for most relief wins in a season and was now sole holder of the club mark. In retrospect, Face can think of "no one game of the streak that stands out," but number 16 must have been a huge win for a pitcher with record-salary aspirations.

Luck had again played a part in ElRoy's success that Sunday afternoon. Weather might have prevented his pitching had the downpour which interrupted play for 40 minutes in the opener lasted a little longer. The slumping Stuart, who in the previous four weeks had accumulated but one homer and seven RBIs, was an unlikely hero before he connected with his game-tying single in the ninth. (As Face recalls today, Stuart had several key hits during his streak, but "of course, he made a few errors that hurt me as well.") And then Furillo offered further proof that baseball is a game of inches. Had his bases-loaded line drive in the tenth been a few feet to the left or right of Skinner, Face's streak might have ended that day.

Face's 16th also marked yet another overtime win for the Pirates, who made it 17 of 19 three days later in a 5–4, ten-inning squeaker against the Giants. Righthander Jack Sanford pitched perfectly for 5⅓ innings and had a two-hit shutout in the ninth, but the Pirates tallied four times to tie it, with Stuart's pinch RBI-double off the wall the key blow. The Bucs might have won it in regulation had Danny Kravitz not hit into an inning-ending, home-to-first double play.

Despite critics' claims that Face's streak of 1959 was a matter of luck, Roy had his share of misfortune as well. Kravitz had pinch-hit for Face, who, having retired the Giants in the top of the ninth, would have picked up his 17th that night had Kravitz come through. Having been removed for a pinch hitter, Face wasn't available in the tenth, making Ron Kline the beneficiary of Mazeroski's game-winning RBI single in the bottom of the inning.

Face remained in the bullpen as the Pirates won their next two games, the second being a battering of Robin Roberts at Forbes Field. Home cooking had been healthy for the Pirates. Going into the getaway doubleheader on August 30, they had won 13 of 17 on the homestand, which pushed their record from three games below the .500 mark to six above, pulling them from 11 to 5½ behind the first place Giants.

The Phils, who had entered the decade like lions with their pennant-whizzing season of 1950, were leaving it like lambs, going into the twin bill at Forbes Field already a remote 20 games behind, destined to finish 23 back by season's close. Philly skipper Eddie Sawyer, who had experienced the thrill of victory in 1950, had been fired three years later, and had returned in 1958 to watch his club finish in the cellar, was accustomed to the agony of defeat by then. Having seen his ace get ambushed the day before, Sawyer turned reluctantly to righthander Humberto Robinson to pitch the twin bill opener, and though the Panamanian performed well in allowing seven hits and two runs in going the distance, Haddix threw a six-hitter in winning 2–1. The game was tied at one when Skinner scorched an RBI single with two dead in the ninth.

The Phillies struck hard and quickly in the nightcap, putting five on the board before Daniels was removed with two outs in the first. The five pitchers that succeeded him shut down the Phils' offense through nine, and Philly starter Ray "Baby" Semproch may have been upset by then. Having thrown six shutout innings, Ray yielded a run in the seventh, saw catcher

Kravitz crack a two-run homer off reliever Dick Farrell in the eighth, and then watched Stuart smash a pinch-blast off Farrell to tie it in the ninth. (Skinner had led off the frame with an out, breaking a streak of reaching base safely 11 straight times. The out left him five shy of Ted Williams' still-standing major-league mark, a record which would be more severely challenged in 1985.)

Face relieved in the tenth with a chance to win his 17th, but when lefty slugger Ed Bouchee connected, ending nine straight scoreless innings for the Phils, it appeared ElRoy's winning streak would be stopped at 16, as it had been for Walter Johnson, Smoky Joe Wood, Lefty Grove, Schoolboy Rowe, Hubbell, and Blackwell. (The Giants' Sanford would join the elite list with a string of 16 in 1962.)

But Face again found reprieve, as it was Stu to the rescue again. Following a Hoak single, a groundout by pinch-hitter Burgess, and a walk to Virdon, Dick drilled a delivery by Farrell over the head of late-game center-field substitute Richie Ashburn. By the time the Whiz Kid could retrieve the drive, Hoak and Virdon had scored, making Face a relief winner for an unprecedented 17th time.

No longer in the company of other greats, Face now stood alone as the holder of 17 straight wins for one season, 22 overall. Only Marquard and Hubbell could claim to have done better, with both record streaks a tantalizing two wins away. Face had looked vulnerable in July, however, and would need more than luck in his quest to be the best as the dog days of August beckoned. He had appeared in 50 of the team's 132 games, throwing over 80 innings, a high total even by today's standards for relievers, so that it was not surprising the slender slinger was beginning to tire and had a more mortal ERA of 2.25. Still, Face's streak had remained unscathed after several recent close calls. It wasn't far-fetched to think he might now begin to settle down.

Face showed no signs of doing so, however, in his next appearance. Following a rainout, the Pirates played two in Cincinnati and were tied at three when Law surrendered consecutive singles to Gus Bell and Frank Robinson. Face relieved and retired Whitey Lockman, the Tarheel who was playing in his last of 15 major-league seasons, and then hoped to dispose of another veteran, Willie "Puddin' Head" Jones, who would end a 15-year career the following season. Jones prevailed with a three-run blast that made Law the unlucky loser when Reds starter Jim O'Toole dismissed the Pirates in the ninth.

Ex-Dodger great Don Newcombe, traded to the Reds the year before, dueled Friend in the nightcap. Both hurlers went the distance, with Newk getting the 2–1 decision. The Reds scored the winning tally in the eighth on Johnny Temple's two-out triple, followed by Vada Pinson's double. Interestingly, Murtaugh chose not to go to Face with the go-ahead run at third. True, he had pitched in the opener, but only to three batters. A month earlier Murtaugh wouldn't have hesitated to use ElRoy twice in a twin bill, but the forkballer's recent flops were making the skipper skittish about doing so now.

The double defeat, coupled with the Giants 4–3 win over Chicago, dropped the Pirates six back and pulled the fifth-place Reds to within a game-and-a-half of the Bucs, who headed to Philly for a three-game series. Haddix pitched well in the opener, allowing one earned run through six, but he received little support from a lineup which produced no runs against the normally mediocre Jim Owens. Face relieved in the seventh and looked shaky as he allowed four hits, a walk, and a run in an inning and a third.

Trailing 3–0 the next night, the Pirates looked like losers again until they scored four in the fifth to take the lead. The Phils answered with a pair in the bottom half, but Stuart tied it with his 23d homer, and after the Phils tallied to take the lead in the seventh, he came through with a clutch RBI double in the eighth. Skinner put the Bucs in the lead in the ninth with a ribby single, and Daniels, not Face, successfully closed out the contest.

Law and Robin Roberts dueled in the rapidly played finale at Shibe Park, their complete-game efforts ending in a win for Robin. Both threw blanks for seven frames until the Pirates pushed one across in the eighth. Face hadn't thrown much that first week of September and might have been used after Roberts' right-field single scooted through the legs of Clemente in right, allowing the tying run to score and Roberts to go to third. But Murtaugh hesitated, and Joe Koppe singled for the go-ahead run. The Bucs had a chance in the ninth, but Clemente's comeback liner with the bases loaded was speared by Roberts and converted into a double play.

Face took the mound the next day in the nightcap of a doubleheader at Milwaukee's County Stadium and pitched scoreless ball for the first time in four outings, allowing no Brave batter to reach base in the final two innings. Unfortunately, he entered in the eighth with the Bucs already trailing 4–1, which is how the game ended. Pirate pennant hopes diminished following the doubleheader loss as they fell seven behind the Giants with three weeks remaining.

The Dodgers were tied with the Braves for second and still had flag aspirations as they trailed the Giants by 2 with 15 to play prior to hosting Pittsburgh in a doubledip on September 11. More than 48,000 fans filled Los Angeles Coliseum (Dodger Stadium was three years away), raising season attendance to 1,900,000, which surpassed the total for 1958 when the Dodgers inaugurated their West Coast play. Although the game would play a vital part in the pennant race, its immediate aftermath would arguably be more significant.

Twenty-three-year-old Koufax took the mound for Los Angeles in the twilight game. Owning an admirable 8–4 record, the southpaw fireballer still hadn't blossomed into the best pitcher in baseball, a rating he would attain during the early-to-mid sixties. Having won 20 of 41 decisions from 1955 to 1958, Sandy remained inconsistent in 1959, entering the opener with an ERA of 3.76. Sandy continued struggling with control in allowing 72 walks in 127 innings pitched, an average of over five per game. Nevertheless, his strikeout percentage was the best in baseball; he was the only starter to have more K's (150) than innings-pitched (127).

Friend and Koufax matched goose eggs until the Dodgers broke through with a run in the fifth. Stuart blasted his 24th homer to tie it, but Wally Moon launched a rocket (as the Soviets would launch a rocket to the moon the next day) to give the Dodgers the lead after six. A Groat single in the seventh again squared the game, and Mejias connected with a man on in the eighth, giving Friend a two-run cushion. When the righty wavered in the eighth by serving Moon's second dinger and then a one-out hit to Norm Larker, Face was summoned.

The appearance marked ElRoy's 99th since his last loss in May of 1958. He hadn't thrown in three days, being inactive during an off day and a two-game set with the Giants which preceded the Los Angeles series. One can hardly argue that fatigue affected his performance that evening, though the suggestion can obviously be made that overwork during the course of the season was a factor. In any case, Face offered immediate relief by retiring Gil Hodges and John Roseboro to end the eighth.

Only three outs from preserving victory, Face succumbed to Maury Wills' third straight hit of the game and Ron Fairly's pinch-bunt sacrifice. Junior Gilliam's next swing resulted in a line-drive triple into the right field corner that scored Wills, tying the game. With the winning run on third, Face was closer to losing than he had been in the last 99 games.

With one out, Charlie Neal might have been purposely passed to set up a potential inning-ending twin-killing, but Murtaugh preferred the prospect of challenging the .280 righty batter against a drawn-in infield over facing the torrid, southpaw-swinging Moon, with taters in his previous two tries. It was a logical strategy, one with which Dodgers manager Walt Alston would have concurred had he been around to watch. (He had been ejected earlier by plate ump Shag Crawford.) It almost worked. Neal hit a weak wormburner, a sure out under normal circumstances, but against the shortened infield, the ball managed to crawl through the left side. Face's glorious streak ended, not with a bang, but with a wimpy grounder.

Today Face has no regrets. "I wouldn't have changed the way I pitched to Neal," he insists. "It was a good pitch. I busted him inside and broke his bat." Although ElRoy was philosophical in the clubhouse that night ("Well, Walter Johnson lost, too," he told reporters), Neal's inadvertent cheap shot annoyed him. Reflects ElRoy, "I think the loss would have been easier to take if it had been on a good, solid hit."

The Dodgers won both games that day, putting them a half-game behind the Giants. Los Angeles proceeded to win 8 of their next 13 games to gain a tie for first by season's end, not with the Giants, who faded to the show position by losing 9 of 14, but with the two-time defending-champion Braves, who closed by taking 9 of 13. It was all Dodgers in the best of three playoffs; they won in Milwaukee and then gave Los Angeles fans their first pennant with a 12-inning thriller at Los Angeles Coliseum. Two weeks later the West Coast had its first Series winner, as the Dodgers took the White Sox in six, with Larry Sherry notching two saves and two wins, including the decider.

As for the Pirates, they finished a disappointing fourth following their promising second place showing of 1958, unaware of their proximity to that proverbial corner of prosperity when they would become the league's first champs of the sixties, outdistancing second place Milwaukee by seven games. Seemingly overmatched against the mighty Yankees in October, the Bucs nevertheless pushed the Bombers to Game Seven, then won it all when Mazeroski ambushed New York in the ninth with a Series-ending clout off Ralph Terry, making hard-luck Haddix the winner of one of the most famous games in baseball history. (Yankee catcher John Blanchard had called for the pitch that Maz hit out and was disconsolate in the clubhouse until fellow backstop Berra told him to forget it, that they'd "be in a lot more of these things." The Yanks did play in the next four Fall Classics.)

After having his streak snapped, Face won in his next appearance on September 19, another extra-inning affair for the Pirates, this one stretching 12 frames. A two-out RBI triple by Maz decided it after Face had appeared a loser in surrendering the go-ahead run in the top of the inning.

In retrospect, Face's 18th and final victory was consequential for two reasons. The Braves took the loss that day, making necessary their unsuccessful playoff with the Dodgers at season's end. And if he failed to reach one record that year, ElRoy's 18 wins in relief is a still-standing major-league mark, one better than the records of Detroit's John Hiller (17–14 in 1974) and Minnesota's Bill Campbell (17–5 in 1976). Face's record of 18–1 gave him a winning percentage of .997, which also remains an unmatched mark for hurlers with 16 or more decisions in a season.

ElRoy put an exclamation point on the incomparable season by fanning the only three batters he faced on September 22, and then hurling a scoreless ninth the next night to preserve a victory for Ron Kline over the Braves in Pittsburgh. He finished 1959 with a praiseworthy ERA of 2.70, and his 18 wins combined with 10 saves accounted for 36 percent of the Pirates' 78 victories.

In spite of his incredible year, Face was overlooked as the choice for the Cy Young Award; the prestigious prize for hurlers went to Early Wynn, who won 22 that year for the pennant-winning White Sox. At the time, only a single award was given each year, the custom of giving one per league not beginning until 1967. Still it is difficult to understand why Face was snubbed, and his not receiving a single vote is thoroughly incomprehensible, even with the knowledge that McDaniel's one tally the following season marked the only ballot for any reliever until 1970. Nonetheless, Wynn's winning was a surprise to no one, including ElRoy. "I wasn't upset. I didn't expect to get it," he recalls. "It used to go to the starting pitchers in those days. If they had given two awards then like they do now, I think I would have been considered."

Face had another fine season in 1960, albeit not as spectacular. He won 10 of 18 decisions, notched 24 saves, posted an ERA of 2.90, and led the league in game appearances with 68. ElRoy saved his best for the Series. He pitched a pair of scoreless frames in preserving Law's 6–4 win in Game One, again saved Law in Game Four, retiring the last eight Yankee batters, retired the last eight the next day in notching his third save, and pitched three innings in the Pirates victory in Game Seven. Says Face, "Winning the World Series was my biggest thrill, even bigger than that '59 season."

Despite his significance to the Series' outcome, Face was bypassed as the MVP choice, which went to the Yanks Bobby Richardson, but the second baseman did perform brilliantly with six singles, two doubles, two triples, and a grand slam in 30 at-bats. Face speaks in a bewildered, not bitter, tone today when commenting on the selection. "I had a hand in all four victories, but they gave the MVP to a losing player. I still don't understand it."

Face believed his playing in Pittsburgh, which at the time lacked access to an AP or UPI news service, prevented the Pirates from attaining as much publicity as teams in cities such as New York, Chicago, and St. Louis and hurt his chances of receiving postseason, and even postcareer, honors, specifically induction into the Hall of Fame. "I was one of the first pitchers in the majors to be used as a closer or late-game finisher," Face reminds us. "I pitched in 802 games with the Pirates. That's good for a tie with Walter Johnson for most games pitched with one club."

Even when excluding that presumably unbreakable record (in this era of free agency) and his marks for most relief wins and winning percent-age, Face's career still rates him consideration as a Cooperstown inductee. He retired in 1969 with 821 relief appearances, which currently ranks ninth on the all-time list for relievers. He accumulated 96 relief wins, placing him sixth on the list. If saves are a better indication of a reliever's worth, Face finished with 193, good enough to be among the top twenty today despite the innumerable relief specialists who have inundated baseball for the past quarter century. The most telling stat for relievers may be wins-plus-saves. ElRoy's 289 ranks among the top twenty and was more than any contemporary achieved except McDaniel (291) and the durable Hall-of-Famer Wilhelm (351). With such revealing statistics, perhaps the Veteran's Committee will someday consider Face for Hall induction.

Although his dream of surpassing Page's pay was eventually realized, it would seem ElRoy had the right idea at the wrong time. Face's highest salary never approached the six- and seven-digit figures enjoyed by mod-ern relief specialists, many of whom are mediocre compared with the stan-dard set by the forkball fireman. After leaving the game, ElRoy worked as a carpenter for the state and would "get up at 6:00 A.M. every weekday" before his retirement in the early nineties.

In the winter following the 1959 season, ElRoy was honored at a ban-quet held in Baltimore. Prior to receiving an award, he met 70-year-old Rube Marquard, one of the two men who held records Face had vainly pur-sued. They began speaking, and if there existed in ElRoy a tinge of disap-pointment prior to the conversation, he walked away feeling differently. "He was so proud of that streak," Face remembers about Marquard, "that it sort of made me feel glad that I hadn't broken it. Even now I'm not sorry I lost the chance."

Some records are better left unbroken.

ElRoy Faces 17 Consecutive Wins of 1959

Date	Opponent (Home/Away)	Score	IP	H	R	ER	BB	SO
4/22	Reds (H)	9–8	2	1	1	1	0	2
4/24	Phils (A)	8–5	2⅓	4	2	2	1	0
5/3	Cards (H)	4–3	3	0	0	0	0	2
5/7	Phils (H)	5–4	1	1	0	0	0	1
5/13	Dodgers (A)	6–4	3	3	0	0	2	5
5/14	Dodgers (A)	7–6	1⅓	2	1	1	1	3
5/31	Reds (A)	14–11	3	1	0	0	0	5
6/8	Giants (H)	12–9	3	3	0	0	0	1
6/11	Giants (H)	12–9	1	2	1	1	0	1
6/14	Dodgers (H)	6–3	2	2	0	0	0	4

6/18	Cubs (A)	4–2	5	3	0	0	0	4
6/25	Giants (A)	3–1	3	2	0	0	2	0
7/9	Cubs (H)	4–3	1⅓	1	0	0	0	1
7/12	Cards (H)	6–5	2⅓	4	1	1	0	0
8/9	Cubs (A)	5–3	3	4	1	0	1	2
8/23	Dodgers (H)	4–3	2	2	0	0	2	0
8/30	Phils (H)	7–6	1	2	1	1	0	0
	Totals		39⅔	37	8	7	9	31

Other Significant Stats Covering Face's 17 Wins:

ERA: 1.59   Games Won at Home: 10   Games Won on Road: 7

Team-by-Team Breakdown:

Dodgers 4   Giants 3   Phils 3   Cubs 3   Reds 2   Cards 2

Seven

What a Difference
a Missed Day Makes

Perhaps no rivalry in baseball history matched the one between New York's slugging center-fielders of the fifties — the Yankees' Blond Bomber, Mickey Mantle, and the Giants' Say-Hey Kid, Willie Mays. From their rookie season in 1951 to 1958 when Giants owner Horace Stoneham moved the club to San Francisco, comparisons between the extraordinarily talented players were made frequently by broadcasters, sportswriters, and fans.

And why wouldn't the gifted duo evoke comparisons? Each played in the same town for rival teams in rival leagues. Fanfare had accompanied both during their rise to the majors. Mantle awed audiences in preseason exhibition games with tape-measure homers and seemingly inhuman speed on the basepaths. Mays was discovered while starring for the Birmingham Black Barons of the Negro National League by scout Eddie Montague, who later said Willie "was the greatest player I had ever seen in my life." The Giants signed Mays for $15,000 and then sent him to Trenton, where he became the first black player assigned to a Class-B Interstate club. Willie responded by hitting .353 in 1950 and was promoted to the Triple A Minneapolis Millers the next year, where he hit .477 in 35 games before being called up by the Giants.

Mantle started slowly in 1951, with frequent strikeouts necessitating a demotion to the minors before he returned prior to the close of the season. Mays too seemed destined for the bush leagues after he went hitless in his first 25 big-league at-bats, causing the distraught Alabaman to break down in the clubhouse. Unlike Mantle's impatient skipper, Casey Stengel, Leo Durocher gave Willie a vote of confidence, promising to stick with him "as long as I'm manager of the Giants." Mays broke his slump with a homer off the left-field roof of the Polo Grounds, and the victim of the blast,

140

Warren Spahn, bemoaned later: "I'll never forgive myself. We might have gotten rid of Willie forever if I'd only struck him out." Mays finished his rookie year with respectable stats — .274 average, 20 homers, and 68 RBIs in 121 games. Mantle ended with a .267 average, 13 homers, and 65 RBIs.

Both players appeared destined for bigger numbers in 1952. For Mays, however, Uncle Sam would intervene. He was drafted and missed most of the season and all of the next. When Willie returned in 1954, Mantle, whose chronic bone condition osteomyelitis resulted in a 4-F classification, had amassed an additional 44 homers and 179 RBIs, along with averages in 1952 and 1953 of .311 and .295 respectively.

Mick continued to be impressive in 1954 with another 27 dingers and a .300 average. He had his first of three 100-RBI, 100-run, 100-walk seasons (Mays never had one), his 129 runs leading the league. But 1954 was Willie's year to do some catching-up. He smashed 41 homers, led the league in batting (.345), slugging (.667), and triples (13), and had his first of ten 100-RBI seasons (Mantle had four). When Mays followed with an equally phenomenal season in 1955 which included leading the league in slugging (.659), homers (51), and triples (13), it appeared his proponents had the advantage, despite Mantle's impressive, league-leading stats of .611 slugging average, 37 homers, and 11 triples.

But Mantle advocates would have the upper hand in 1956. He topped the majors in batting (.353), homers (52), and RBIs (130) and became the ninth player to achieve the Triple Crown, while also leading baseball in slugging (.705) and runs (132). Mays's .296 average, 36 homers, and 84 RBIs paled in comparison.

The Giants' move to the Bay area didn't end debate over who was the better ballplayer, and prior to the 1960 season it was anyone's guess. Listed below are Mantle's and Mays' figures for the years 1951 to 1959:

	Games	AB	BA	SA	HR	RBI	R
Mantle	1246	4478	.311	.569	280	841	994
Mays	1065	4074	.317	.590	250	709	777

In terms of the stats, Mays appears the slightly superior batter, considering his two-year layoff during military service. His batting and slugging averages were higher during the period covered by the table, while his homer and RBI rate were comparable to Mantle's. Still, while each had taken one batting championship by 1960, Mantle had three homer crowns to Mays' one, one RBI title to Mays' none, and two MVP Awards to Mays' one. Mantle appeared to be the more feared batter, leading the league in walks three times during the fifties and surpassing the 100-walk plateau each year from 1954 to 1958. Mays wouldn't reach the 100 mark until 1971, when he led the senior circuit in passes for the first and only time of his career.

Mick and Willie continued their rivalry as the sixties unfolded. The Yank surpassed the Frisco Kid in homers in 1960 and 1961, and though Mays outhomered his counterpart 49 to 30 in 1962, injuries prevented Mantle's playing in nearly forty games that year. His injuries didn't prevent, however, his taking a third MVP. A more serious injury led to Mick's playing in only 65 games in 1963, while Mays batted .314, walloped 38 four baggers, and drove in over 100 runs for the fifth consecutive season. (He would stretch the streak to eight.) Nineteen sixty-four was another banner year for Willie, who led the league with 47 homers and a .607 slugging percentage, while Mick made a comeback by belting 34 homers, driving in 111, and reaching the .300 mark for the tenth and final time of his career. (Mays would have an equal number of such seasons.)

By 1965, many may have been wondering if the productive pair would ever slow down. Mick was off to a quick start, hitting four homers in the first couple of weeks, but chronic disease along with a weak Yankee lineup hindered his effectiveness the next few months. Pitchers, aware of his vulnerable legs which had to be completely wrapped before each game, began throwing low-inside, while wasting pitches outside. The keep-him-off-the-plate-then-make-him-reach strategy worked. Mantle saw few strikes but kept swinging the stick, realizing that taking walks would merely result in higher left-on-base numbers for the team by game's end, not additional tallies. As the Yanks' scoring struggles persisted, the pressured Mantle's frustration at the plate intensified.

By August, Mickey's name could be found not near the top of the leaderboard but in the unaccustomed middle position of the batter-stat list. His woeful .263 average placed him 40th among AL hitters, though it was good enough for second among Yankee regulars, with Tom Tresh's .266 leading the Bombers. Mick's 14 homers by August 8 put him on a pace to sock about 20, which would be the lowest total since his rookie year, when he socked 13 (discounting the injury-plagued 1963 season when he managed merely 15).

In conspicuous contrast, Mays began 1965 splendidly and was among the top five in most offensive categories by the Fourth of July, including being first in homers with 22. He reached a career milestone on July 8 when he rocketed his 476th homer, surpassing Cardinals-great Stan Musial, who had retired in 1963 after 22 years in the majors. If there existed some secret to the enduring success of the 34 year old, Willie wasn't aware of it. His strategy had always been refreshingly uncomplicated, to "just go up there and look for any pitch over the plate and if it's something I think I can hit, I swing," as he advised teammate Len Gabrielson in June.

Mays fans may have been celebrating their advantage over Mantle supporters, but their glee seemed premature in the games following the All-Star game of July 13. After starring in the midseason classic by homering off starter Milt Pappas in the first frame and then preserving a 6–5 victory with a leaping, backhand catch to thwart an eighth-inning AL rally, Mays fell into a horrendous slump reminiscent of his dreadful debut in 1951. Following his July 8 homer, he failed to get another round tripper or RBI for the next three weeks. He broke the homer and RBI drought as well as an 0-for-24 slide when he connected off the Braves' Bob Sadowski on July 30. Willie finished the month with an 0-for-four collar at Milwaukee's County Stadium. (The Braves would move to Atlanta and into the batter's paradise, Fulton County Stadium, in 1966.) He had hit two homers for July, after averaging better than seven per month the first three months of the season. Mantle fans jeered that Willie was fading fast, unaware that the following month would prove the most productive of Mays' career.

Willie's work in the Giants-Braves twin bill of August 1 would be but a hint of what lay ahead. He drilled three hits off winning pitcher Tony Cloninger (who would win 24 that year) and then stroked another pair in the nightcap off complete-game winner Wade Blasingame. Yet all the safeties were singles, and he failed to gather any RBIs. The doubleheader drop dropped the Giants to fourth in the standings, four games behind front-running Los Angeles.

With Giant spitballer Gaylord Perry "loading 'em up" throughout, despite frequent but futile inspections of the ball by umpires, the Braves overcame Vaseline and Mays' 25th circuit to once again defeat Frisco on August 2. Perry was given a warning in the eighth inning, and had the umps caught him in the act, he could have been ejected and suspended for ten days according to a rule adopted in 1957 which specified various illegal pitches and penalties. The rule was amended in 1968, and again in 1974 when wet ones would be automatically called a ball on the first offense, with the hurler given a warning. If the offense was repeated, the pitcher was to be ejected and "subject to such action as may be imposed by the league office." Judging by the scarcity of penalties imposed today, one can conclude that modern pitchers are more honest, clever, or scared than in the past or that umpires are either more reluctant to make the spitball call or less observant.

Willie regained the homer lead with a pair in a wild affair against the second place Reds at Crosley Field on August 5. With two on in the open-ing inning, Willie crushed a delivery from Cincy righthander John Tsi-touris, the ball clearing the center-field fence 387 feet from home plate. Mays hit another with no one aboard in the next inning, victimizing righty reliever Bobby Locke and giving the Giants a lead of six runs, which had been extended to ten by the time Willie stepped to the plate in the sixth.

Whether on his own initiative or under orders from Red skipper Dick Sisler, lefty Roger Craig fired a knockdown pitch which sent Mays sprawl-ing to the ground, to the delight of the Crosley crowd. It was Craig's sec-ond wild toss of the inning; he had nailed pitcher Bobby Bolin earlier. By the eighth, Giants batter Hal Lanier knew better than to "dig in" at the plate with an 18–5 Frisco lead and he was able to evade a Bill McCool fast-ball aimed at his back. Umpire Doug Harvey reacted by fining McCool fifty dollars.

Annoyed by the arbiter's interference, Red slugger Frank Robinson purposely stalled prior to leading off the bottom of the eighth. After his order to step in the batter's box was twice ignored, Harvey instructed the Giants' reliever to deliver the pitch. Masanori Murakami, the first Japanese ever to play in the big leagues, obeyed. (In 1964 it appeared the Giants had landed a rising star, but Murakami returned to the Land of the Rising Sun in 1966, obeying orders from his father.)

Robby began arguing while remaining out of the box, and Harvey again motioned to Murakami, who was more than willing to toss strike two. Robinson became livid and, following his ejection, needed to be restrained by Sisler and teammates. Before departing, the irate Robinson threw assorted equipment onto the infield as a final gesture of protest. He was handed a two-game suspension and $150 fine by NL president Warren Giles the next day.

Robinson finished the season with 33 homers and 113 RBIs, but the future Hall-of-Famer, who today holds fourth place on the all-time home-run list, was traded that winter by Cincy president Bill DeWitt for pitcher Pappas because he thought Frank was an "old thirty." The youthful Pap-pas had a record of 12–11 with the Reds in 1966 and was 99–90 with three clubs from 1966 to his final season in 1973. Robinson won the Triple Crown and MVP in 1966 playing for the world-champion Orioles and was the MVP in the World Series as well. Playing an additional nine full seasons from 1966 to 1974, Robby averaged 25 homers per season, including four years with 30 or more. His combined batting average for those years, which included several lean ones for batters, was a healthy .286, six points fewer than his career mark. His ribby rate for his post–Red career was 79 per sea-son, including two seasons with 100 or more, one with 99, and another with

Willie Mays takes a swing at a Milt Pappas delivery during the 1965 All-Star Game in July. The following month he would enjoy his finest homerun spree (AP/Wide World Photos).

97. DeWitt's blunder may not, however, have matched that of Red Sox owner Harry Frazee; in 1919 the money-starved theater producer sold a fellow named Ruth to the Yanks.

The Giants traveled to St. Louis on August 6, where they won their fourth straight and edged to within two of the Dodgers, with Mays contributing a pair of singles in the 3–2 squeaker at Sportsman's Park. (The Cards would move into Busch Stadium the following season.) Mays connected for his fourth and fifth of August in the nationally televised game the following afternoon, both being two-run blasts. The first was a mammoth wallop hit off starter Tracy Stallard, with the ball settling in a back row of the left-center bleachers, traveling approximately 450 feet. His more modest second drive landed in the same bleachers and was yielded by rookie reliever Nellie Briles, who would distinguish himself as a starter with the Cards and other clubs during the sixties and seventies. The pair of round trippers marked Willie's 53d multiple-homer game, a feat he would perform ten additional times before retiring. His 63 games with two or more homers is a still-standing National League record.

Adding an RBI single, Willie's five ribbys gave him 70 for the year, a distant 20 behind league-leader Deron Johnson. Willie's RBI slump of July was costing him a legitimate shot at the Triple Crown because his 29 homers led the league and his .328 average was second only to Roberto Clemente's.

With help from Mays' three hits, including his sixth August homer, the Giants completed a sweep of the Cards with a 6–4 triumph on August 8. Willie's poke came off righthander Bob Purkey with two outs and none on in the sixth and marked the 10th time in 13 seasons he reached the 30-homer mark.

The winning pitcher was a lefty starter named Warren Spahn. Spahn had been picked up by the Giants in July, having been released by the Mets after losing 12 of 16 decisions, including 8 straight. In his Giant debut at Candlestick Park on July 22, 30,000 fans gave the 21-year veteran and winner of 360 major-league games a standing ovation as he took the mound. Baseball dramas don't always end, however, in storybook fashion. Although San Fran won, Spahn failed to notch the win when he was pulled by manager Herman Franks while trailing 3–2.

Many believed Spahn was over the hill by 1965 and wondered why he hadn't already retired. Hall-of-Fame hurler Bob Feller was one of them. In a wire-service story prior to Spahn's next start on July 27, the former Indian fireballer was quoted as asking, "What is he out to prove?" When informed of Feller's query, Spahn reacted by wondering why an "outsider should be telling me when to quit" and then suffered a complete-game 3–0 loss to Purkey and the Cards despite surrendering only four safeties.

Spahn's victory in St. Louis was his third try, and though he needed help from Murakami and Jack Sanford, the 44 year old offered proof that pitching experience is an advantage, not a detriment, that finesse and guile are adequate substitutes for a blazing fastball. Forthcoming decades would furnish further evidence of that theory in the form of such wily hurlers as Don Sutton, Phil Niekro, Tommy John, and Jim Kaat. Even reputed fireballers such as Tom Seaver and Frank Tanana enjoyed lengthened careers by learning to "set up batters" when merely "blowing them away" was no longer feasible. How many of baseball's current crop of pitchers possessing ninety-mile-per-hour fastballs and trick pitches, but lacking the ability to control them, will attain equal success and longevity?

Spahn would win only two more with Frisco before retiring at the close of the season, settling for a career which included 363 lifetime victories, still the most by a left-hander in baseball history. His victories included thirteen 20-win seasons, two coming after the age of forty; nine seasons with an ERA under 3.00; 63 shutouts, second to Eddie Plank on the all-time lefty list; and two no-hitters, both coming late in his career. Not bad for a hurler who missed three seasons while serving during World War II. Spahn's accomplishments were realized despite his amassing 150 or more strikeouts in only five seasons. As a youth, he had relied on rising fastballs but continued winning when the power vanished, becoming a "pitching scientist, an artist with imagination," as Stan Musial once described him.

After an off day for travel, another pitching virtuoso made his appearance for the Giants at Candlestick on August 10. Juan Marichal's career wouldn't be as lengthy or impressive as Spahn's, but by 1965 he was the closest thing to perfection on the mound, with the exception of Sandy Koufax, the darling southpaw of the Los Angeles team. Marichal won 18 in 1962, 23 the following season, another 21 in 1964, and was on target for a third consecutive 20-win season as he entered the game against the Pirates that day with a 17–8 record. The right-hander's distracting high kick, overhand delivery, and reputation for brushing back batters made him equally effective against righty and lefty batters.

Despite being a questionable starter because he had developed a sore elbow in his previous outing, Juan pitched effectively and, thanks in part to a Mays RBI single, had a 4–1 lead going into the ninth, having allowed only two hits to that point. The Bucs' Bill Virdon ambushed the Dominican Dandy for a wind-blown, opposite-field, two-run homer, but Marichal hitched up his trousers and retired Roberto Clemente, Willie Stargell, and Donn Clendenon on strikeouts.

Mays connected for numbers seven and eight of the month as the Giants stretched a winning streak to eight in the twin bill opener of August 12 before having it snapped by the Pirates in the nightcap at Candlestick. Willie's solo homer off Bob Friend in the sixth was a key blow in the Giants 4–3 win, as was his brilliant defensive play in the fourth, when he ran down a Jim Pagliaroni double to prevent an apparent run. Mays' homer in the second game was surrendered by Vernon "The Deacon" Law and was Willie's eighth in ten games. Predicted sportswriter Bob Stevens, "August promises to be a vintage homerun month for the Giant center fielder."

Spahn lost 3–2 to Philadelphia the next day, all three Philly runs being unearned, as Mays was held hitless for the first time in the thirteen August contests. The winning pitcher was Bo Belinsky, who threw two innings of perfect ball, save for a walk to Mays in the fifth. Asked afterwards what his pitching selections to Willie had been, Belinsky joked, "I was desperate. I'd even throw Mamie Van Doren up there." (Bo and the voluptuous actress had been a hot item while he was a member of the Los Angeles Angels from 1962 to 1964.)

Mays again drew the collar against the Phils on August 14, as Marichal surrendered a two-run, opposite-field homer to sophomore slugger Richie Allen in the eighth that proved to be the game-winner in the 4–2 Philly win. After yielding the blast, Marichal stormed toward home plate in a rage, screaming at umpire Lee Weyer for what Juan interpreted as a missed third-strike call to Cookie Rojas earlier that inning. Weyer shouted back, and the two were face-to-face before manager Herman Franks and Giants teammates forcibly restrained Marichal, while Mays played peacemaker by gently placing his hand on Weyer's shoulder and coaxing him away from the irate right-hander. Marichal's temper may have surprised some among the 23,000 Candlestick spectators, but eight days later the hurler's hot-headedness would be made apparent to millions of baseball fans through-out the country.

Although better able to control his emotions, Mays too was becom-ing frustrated. He failed to get a hit for the third consecutive game in the Sunday afternoon finale with the Phils on the 15th, which was won by the Giants 15–9. The victory drew Frisco to within 2½ of the Dodgers, and with the beatable Mets coming to town for a trio of games while Los Angeles was hosting the combative Phils, Franks and Company hoped to pull closer by the end of the week.

Casey Stengel was in his fourth year as Mets helmsman but wasn't with the ballclub in Frisco, having fractured his hip in a fall at the All-Star banquet in July. In Casey's absence, Wes Westrum was managing the club that had claimed the cellar spot the past three seasons and was doing its best to take it again. The Mets trailed their fellow expansion club from 1962, the ninth place Houston Colts (renamed Astros the following sea-son), by 13 games.

New York would find no reprieve at Candlestick. A Mays opposite-field dinger off Tall Tom Parsons (6' 7") was the difference in a 3–2 Met loss on August 16, and they fell by the same score the next day. The Mets were no match for Marichal in the closer. Going into the game, Juan had beaten them 13 straight, holding them to a lifetime ERA of 0.87. When Mays hit his tenth tater of August off lefty Larry Miller with two down in the first, it was all Marichal would need. He improved his impressive stats against the young franchise by throwing a 5–0 whitewash. It put him in a positive frame of mind prior to facing his next opponent — the Dodgers — who had lost two of three to Philly and were coming to town for a four-game fight for first.

The Mets hadn't left their heart in San Francisco upon their return to New York on August 19. They kept trying and even took three of four from the world-champion Cardinals that week. They finished last for the fourth straight season but moved to ninth place in 1966 and after becoming cellar-dwellers the next season, they again grabbed ninth in 1968 before shocking the universe with their miracle world championship in 1969.

Although Mays had done well with a pair of homers against New York, he missed a chance for more when he was removed from the lineup prior to the start of the second game. Willie's leg was sore, and though he wanted to play, Franks decided against using him, saying to reporters afterwards: "I thought, 'What the hell am I doing? If he hurts it some more, he might be finished for the Dodger Series this weekend.'" The conservative strategy was logical. The Mets could be beaten with or without Mays, as was shown, and the upcoming set with Los Angeles carried greater importance. In retrospect, Willie's missed opportunity was consequential because he failed by one to match Rudy York's still-standing record 18 homers in one month, set in 1937, and the Giants failed to take the flag in 1965 anyway, with the Dodgers prevailing.

Over 35,000 fans attended the Thursday afternoon opener, and though the result — an 8–5 Giants setback — wasn't satisfying, few could have complained of not getting their money's worth. As with many Giants-Dodgers confrontations of the sixties, the game was characterized by a stubborn refusal by both clubs to accept defeat. The 15-inning thriller featured a Mays four bagger, and right-fielder Matty Alou three times threw out Dodger baserunners. Pitcher Don Drysdale hit his 6th homer of the season and 26th of his career. (He would hit another before season's end; his seven is a still-standing NL record for pitchers, and his 29 career homers mark is second to Spahn's 35.) Tom Haller hit a two-out, ninth-inning, game-tying homer, and an apparent go-ahead run by the Dodgers in the twelfth was thwarted when Willie Crawford failed to touch third while charging home.

The game began as a promising pitching duel between the experienced Spahn and the Dodgers' Drysdale. A Cy Young Award winner in 1962, Big D was having a good but not spectacular season, bringing a 16–11 record into Candlestick. He would go on to win seven of his last eight decisions and was the key to L.A.'s successful pennant run in late–August and September. Drysdale (23–12) and Koufax (26–8) combined to provide half of the team's 97 victories in 1965 and then combined to form a bargaining team during the winter, each refusing to negotiate with the Dodgers' front office without keeping the other informed.

Spahn was given an early 2–0 lead when Mays cracked his 11th of the month off Drysdale in the first, the ball traveling 330 feet before clearing the ten-foot wire screen in left. He was removed in the seventh as the potential winning pitcher, but when Murakami tried slipping a fastball past Johnny Roseboro, the resulting single knotted the score at three apiece.

Los Angeles scored two in the eighth, then twice had victory elude them when Haller homered and Crawford blundered on the basepaths. In the 15th, Perry's spitballs weren't sufficiently moist to prevent three Dodgers' runs. Reliever Ron Perranoski pitched his fourth shutout inning (Drysdale had been lifted for a baserunner in the 12th) to clinch the victory.

That gamesmanship and bench-jockeying were used by both clubs should have surprised no one. In the fifth inning, the Dodgers' Maury Wills was awarded first when it was ruled catcher Tom Haller had interfered with his swing. Screams of protest came from the Giants, who claimed that Wills intentionally made contact with Haller's mitt. In the Giants' half of the inning, Alou unsuccessfully tried the same tactic and, after being retired, teamed with Franks in the dugout in a shouting match with catcher Roseboro. The combative marathon set the tone for the remaining three games. The Dodgers had drawn first blood but would see some of their own spilled — literally — before the Series' completion.

The Giants tied the Series the next night before more than 41,000 fans, the largest home crowd of the season. Right-handers Bob Shaw and Howie Reed each surrendered second-inning runs. Alou doubled with one out in the third, and Mays then crushed a Reed fastball over the right-centerfield screen, the deciding blow in a 5–1 decision.

On Saturday afternoon, attendance topped that of the previous night, with the 42,283 setting a Candlestick record while falling only a couple hundred short of capacity. Mays delighted spectators with his third circuit of the Series. The Giants trailed 4–3 in the eighth, one Dodgers run being a result of Mays overrunning a Wills single and being charged with a two-base error. Willie made amends when he timed a 3–1 Bob Miller pitch and sent a fly ball to right which, with help from the wind, carried over the fence. His 13th August blow was also the 490th of his career, putting him within 3 of Lou Gehrig's lifetime total.

The game went to the 11th inning. Lefty-swinging first baseman Wes Parker failed to bunt for a hit and then brought two home for the Dodgers with a two-out homer off Frank Linzy. Veteran southpaw Johnny Podres had replaced Perranoski after the fireman turned an ankle while covering first base on a putout to end the ninth. Podres threw his second straight perfect inning to end it, fanning the final two batters. The loss again put Frisco 1½ behind the Bluebloods, and a game behind the sizzling Milwaukee Braves. The Giants felt obligated to take the Series closer which featured, as sportswriter Stevens put it, "the greatest left-hander of the day against the greatest right-hander."

It was a dream matchup. Former Cy Young Award winner Koufax had a record of 21–4, Marichal a 19–9 mark. Both hurlers had ERAs below 2.00. Sandy led the league in strikeouts, Marichal was among the leaders. Koufax had exceptional control, Marichal's was even better. A Sunday afternoon overflow crowd of 42,802 jammed into the Stick to watch their first confrontation of the year. It would be their last.

The Dodgers jumped on Marichal quickly. Wills opened the game by bunting for a hit and was chased home on a two-out Ron Fairly double. In the second, Parker doubled and then scored on a John Roseboro single, and two outs later, Wills stepped to the plate for his second try. There was no love lost between Marichal and the Dodgers' speedy second baseman, who many regarded as their most valuable player. Lingering thoughts of Wills' tricky tactics in the series opener and irritating infield hit to open the finale motivated Marichal to let one fly in the direction of Maury's chin. "I don't know how I got out of the way," Wills would wonder after the game.

The war had begun. Mays led off the second and felt the breeze from a Koufax counterattack that sailed over his head. Marichal renewed the offensive in the third by sending Fairly to the dirt with a number one. Considering the atmosphere, it wasn't paranoia that made Marichal feel uneasy as he stepped to the plate for his first at-bat in the bottom of the third. Juan had reason to be nervous.

Koufax fired the first pitch down the middle, but his next fastball was perceptibly closer to the batter than to the dish. As Marichal stared at Koufax, Roseboro rifled the return throw, which either nipped Juan's ear or came close enough for him to blurt out a threatening remark to Johnny. Despite the hostile surroundings, the backstop wasn't about to back off and moved towards Marichal in a challenging manner. No longer having a baseball as a weapon, Juan used what was available, clubbing Roseboro on the side of the head with his bat.

Recalling the incident for interviewer Jay Johnstone thirty years later, Marichal still claimed innocence, saying, "I wasn't the person who started the whole thing." He told Johnstone that Koufax later admitted to him that he had been ordered to nail Marichal but that Roseboro volunteered to do the job instead. Even if true, Marichal's defense is difficult to accept. Roseboro was fortunate in escaping serious injury or even death from the near-the-temple blow.

As blood spilled from the side of Roseboro's head, players spilled onto the field from both benches. Understandably, most of the Dodgers' efforts were focused on reaching Marichal, though Koufax was restraining a revenge-minded Roseboro. Rookie Dodgers hurler Mike Kekich had Marichal in a headlock underneath a pileup, but was unable to land any damaging blows. L.A.'s muscular moundsman Howie "Diz" Reed went berserk, pulling players from the pile in an effort to reach Marichal. Len Gabrielson outweighed the Dodgers' John Kennedy by forty pounds and met little resistance while carrying him away from the free-for-all. Dodgers coach Danny Ozark wasn't as easily restrained, breaking away several times and rushing towards the hated hurler. Giants Tito Fuentes and Orlando Cepeda had bats in their hands but refrained from using them.

There were some who played peacemaker in the chaos at Candlestick. Plate umpire Shag Crawford dragged the maniacal moundsman to the ground prior to the pileup. No Giants player dared approach Roseboro, save for Willie Mays, who physically prevented his friend from fighting while pleading, "You're hurt. Get out of here." Koufax and Dodgers manager Walt Alston coaxed Roseboro to the dugout, while police descended from the stands and put an end to the 15-minute fracas.

Marichal was ejected (he was suspended for nine games the next day by NL president Warren Giles), Roseboro was removed from the game for medical attention, and the game resumed. Koufax appeared unshaken by the incident, fanning pinch-hitter Bob Schroder and then retiring Fuentes on a fly ball. Needing one out to end the long inning, the Sandman fell asleep, walking Jim Davenport, then Willie McCovey. Koufax's next pitch was a high heater, but wonderful Willie was waiting. He crushed the ball well over the left-center field fence and into the bleacher seats, giving the Giants the lead. After the Dodgers were retired by reliever Ron Herbel in the fourth, Mays sprinted from the outfield, scurried through the dugout, and entered the enemy clubhouse to check on Roseboro's condition. Informed that his friend had merely a superficial slash, the relieved outfielder rushed to rejoin his mates.

The Dodgers died easily against Herbel's slants until tallying in the ninth. With the tying run on, Murakami relieved, and he disposed of Wills on a fly ball before ending it by whiffing Junior Gilliam. Koufax was charged with his fifth defeat despite yielding only four hits, two by Mays. He would win 5 of his next 8 decisions, giving him 26 by season's end, a league best, as was his 2.04 ERA and 382 strikeouts, which set a modern record for most in a season. It was broken by Nolan Ryan's 383 in 1973.

Mays' crack off Koufax carried much significance. It was the game-winner which enabled the Giants to gain a split of their most important series to that point. It was his 14th of the month, putting him within 4 of York's record and within 2 of the National League mark, then held by Ralph Kiner who smashed 16 in September of 1949. It was his sixth straight game with at least one homer, putting him within two of Dale Long's major-league record. It was his 38th homer of the year, only 2 shy of the prestigious 40 plateau, and it was his 491st career blast, pulling him within 2 of Gehrig's total.

One Mays quest ended in failure on August 23. While Marichal was complaining about the severity of his suspension and others bemoaned its leniency, the Giants traveled to Pittsburgh, where the Buccos played poor hosts in winning 5–2. Veteran Vernon Law issued only six hits in going the distance, while shutting down Frisco's leading slugger in three plate appearances. Mays was robbed of another chance when he injured his groin in the seventh inning and was removed from the game, ending his consecutive-game homer streak.

Willie's injury resulted from what was described as "the greatest throw ever made in ancient Forbes Field." The dazzling defensive gem began when Mays ran down a Donn Clendenon drive at the base of the center-field fence. He then whirled and launched a missile to the plate that arrived in Haller's glove on one bounce. The catcher tagged out an incredulous Willie Stargell who had tried to score.

Predicted a pessimistic Franks in the clubhouse, "I doubt if Willie can make it for several days." He wasn't in the lineup the next night, but rookie Ken Henderson seemed an adequate replacement after he made several exceptional defensive plays before drilling a triple and scoring the go-head run in the ninth. The 3–2 Giants lead vanished when right-fielder Alou threw behind baserunner Clendenon, who had taken a wide turn at first following a single. Alou's heave eluded McCovey, allowing Clendenon to reach second and then score on a Jim Pagliaroni hit.

The unearned run proved crucial when the Giants tallied twice in the tenth but were denied victory by rain and the rulebook. Reliever Linzy retired the first Pirates batter before a downpour forced plate umpire Ed Vargo to call time. The delay stretched to an hour and forty minutes. With the field unplayable by then Vargo postponed the game. Since Pittsburgh hadn't completed their at-bats in the bottom of the tenth, the Giants' two runs in the top half were nullified and the score reverted to a 3–3 tie.

The Giants were furious, not at Vargo, but at the Pirates' groundscrew who, it was claimed, purposely stalled before covering the field. Since the rain ceased shortly after the game's postponement, the tarpaulin delay had a significant effect on the game's outcome. Giles reviewed the protest and of course rejected it.

If Frisco was burned by the tie, Mays was helped by it. The game he sat out was replayed the next day, with Willie back in the lineup. Some might argue that Mays still lost an August opportunity, since all stats derived from ties are counted anyway. Had Willie played, however, the game might have ended in a decision before storm interference and groundscrew skullduggery made its replay necessary.

On August 26, rookie Met screwballer (and screwball) Frank "Tug" McGraw was making a believer of Los Angeles by besting its best hurler, Koufax, 3–2, enabling New York to take three of four from the dumbfounded Dodgers. Meanwhile, the Giants were dropping a doubleheader to the Pirates and dropping to fourth in the standings, despite remaining 1½ away from the still-first Dodgers. Mays was held hitless in the replayed game but socked his 15th of the month in the nightcap's ninth, a two-run, opposite-field shot off winner Al McBean.

Met broadcaster Ralph Kiner was particularly interested in Mays' efforts the next night as the Giants opened a three-game set in New York. Kiner held several homerun records but cherished none more than his NL mark for the most in one month. With five scheduled Giants games in the five days remaining in August, Kiner hoped Willie could be stopped and told him so on his television pregame show.

A record crowd of 56,167 packed two-year-old Shea Stadium and marveled as ex–Met Spahn dazzled batters for seven innings, allowing seven hits and no walks in notching his 362d career win. Although the Mets trailed badly by the eighth, Kiner may have been pleased to know that Mays had failed to reach the seats. Ralph needed to sweat out one last at-bat.

Kiner's heart sank when Willie, facing reliever Tom Parsons off whom he had homered in their last confrontation at Candlestick, connected for his 16th circuit of August, 493d of his career (tying Gehrig's lifetime total), and 40th of the season. (It was the 6th time he had reached the 40 mark, which set a new NL record that replaced the old one that had been shared by three others, including Kiner.) Willie had yet another plate appearance in the ninth, but Kiner breathed easily after righty Jim Bethke walked him.

Galen Cisco and Al Jackson combined to thwart Mays and the Giants the next night, though Willie managed a single and double against the Cisco Kid. Game-delaying swirling winds which circulated dust and hot dog wrappers around the infield should have made the Candlestick residents feel at home, but perhaps the 48,000 banner-waving Met fans, or "kooks" as they were labeled by Stevens, were too much of a distraction. The Giants were blanked 3–0 by a team they had beaten nine straight times. If only Casey could have been watching from the dugout.

Although he was out of the hospital by then, Stengel still suffered from his broken hip. On August 30 the Mets called a press conference in which the Ol' Perfessor, with uncharacteristic eloquence, made it official, terminating a 25-year career as helmsman. "In fairness to myself and the club, I thought it best, when I could no longer strut out to the mound to yank a pitcher, that I should not return as manager," Stengel stated, being careful to add, "I had not intended to retire until I got hurt." His use of "yank" was appropriate for the skipper who had guided the Bronx Bombers to ten pennants and seven world championships.

Met fans set another attendance record on Sunday, August 29, as the two clubs closed out the series. It would be a battle of tall, hard-throwing right-handers. The Giants Bobby Bolin had seven wins, one fewer than Met starter Jack Fisher. But Fisher also had 16 losses which, as Stevens mocked, was "not abnormal, if you're a Met." Fisher would fail to increase his win total by season's end, but his losses would increase to 24, tying Roger Craig for the still-standing seasonal club record.

The game was close for two frames. In the third the Giants pushed two runs across and had two on when Mays took his second swings against Fisher. Surrendering landmark homers was nothing new to the former Oriole who had served up Roger Maris' 60th in 1961. Fisher's notoriety was enhanced when Mays drilled a fastball that easily carried over the left-center fence, traveling approximately 450 feet. As he circled the bases, the record-setter received a standing ovation from the crowd, many of whom still remembered Willie's homer heroics when he played for the New York Giants.

In the clubhouse, Mays was happy over his clout which set the monthly NL mark and allowed him to surpass Gehrig's total, but he claimed to be prouder of his first homer, hit off Spahn in 1951. He set his sights on another milestone, telling reporters, "The thing I want the most is to hit 535 of them." Jimmie Foxx had hit 534 which, at the time, was the most by any right-handed batter.

Commenting on his monthly homer mark being surpassed, Kiner admitted: "Sure, it hurts a little. I get a kick out of all these guys who claim they don't mind when someone comes along and breaks one of their records. They all mind." Ralph reiterated those feelings to the record-setter on his *Kiner's Corner* postgame show. Smiling, Mays apologized for being the one to break it. Still a broadcaster with the Mets today, Kiner remains the proud holder of the major-league mark for most homers in four straight games (8) and is one of two players in history to hit four consecutive homers on two occasions, the Phils' Mike Schmidt being the other.

The question remained whether Willie could sock another and match

Willie Mays and Ralph Kiner, after Willie's number 17 of August (UPI/Bettmann).

York's 18 homers in a month. Following an off day on Monday, the Giants visited Philadelphia on the final day of August for a doubleheader. The Phils had a formidable starting duo that day in Jim Bunning and Lew Burdette. Now in his 11th major-league season, Bunning had won 20 games in 1957 and 19 in 1962 and 1964. He would finish the 1965 season with another 19 victories, and he won another 19 in 1966. His greatest single-game achievement was his perfect game against the Mets on June 21, 1964, when he became the first NL hurler to win a perfecto in the century. (In September of 1965, Koufax would become the second.)

Bunning was stingy in yielding eight hits and one run before leaving after the tenth in a 1–1 deadlock. Mays, held to a walk in four plate appearances, was the first batter to face rookie righty reliever Gary Wagner in the 11th. Willie whistled a drive toward the left-field corner that fell just short of the wall for a double. A passed ball and a forceout brought Mays home with the eventual winning run.

Spahn faced his former Milwaukee pitching partner Lew Burdette in the nightcap. The crafty Burdette was in the twilight of an 18 year career that included two twenty-win seasons with the Braves and two Series appearances against the mighty Yankees in 1957 and 1958. In 1957, Burdette beat the Bombers three times, the last two being shutouts, as the Braves took the seven-game Series. The pinstripers had their revenge in the following Fall Classic, defeating Burdette twice and taking the Braves in seven.

If both hurlers were past their prime, it wasn't apparent during their performance in the nightcap. Burdette was brilliant in allowing six hits and three walks in nine innings. Spahn was even more masterful, yielding only three safeties while walking one in going the distance. Unfortunately for Warren, two of the Philly hits were homers, and he lost 2–0.

The cautious Burdette pitched carefully to Willie in his four plate appearances, walking him twice. In Mays' last chance in the eighth inning, he caught a Burdette pitch squarely, the ball chasing Adolfo Phillips to deep center. The Philly ballpark being ancient Shibe Park, with its 447-foot center field, and not yet Veterans Stadium which, with its more reachable distances, was inaugurated in 1971, Mays's bid for history ended in a 420-foot out.

Marichal rejoined the Giants in September, gained his 20th win for the third straight year, and won another two before season's end. Unlike Koufax, whose arthritic elbow limited him to one additional big-league season, Juan continued to thrive in the sixties, leading the majors in wins (26), complete games (30), and innings-pitched (326) in 1968 and topping the NL in ERA (2.10) and shutouts (8) in 1969 while notching another 21 victories. Manito's lifetime winning percentage (.631) is among the top twenty of the century, his 2.89 ERA only 13 points higher than that of his contemporary Koufax. He retired after the 1975 season, and though he was eligible for the Hall of Fame by 1981, he wasn't elected until 1983, his notorious act of 1965 perhaps being responsible for the delay.

Juan's violent temper cost more than a two-year hiatus between eligibility and election to the Hall. He lost two starts to his suspension in 1965, and Frisco lost the pennant by two games, settling for second despite winning 23 of 33 after August. It would be a heartbreaking decade for Giants fans, who saw their team finish runner-up five times and finish within three games of the top four times.

The Mantle-Mays rivalry was a one-sided affair in 1965. Mantle suffered his worst season, accumulating 19 homers and 46 RBIs while batting .255 in 122 games. He enjoyed a mild comeback in 1966, socking 23

homers in two-thirds of a season, while batting a respectable .288 in a year
in which the American League boasted but two .300 hitters. Manager Ralph
Houk's moving the center fielder to first in 1967 enabled him to play in 144
games, but Mick managed only 22 homers, while his average dropped to
.245. When it fell to .237 in 1968 and, sadly, pushed his lifetime mark below
.300, Mantle called it a career.

Mays finished the 1965 season as the league leader in slugging and
homers, his 52 round trippers enabling him to reach the 50 plateau for the
second time. He belted another 37 in 1966, but his .288 average should have
been an indication that Willie, too, was feeling his 35 years. Mays hit .263
in 1967, while his homer count fell to 22 (the same as Mantle's). He never
again reached the thirty-homer mark, nor batted .300, nor drove in 100 runs.
As with his rival, the second half of the sixties was not kind to Mays.

Willie was traded to the Mets in 1973, a sentimental gesture that
enabled the beloved star to return to New York. Playing as a part-timer, he
accomplished little for the Mets, managing only six homers and a .211 average, though he had a pair of hits in seven at-bats in the World Series. As
mentioned in a preceding chapter, the trade hurt his career more than
helped it because it prevented his joining a select group who played 20 or
more seasons all with the same club.

Mays' accomplishments are too numerous to list here but except for
his 22 career extra-inning homers, he owns no major-league records. York's
prestigious mark might not have eluded Willie in 1965 had he played in all
31 Giant games of August (not including the tie he missed). That Willie sat
on a day when the Mets, with their highly hittable pitching staff, were the
opponents makes the missed opportunity even more significant.

Albert Belle turned on the power in September of 1995, as did Juan
Gonzalez twelve months later, but their 17 homers also fell one shy of York's
big-league mark and, being American Leaguers, they did not reach a league
record either. At least Mays can boast that his 17 in a month is the best any
National Leaguer has ever achieved. Considering the senior circuit's long
history, that's saying a lot.

Willie Mays' 17 Homers in August of 1965

Date	Opponent	Ballpark	Opp. Pitcher (lefty/righty)	Score
8/2	Braves	County Stadium	K. Johnson (R)	4–2 (Mil)
8/5	Reds	Crosley Field	J. Tsitouris (R)	18–7 (SF)
(2)			B. Locke (R)	
8/7	Cards	Sportsman's Park	T. Stallard (R)	10–4 (SF)
(2)			N. Briles (R)	

Date	Opponent	Ballpark	Opp. Pitcher (lefty/righty)	Score
8/8	Cards	Sportsman's Park	B. Purkey (R)	6–4 (SF)
8/12	Pirates	Candlestick Park	B. Friend (R)	4–3 (SF)
8/12	Pirates	Candlestick Park	V. Law (R)	5–2 (Pit)
8/16	Mets	Candlestick Park	T. Parsons (R)	3–2 (SF)
8/18	Mets	Candlestick Park	L. Miller (L)	5–0 (SF)
8/19	Dodgers	Candlestick Park	D. Drysdale (R)	8–5 (LA)
8/20	Dodgers	Candlestick Park	H. Reed (R)	5–1 (SF)
8/21	Dodgers	Candlestick Park	B. Miller (R)	6–4 (LA)
8/22	Dodgers	Candlestick Park	S. Koufax (L)	4–3 (SF)
8/26	Pirates	Forbes Field	A. McBean (R)	6–5 (Pit)
8/27	Mets	Shea Stadium	T. Parsons (R)	9–2 (SF)
8/29	Mets	Shea Stadium	J. Fisher (R)	8–3 (SF)

Eight

Nolan's Near No-Hitters

On April 18, 1970, Richard Nixon, in his second full year as president, was in Honolulu congratulating three astronauts for their just-concluded space venture. The journey was supposed to have included a moon landing, but an explosion of a liquid-oxygen tank resulted in damage to the Apollo 13 spacecraft. The mission was then aborted. "Greatness comes not simply in triumph but in adversity," Nixon exclaimed. "It has been said that adversity introduces a man to himself." His words were prophetic in regards to his own political career.

That same day, approximately 5,500 miles distant, Nolan Ryan was being congratulated by his teammates in the locker room of Shea Stadium in New York. The 6' 2" hard-throwing righthander had just thrown the first shutout of his three-year career. While doing so, the Texan fanned 15 Phillies, setting a new club record for strikeouts, a mark teammate Tom Seaver would surpass only one week later. The day was not without adversity for Ryan. Denny Doyle's opposite-field single to open the game became both the first and last hit for Philadelphia. The "Ryan Express" ran at full speed the rest of the way, but Doyle's dinker prevented Nolan from fashioning his first no-hit effort.

After the game, some of the still-dazed Philly batters were asked their opinions of the young phenom. Slugger Deron Johnson commented, "He's the best. Nobody throws the ball like that." Catcher Tim McCarver agreed about Ryan throwing the fastest, saying, "He's No. 1, definitely." Doyle, who along with posting the sole hit for his club, was one of only two Phils to avoid whiffing, recalled facing the fanning machine in his first at-bat in pro ball. "I dribbled the ball somewhere," Denny declared. "I thought at the time maybe I should have taken up soccer or something."

No doubt Ryan had many batters second-guessing their professions throughout his career, which spanned four decades. Upon his retirement, he would join others in being classified a pitching legend — a title reserved for such stars as Cy Young, Christy Mathewson, Walter Johnson, and Grover Cleveland Alexander. It is an honor few if any of his contemporaries could claim.

Besides being known as the national pastime's all-time strikeout artist, Nolan Ryan is best remembered as the no-hit man. That no one will ever match his seven career no-hitters is not a certainty, but it's as close to a sure bet as anyone can find. It follows that if allowing a team no hits in a game is a remarkable achievement, then limiting it to only one isn't much less admirable, especially if, as Ryan once admitted, "A lot of luck goes into throwing a no-hitter." Yet when Nolan mowed down the Phils and wowed the 24,000 fans at Shea on that Saturday afternoon in 1970, his near no-hitter was overshadowed by his record-breaking K mark and first-ever shutout. Just as ignored would become the record dozen one-hitters Ryan threw before retiring after the 1993 season. Only the American League's Bob Feller would come so close and fail as often, and Nolan's 19 low-hitters (which include both no-hit and one-hit games) remain a major-league record.

Ryan's next near no-hitter came two years later and in a different uniform. His trade to the California Angels for infielder Jim Fregosi after the 1971 season may not be the biggest swapping blunder in baseball history, but it's probably the Mets' worst. In his first three years with the Halomen, Nolan would average over 20 victories and 360 strikeouts per season, with an ERA of 2.70.

On July 9, 1972, bickering Democrats prepared for their convention in Miami to decide who would challenge Nixon's attempt for a second term. Three weeks earlier five men had been arrested for an illegal break-in at the Democratic headquarters at the Watergate complex in Washington, D.C. Their connection with top officials in the Nixon administration had not yet been proven, and the president won in a landslide reelection. It wouldn't be long, however, before Nixon would be introduced to personal adversity more formidable than has been experienced by any American politician before or since.

While Miami was hosting Democrats on July 9, California was hosting the Red Sox. The Angels' starter, Ryan, in only half a season with his new ballclub, was already making the Mets' management regret their trade because he had accumulated a 10–5 record and 2.34 ERA to that point. Nolan was also having his share of regrets. While his former club was in second place and still in the hunt for the pennant, California was in fifth position, atop only Texas in the standings and a distant 14 games behind league-leading Oakland.

As was the case two years earlier, Nolan's chance for his first career no-hitter ended quickly against Boston that Sunday afternoon. After leadoff batter Tommy Harper drew a base-on-balls, Ryan retired Doug Griffin and then faced Sox superstar Carl Yastrzemski. Carl pulled a Ryan curve, and as *Los Angeles Times* sportswriter Ross Newhan reported the next day, "Yaz's clean shot to right deprived Ryan of a plaque in Cooperstown," while correctly adding, "but that still may be the final destination for the 24-year-old righthander who rubs snake oil on his arm and has venom in his fastball."

Harper and Yastrzemski would be the only Bostonians to roam the basepaths. Ryan retired the next two hitters, Reggie Smith and Rico Petrocelli, on strikes. He then dismissed the remaining 24 Red Sox as effectively as Stan Smith had dismissed tennis's badboy Ilie Nastase earlier in the day, becoming the first American in 17 years to win at Wimbledon. The Angels scored in only one inning, the fourth, but the three runs proved more than sufficient.

While retiring 26 in a row en route to his one-hitter, Nolan fanned 16, which matched the club record he had set only a week before. Of more significance was the fact that half of his strikeouts were accomplished in consecutive fashion. His eight straight K's set a still-standing American League record (since tied by the Bosox's Roger Clemens and the Yanks' Ron Davis) and fell two shy of former teammate Seaver's major-league mark. Ironically, it was the same player who had broken up his no-hit chance earlier who snapped Ryan's strikeout streak.

After fanning Smith and Petrocelli to end the first, Nolan faced Carlton Fisk, Bob Burda, and Juan Beniquez in the second. Not only did each of the trio fan, but all went down on only three swings. By whiffing the side on nine pitches, Nolan joined 14 other former hurlers who had turned the trick, and Seaver wasn't one of them. For the first time, Ryan had a K mark which his former rival moundsman couldn't match.

When the Angels artist burned third-strike fastballs past Sonny Siebert, Tommy Harper, and Doug Griffin in the following frame, Ryan's whiff streak reached eight, surpassing the AL mark of seven previously shared by six others. In the fourth frame, Nolan set his sights on Seaver's ten in a row, but Yaz put a quick end to those hopes with a leadoff, fly-ball out.

"I had more confidence today than I ever had," the fireballer revealed afterwards. "I have a feeling now that I can throw to spots." His claim was verified by the fact that only 38 of the 128 pitches thrown were out of the strike zone and Ryan issued only one walk, compared to six in his first one-hitter two years before.

Manager Del Rice, flabbergasted by his fireballer, told reporters, "He was throwing so hard that he made my own arm hurt." Pitcher Clyde Wright was due to start the next day, but had reservations. "There's no way I can follow that. I'm not going to show up tomorrow." A couple of former Dodger catchers compared Ryan to another great strikeout artist. "He's as fast as Koufax. I'm sure of it," said Jeff Torborg. Johnny Roseboro wasn't ready to make that claim yet, but did admit, "He can be as great if not greater than Koufax."

Ryan must have agonized over his two near no-hitters, and when the 1972 season ended, he may have been wondering whether he would ever hurl one. His answer came early in 1973, when the Kansas City Royals became the first of Nolan's no-hit victims on May 15. Exactly two months later the tall Texan gunned down the Tigers for his second career no-hitter. With two-thirds of the season remaining, Californians were dreaming of Ryan firing an unprecedented third no-hitter in one year. In August their dream almost became reality.

The Yankees entered Anaheim on August 29, the same day still-president Nixon had decided to appeal a decision made by John Sirica. The judge had ordered him to turn over recorded conversations made in connection with the emerging Watergate scandal. The tapes were eventually submitted, and a mysterious 18-minute gap in one of them became evident. An expert later testified that the erasure had been done deliberately.

The Yanks were having their problems as well. It had been nearly nine years since the proud franchise had claimed a pennant flag in 1964. Nineteen seventy-three would prove just as frustrating, with the Bombers struggling to a fourth place finish in their six-team division and an 80–82 record. It would take another two years before the combined excellence of Thurman Munson, Chris Chambliss, Roy White, Ron Guidry, and Catfish Hunter would end an eleven-year drought for the franchise considered by many to be the most successful in sports history.

Although Munson's best years awaited him, he had some fine seasons, memorable games, and key hits prior to 1976. In his rookie season in 1970, he batted .302, he finished at .301 in 1973, and he had a career-high .318 in 1975 with 102 RBIs. The plane crash that took his life in August of 1979 robbed him of several more productive seasons as a Yankee superstar. It would appear, at least at the time of this writing, that it robbed him of his chance at Cooperstown as well.

Thurman would play a key role in the midweek matchup between the Yanks and Angels. Not that his efforts had much effect on the final score. The Angels won handily, scoring five runs off Doc Medich while Ryan was blanking the Bombers. It was Munson, however, who accounted for his team's sole safety, a "lucky" hit which landed in short-center field for a single. The ball should have been caught, but confusion between second baseman Sandy Alomar and shortstop Rudy Meoli caused it to fall.

The scoreboard tells the story as Nolan Ryan disposes of the Royals' Amos Otis for his first career no-hitter on May 15, 1973 (UPI/Bettmann).

Both players agreed it should have been called an error, but official scorer Dick Miller was quick to defend himself. "If one fielder had been involved, the fly could have been caught with ordinary effort," Miller acknowledged. "But with two going for it, both calling at the same time and concerned about running into each other, more than ordinary effort was involved."

In all likelihood, the call would have gone unchallenged had it not resulted in the only hit off Ryan. That it came, once again, in the opening frame eased the agony of Nolan's coming so close to a record third no-hitter in one season. "I don't think you can get upset losing a no-hitter in the first inning," Ryan philosophized later. "If I've got a chance for one in the seventh or eighth, that's a different story." Munson, meanwhile, showed no remorse for his part in spoiling the show, saying, "No, I'm not sorry it was a cheap hit. I tried to bunt in the ninth for a second hit."

Although Ryan failed in his attempt for three no-hitters that season, he couldn't have been too disappointed. Nineteen seventy-three may have been his most overpowering year. Appearing in 41 games, the second highest total of his career, Nolan won 21 games and had an ERA of 2.87. He struck out ten or more batters in a game 23 times, breaking the major-league mark of 21 held previously by Sandy Koufax.

Ryan challenged another Koufax mark that season. Sandy had fanned 382 batters in 1965. Ryan's ten against the Yanks during the one-hitter in August gave him 314 with about six starts remaining. The race to top the K mark coincided with Hank Aaron's attempt to overtake Ruth's career homer mark that year. As Angels general manager Harry Dalton said on August 30, "We have the two most dramatic individual races I can remember, both coming down to the wire at the same time. It's a case of classic extremes — pitcher and hitter — the two basic ultimates of the game." Ryan was successful, topping the total of the Dodgers Hall-of-Famer by one by season's end. As for Aaron supporters, they would have to wait another year before crowning him the new homerun king.

President Nixon's possible impeachment loomed closer in 1974, as 21 Democrats on the House Judiciary Committee indicated on June 27 their readiness to vote for his removal. On that day, Ryan came close to his third career no-hitter in a home game witnessed by only 8,000 fans. No doubt California's last place position had something to do with the tiny turnout, that and the fact that the club had finished no better than fourth the previous three years and was looking for its first pennant since joining the American League during the expansion year of 1961.

Angels followers weren't the only ones who were becoming annoyed at their club's consistent failing. Angels owner Gene Autry, known for

singing cowboy songs during his television days, was now singing the baseball blues. When free agency opened the doors of monetary opportunity
for ballplayers a few years later, Autry, along with the Yanks' spendthrift
George Steinbrenner, opened their vaults and went on shopping sprees for
the next two decades. Although George's money bought early success, Gene's
spending did little to help; the Angels were still looking for their first pennant when Autry finally sold the team to the Disney Group in 1996.

With free agency not yet in full force, Autry was doing other things
to shake up his club. Before Ryan faced Texas that night, California manager Bobby Winkles had been fired, with former Oakland A's skipper Dick
Williams chosen to replace him. Frank Robinson looked forward to playing for the leader of the World Champion Oakland teams of 1972 and 1973,
though he had been harboring thoughts of being picked for the post himself. Robby shrugged off the snub by saying: "I'm not disappointed. To be
disappointed you have to hope to be considered. This has gone on for
years." Robinson's cynicism proved to be unwarranted. When the 1974 season ended, he was hired by the Cleveland Indians, breaking the color line
for managers on October 3.

As a welcoming gift for Williams, Ryan threw his fourth career one-
hitter that night. Amazingly, the potential no-hitter was again spoiled in
the first inning. Nolan's location on a pitch to ex–Angels player Alex Johnson cost him. Johnson went with the outside fastball and sent a liner to
right field. Joe Lahoud charged in and at the last second decided to play
the ball on one hop, conceding the hit. By game's end, Lahoud may have
been second-guessing his judgment.

When Toby Harrah walked in the sixth frame, he became the second
and last baserunner for Texas. Ryan's control was superb once again, and
he threw only 34 balls out of 99 pitches. Although he struck out only six,
Nolan's effectiveness that day is verified by the fact that only four balls were
hit to the outfield by the Rangers, whose .285 batting average was the best
in the league.

Nixon's presidency became history on August 4, when the pressure
from the Watergate investigation forced him to resign. The following month
Ryan ended his season by making history — throwing another no-hitter
against Minnesota on September 28. His third was the most by an American Leaguer, and whether Nolan could equal Koufax's career total was a
question asked by many.

It wasn't long before Angels fans had the answer they were looking for.
Two months into the 1975 season, Ryan conquered Baltimore with a 1–0
no-hitter, forcing Sanford to share his cherished record.

California partisans had grown accustomed to the possibility of a no-hit performance whenever Ryan took the mound. Now that their hero had a chance to have the record for himself, they became even more eager to see one. But Ryan didn't come close in his remaining starts in 1975 and again failed to notch a no-hitter the following year.

On April 15, 1977, the largest crowd to witness a home opener in Anaheim watched Nolan take on the newly formed Seattle Mariners for the first time. Ryan was looking to end an early-season, four-game losing streak by his club. He was unhittable until the fifth. The Mariners' lefty-swinging catcher, Bob Stinson, then lined a low-outside curve to

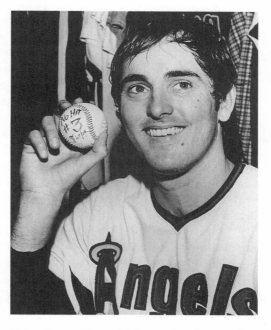

Nolan Ryan, after no-hitter number three against the Twins on September 28, 1974 (National Baseball Library & Archive, Cooperstown, N.Y.).

left that produced loud groans and sighs from the disappointed crowd. It was the sole Seattle hit, resulting in Ryan's fifth career close-call victory.

Although the single had robbed him of a record fifth no-hitter, Ryan didn't seem too displeased in the locker room, saying he probably didn't deserve it anyway. The stats justify his claim. Nolan's wildness resulted in six walks, including three to load the bases in the sixth. His lack of control would become a trend that year, with Ryan leading the league in base-on-balls with a career-high 204. It fell 4 shy of Bob Feller's unenviable 1938 major-league record.

Ryan teased Angels fans with another near no-hitter in 1978. Pitching before a home crowd of over 17,000 on May 5, he set down the Cleveland batters without a hit through the first five innings. In the sixth the Indians' last place hitter, Duane Kuiper, faced Ryan for the second time. The southpaw swinger, batting a paltry .193 at the time, ran the count to 1–1. He then whistled a liner which went over the head of Angels third sacker Carney Lansford for the Tribe's only hit. Teammate Terry Humphrey handed Nolan the game ball in the clubhouse, and the unpretentious pitcher tossed it into his locker, joking, "I'll give it to my dog."

With his modest demeanor, Nolan probably wasn't too perturbed the next day when the *Los Angeles Times* chose another baseball event as its lead story. While Ryan had just missed a milestone in Anaheim, Pete Rose had successfully reached one in Cincinnati. Pistol Pete bulleted a fifth-inning hit to left against Montreal's formidable hurler Steve Rogers. It was his 3,000th career safety, making him only the tenth player to reach the esteemed plateau.

A natural question for reporters to ask afterwards was whether the scrappy 37 year old thought he could reach the 4,000-hit mark before retiring. Said Charlie Hustle, "No, no way." With that response, the normally confident superstar underestimated both his ability and durability. Seven years later he would surpass Ty Cobb and become the all-time hit leader. Pete retired in 1986 with an astounding 4,256 safeties.

"I was close to tears," Rose admitted, referring to the five-minute standing ovation he had received from the 37,000 appreciative fans after number 3,000. Pete would be brought to tears a decade later for different reasons. His alleged involvement in gambling while a player-manager with Cincinnati, a charge the baseball hierarchy has yet to prove, resulted in his banishment from baseball — a game he loved so dearly that he once said, "Playing baseball for a living is like having a license to steal."

Nolan Ryan may have experienced the greatest mental pain of his long career in a game against the Yankees the following season. The Bombers had fared much better since Munson had spoiled Ryan's no-hit bid in 1973; they had won three consecutive pennants from 1976 to 1978, including the previous two World Series. Steinbrenner's two maneuvers during those years — hiring the fiery, though sometimes explosive, Billy Martin as manager and then acquiring the power-hitter with the equally powerful personality, Reggie Jackson — may have been the catalyst the Yanks needed.

Some, including this writer, argue that New York had significantly improved by 1975 so that the club would have won without both Martin and Jackson. Munson had emerged as one of the game's top backstops by then and was clearly the leader of the team. Pitchers Guidry and Hunter were already on the roster, primed and prepared for outstanding seasons; and newcomers Chris Chambliss and Lou Piniella, who had joined the team in 1974, were ready to deliver numerous timely hits for several subsequent seasons. Martin was a respected skipper, but so was Ralph Houk; he could have won with the talent given Billy had he not been chased by George in 1973. As for Jackson, he delivered many long balls, but struck out with alarming frequency, and his fielding was suspect at best. Reggie was a key to winning the Series in 1977 and 1978, but there were others on the team who had played a more vital role in getting there.

Ryan was still looking for that elusive fifth no-hitter when he took on Reggie and Company on July 13. When he strong-armed the Bombers for seven frames without a hint of a safety, many in the crowd of 41,000, along with millions more watching the nationally televised contest at home, were optimistic. After the Yanks' Jim Spencer scorched a one-out liner to center in the eighth, however, which then trickled off the glove of the charging center-fielder Rick Miller, the spectators' spirits simultaneously sank. Their hopes were renewed a few moments later. Official scorer Dick Miller, whose controversial decision on Munson's blooper had denied Ryan a no-hitter six years earlier, made amends in the eyes of Angels fans. He ruled that Spencer's drive should have been caught. With the error call, the no-hit possibility remained alive.

The Yankees reacted defiantly. Several of the players' heads could be seen popping out of the dugout, their eyes glaring in the direction of the scorer's box. Jackson showed his disapproval by making a threatening movement with his hand. But Miller defended the call afterwards, saying, "The first hit in a game of this nature has to be completely clean." You couldn't convince the New Yorkers. "I can't remember a worse call than that when there's been a no-hitter on the line," barked the outspoken Martin later. Spencer, who had also made an impolite gesture towards Miller after the decision, complained, "If they want to give him a no-hitter, we shouldn't even go out on the field." Even Angels executive Buzzie Bavasi was angered by the ruling, yelling at Miller, "You've embarrassed us all."

That other on-the-spot Miller, outfielder Rick, agreed with his name-sake that the ball should have been caught. "I've made that play before," he admitted. "It ain't easy, but it was there." Teammate Rod Carew was more upset with the Yankees' reaction than with the call, arguing: "The man pitched a hell of a game. Let 'em get a clean hit and then they can pop off. That's bush!" As for Ryan, he admitted Spencer's liner and the controversial call that followed affected his concentration. "I was kind of let down because of that play. The fan and Yankee reaction prevented me from getting back to where I wanted."

When shortstop Jim Anderson couldn't handle a Munson grounder leading off the ninth, Miller's ruling an error went unchallenged. Nolan then retired Graig Nettles, and no-hit history was only two outs away. But Reggie Jackson, who thrived on clutch situations in front of national audiences, further fed his ego by drilling a wormburner past the mound between second and short. Miller's error call of the previous inning had allowed Jackson to be the man of the hour.

Ryan's chance had literally slipped past him. "I just didn't get my glove down," the unperturbed Ryan explained in discussing Jackson's hit. "I'm disappointed, but I've been there before, so it's no big do-or-die letdown. It just wasn't meant to be a no-hitter tonight."

Nor was it meant to be for Steve Renko. The Boston free-agent hurler flirted with a no-hitter in a California city that same night. He lost it on a ninth-inning, one-out single by another future showman of the game — Oakland's fabulous rookie, Rickey Henderson.

Although Ryan said he had been there before, this was the first of his no-hit attempts that became a one-hitter in the ninth. It was also the first of his one-hitters which did not result in a shutout. After Munson raced to third on Jackson's single, he scored on a sac fly by Piniella for the Yankees' only run. Three weeks later time would run out for Munson. The catcher's life ended in a fiery plane crash near Canton, Ohio, on August 2. The grieving Bombers were a different club without their leader, and the defending champs finished the season in fourth place. The Yanks wouldn't win another world championship for another 17 years.

Koufax had been in attendance in Anaheim and had watched Ryan's close call with New York. Although Sanford said later that he had been prepared to congratulate his rival, the sight of Jackson's grounder skipping past Ryan and into the outfield must have been partly pleasing to the Dodgers demon. On the other hand, he may have thought the hit simply delayed the inevitable and that the 32-year-old Texan had enough steam left in his arm to eventually throw no-hitter number five. It was a feeling many in Anaheim had. Sure, the missed opportunity was disappointing, but with the kind of "stuff" their hero had, he would come through for them sooner or later.

It was not to be. Or, to put it more accurately, not to be for California fans. Having accumulated a 16–14 record in 1979 with a high ERA and a low number of strikeouts (for Ryan that is — his 223 K's still led the league), Nolan's best years appeared over in the eyes of the Angels brass. When the 1980 season began, Ryan was throwing his beebees for the Houston Astros. What a bitter disappointment it must have been for Angels rooters that their hero threw his coveted fifth career no-hitter on September 26, 1981, for a different team. That the victim was Koufax's former club, Los Angeles, made it ironic for Californians as well.

If Ryan believed that the trade would result in his being on a pennant contender, he was right. Houston grabbed the flag in Ryan's first year with the club in 1980 and came close again in 1981. Nolan played a key role, winning eleven games each of those seasons, with a combined ERA of 2.74.

Nineteen eighty-two was a different story. Skipper Bill Virdon had trouble getting his club untracked, and by August the Astros were entrenched in fifth place, a dozen games behind Tom Lasorda's league-leading Dodgers.

Ryan, for his part, was having a good year. When the Astros visited San Diego on the 11th, the no-hit master took the mound with an 11–9 record and was among baseball's leaders in strikeouts.

Baseball owners that day were wrestling with the idea of removing Bowie Kuhn as commissioner, but Houston owners had come to a decision regarding Virdon two days earlier. Bob Lillis was the newly appointed leader, and just as Ryan had given Dick Williams a welcoming gift in his first start under the new manager in 1974, the 35-year-old hurler gave Lillis a similar one.

Nolan started the game against the San Diego Padres by retiring the first 13 batters. Uncharacteristically for Ryan, none of them were K victims. His club had given him a 3–0 lead when he took the mound in the fifth. With the Padres still looking for their first safety, no doubt some at the park were thinking no-hitter, but Ryan wasn't one of them. "No hitter? No way I was thinking that," Ryan professed afterwards.

Terry Kennedy faced Nolan with one out in the fifth. A la Reggie Jackson, Kennedy drilled a grounder towards the mound. It was déjà vu for Ryan. The ball eluded him and then shortstop Dickie Thon for San Diego's first hit. It was also their last.

Although Jackson's grounder had been hit hard, it appeared Ryan had a chance to spear Kennedy's. "I tell you why I didn't," Ryan explained in the locker room. "It was a changeup off the end of his bat and it had some spin on it. I quit on it."

The excitement of a possible no-hitter had vanished, but the game would provide more thrills, and anxiety, for manager Lillis. Gene Richards opened the bottom of the ninth with a walk. Rookie Tony Gwynn, who was 0–3 to that point, scorched a rapid Ryan release towards right field. But Ray Knight prevented its getting there with an acrobatic catch and then whirled and fired a strike to second, doubling up the bewildered Richards.

The first baseman's effort would prove vital to the game's outcome. Ryan nailed the following batter with a pitch and then walked the next. Terry Kennedy came to the plate representing the potential tying run. Nolan made the lefty swinger pay for getting the first Padre hit by making him the game's final out. The shutout, and Ryan's eighth one-hitter, were preserved.

The same cast of characters put on a repeat performance almost a year later. On August 3, 1983, the Astros revisited San Diego, with Ryan on the hill. Earlier that day Bowie Kuhn had reluctantly submitted his resignation after a 14½-year reign as commissioner. Kuhn's contract was due to expire in a week, and with the owners still haggling over whether to renew it, Bowie didn't give them the chance to say no. Kidded Kuhn, "The fact that it [his decision to resign] was unanimously accepted shows that I could get them to agree unanimously at least on one proposal."

Houston gave their ace an early lead when Terry Puhl hustled a ground ball into a hit with one out in the first and then scored on a triple by Thon. It was all the veteran thrower needed and would get. He ended a personal four-game losing streak with the 1–0 whitewash, after winning ten of his first eleven starts that year. In doing so, Nolan whiffed ten Padres to increase his lifetime total to 3,606, leaving him at the time only 3 behind Steve Carlton's major-league leading amount. Of most significance that day, however, was Ryan's ninth near no-hitter. Tim Flannery hit a seeing-eye one hopper in the third which skipped between second and first for San Diego's only hit.

It wasn't until six years later that Ryan would excite his followers with another near no-no. The 42 year old was still throwing in the Lone Star State, but for a different town, having switched from Houston to the Texas Rangers in Arlington before the 1989 season began.

Ryan split his first two decisions as a Ranger before entering Toronto on April 23 for a Sunday matinee contest against the Blue Jays. Texas had lost the first two games of the series and was hoping its newly acquired fireball flinger could salvage the final game.

While Chinese students planned protests to demand government reform and greater freedom half-a-world away, Ryan bullied the soon-to-be division champs with one of his most overpowering displays. The tall Texan hurler entered the ninth having fanned a dozen and allowed only three walking Blue Jays to reach base. The chance for Ryan's no-hitter was so near he could taste it. Said Nolan afterwards, "Every time you get into the ninth, the attitude is, 'I'm not going to let this one get away.'"

While taking his warm-up throws, Nolan received a standing ovation from the appreciative Toronto crowd. He then inched closer to his goal by retiring leadoff hitter Lloyd Moseby on a foul popup. Nelson Liriano, who had one of the walks surrendered by Ryan, then came to bat. As Texas catcher Geno Petralli later explained, their strategy was to pitch away from the plate to the pull-hitting switch-hitter. The outfield played shallower than normal to prevent a bloop hit from falling.

Robert Burns warned us about plans of mice and men going awry. He might have included ballplayers as well. Unfortunately for Ryan, one of his pitches went awry. The ball found the fat part of the plate and the fat part of Liriano's bat. He blistered a drive over the head of first baseman Rafael Palmiero. Right-fielder Ruben Sierra gave chase but knew all along he had no chance.

For Ryan, it was the most aggravating of all his close calls. After the hit, he hung his head and cursed his bad luck. "My goal each start is to win the game," Ryan lamented later. "But when you get that close…." Nolan paused and then finished by admitting, "I'm disappointed about it."

Like Munson in 1983, Liriano didn't feel guilty about his triple that ended the dream of Ryan and the 31,000 spectators, who gave the visiting legend another standing ovation after the hit. "I heard the people cheering, but I was doing my job," he said. "I'm not sorry. I don't feel like a bad guy."

In China, seven weeks after the prodemocracy movement had begun in April, the government showed patience no longer. Soldiers viciously crushed student protests at Tiananmen Square in Beijing on June 3, spraying the area with bullets and leaving blood and bodies on the streets as a grim portrait of their day's work. Although the tyrant Ayatollah Khomeini died that day, the Chinese reaction was a reminder that numerous ruthless regimes still held power over helpless citizens outside the United States.

Baseball's beauty is that it allows its followers to escape from the madness of the world by attending a game. There were 24,000 fans at the Kingdome in Seattle on June 3, and the postgame talk no doubt centered on the extraordinary efforts of a seemingly ageless hero.

Ryan got off to a shaky start. The first batter for the Mariners, Harold Reynolds, smacked a grounder which eluded second sacker Julio Franco for a single. After stealing second and advancing to third on another ground ball, Reynolds scored on a sac fly. The one run and one hit that inning would be the only offense Seattle would put together. Nolan breezed to a 6–1 victory, retiring the last 22 batters (he walked a couple in the second inning) while fanning 11. The strikeouts lifted his season's total to 100, the 21st time in his career he had reached that plateau. Nolan would repeat the feat the following season, breaking Don Sutton's major-league mark.

The one-hitter was Ryan's fifth in which the sole safety had come in the opening frame, but Ryan wasn't finished displaying more of his wonders to the baseball world. He ended the 1989 season with 16 victories and a respectable 3.20 ERA. He collected 301 strikeouts to lead the majors for the seventh time. In 1990 he fell one shy of David Cone's major-league high, but his 232 K's were still good enough to lead the league for the eleventh time. Ryan won another 13 games that season and another 12 in 1991, the 20th time he finished in double figures in victories. Nolan's 203 strikeouts in 1991 marked his fifteenth season with 200 or more whiffs, while his 2.91 ERA was the eighth time he had finished under 3.00. Yet his greatest accomplishments during his final three seasons undoubtedly occurred during three mind-boggling games.

After winning his first three decisions in 1990, the ageless wonder faced the White Sox in Arlington on April 26. He retired the side in the first and then threw to the Chicago's bespectacled strong-boy Ron Kittle, leading off the second. Ryan went ahead on the count 1–2 and then tried to get Kittle to chase a bad one. "I didn't make it bad enough," Ryan acknowledged later. The long-armed slugger took an "excuse-me" swing at the outside breaking ball and blooped the ball to shallow right field. First baseman Palmiero appeared to have a play but slipped on the wet infield and lost his chance. The ball fell for the first hit of the game, which turned out to be the only hit off Ryan. The workhorse allowed only two other baserunners, both on walks, and fanned an incredible total of 16 batters.

Ryan's mound opponent was pretty great himself that day. Melido Perez had a no-hitter and shutout broken up in the fifth frame and surrendered only two other hits afterwards. A comment often made by broadcasters and sportswriters is that fans love to see slugfests. Nevertheless, the 20,000 at Arlington couldn't have been too disappointed with the brilliant pitching, which combined to allow only four hits and one run.

Ryan wasn't too disappointed with his twelfth, and what would be his last, one-hitter. Said Nolan, "I've been in that position enough to know everything has to be perfect." Ryan fans were probably more upset, realizing that the chance for their hero to notch another no-hitter had gone by and few opportunities remained.

But later that year the veteran proved to all that even in the age of the so-called "superior athlete," a 43-year-old legend could still dominate the best batters. On June 11 in Oakland, Nolan dismissed the defending world-champion A's with his sixth career no-hitter, handing out "oh-fors" to the likes of Mark McGwire, Rickey Henderson, Carney Lansford, and Jose Canseco. As if to prove it wasn't luck, Ryan celebrated another birthday the following January and then threw his seventh and last no-hit ballgame against the soon-to-be division champions, the Toronto Blue Jays, on May 1, 1991. That his final masterpiece was performed in front of a sizeable audience at Arlington was appropriate.

Sadly for baseball followers, Nolan called it quits after the 1993 season. Not so sadly for major-league hitters. In 1975, Reggie Jackson explained, as only Reggie can, what it was like facing the strikeout machine. "Every hitter likes fastballs, just like everybody likes ice cream. But you don't like it when someone's stuffing it into you by the gallon. That's how you feel when Ryan's throwing balls by you."

Nolan left career stats for others to try to match which are best described as untouchable. It's not a question of whether any future hurler will again be able to accumulate 5,800 strikeouts or seven no-hitters, but how close anyone can come.

Yet Nolan's greatest achievement came with his failures. The dozen one-hitters are impressive enough, but even more so when you consider that in half of them he came within inches of adding to his no-hit list. There was the confusion leading to Munson's popup falling, the ground balls by Jackson and Kennedy which barely escaped Ryan's glove, the indecision by teammate Lahoud, Kittle's apology-single, Liriano's last-inning liner. Although the records show Nolan having seven no-hitters and twelve one-hitters, with a little luck those numbers could easily have been reversed. Perhaps it's for the best, however, that they aren't. Those who would challenge Ryan's seven no-hitters have a large enough task as it is.

Nolan Ryan's Dozen One-Hitters

Date	Opponent	R	BB	K	Opposing Starter	Only Hit
4/18/70	Phils (H)	0	6	15	Bunning	Doyle
7/9/72	Red Sox (H)	0	1	16	Siebert	Yastrzemski
8/29/73	Yanks (H)	0	3	10	Medich	Munson
6/27/74	Rangers (H)	0	1	6	Brown	Johnson
4/15/77	Mariners (H)	0	6	8	Abbott	Stinson
5/5/78	Indians (H)	0	5	12	Wise	Kuiper
7/13/79	Yanks (H)	1	5	9	Tiant	Jackson
8/11/82	Padres (A)	0	3	6	Show	Kennedy
8/3/83	Padres (A)	0	6	10	Lollar	Flannery
4/23/89	Blue Jays (A)	1	3	12	Stottlemyre	Liriano
6/3/89	Mariners (A)	1	2	11	Zavaras	Reynolds
4/26/90	White Sox (H)	0	2	16	Perez	Kittle

Nine

A Wee Bit Short

Although they played eight decades apart, National Leaguers William Keeler and Pete Rose shared numerous attributes. Both were considered among the best batsmen of their day, hitting the ball to all fields, or "where they ain't," as Keeler once described his strategy. Neither displayed exceptional power nor ever amassed as many as 100 RBIs in a season, but both scored often, Rose leading the league in runs ten times, Keeler eight. Rose won three batting titles and had a still-standing major-league record of 10 seasons with 200 or more hits; Keeler took two batting crowns and surpassed the 200-hit mark eight times. Keeler finished his career with 150 triples; Rose collected 135, many ending in rousing, if at times flamboyant, head-first slides. Rose had 10 five-hit games during his career, a modern league record, while Keeler had 8 such games.

Both were reliable though not exceptional fielders and played several positions before retiring. Both were considered below average in size during their era — "Wee" Willie at 5' 4", 140 pounds while playing during the end of the nineteenth century and the beginning of the twentieth century; Rose at 5' 11", 190 pounds playing during an age of the bigger, stronger ballplayers of the seventies and eighties. Both played for clubs which were arguably the best of the decade — Keeler for the rough-and-tough Old Orioles of Baltimore during the 1890s, Rose for Cincinnati's Big Red Machine during the 1970s. Both were well liked and respected by their peers, and though Rose's work ethic and spirited play earned him the nickname "Charlie Hustle," Keeler, too, must have played with inordinate passion on an Oriole team notorious for doing anything to win, including breaking a few rules, or a few arms, legs, and skulls. Keeler was elected to the Hall of Fame in its inaugural year of 1939. Rose hasn't been elected, but he deserves to be there.

With the two players having much in common, perhaps it's fitting that Rose merely matched Keeler's 1897 NL-record, 44-game hitting streak.

The year 1978 had its share of emotional highs and lows for the Cincy-born switch-hitter who, as teammate Johnny Bench once pointed out, was "goal-oriented." Two days after reaching the 3,000-hit plateau on May 5, Rose's streak of playing in 678 consecutive games came to an end. The year marked Pete's 16th with the Reds since his rookie season of 1963, but he would be playing for Philadelphia the following season. Two hundred hits was a professed goal for Rose, and despite a month-long slump, he had a realistic shot after his hitting streak. He finished with 198. The Reds had faltered in 1977 following two world championships so that Rose and Company thirsted for clubhouse champagne in 1978, but they were left dry by the division-winning Dodgers, who edged them out by two games.

Yet it was Rose's failure to break Keeler's streak that was most disheartening. As it reached the midtwenties, the streak had the attention of most baseball fans. By the time it approached the forty mark, all America was captivated by this most formidable challenge to immortal Joe DiMaggio's famed 56-game string. As the *New York Times* Joseph Durso commented near the end of July, "Streaks, up or down, fascinate people as abnormalities of human behavior."

After Pete's streak was snapped, a reporter wanted to know if he was relieved. Rose blurted bitterly, "No. I'm not relieved. I'm teed off," and hinted that the pitcher who had stopped him, Gene Garber, could have gone a little easier, saying, "Garber was pitching like it was the seventh game of the World Series." Even in his autobiography, written ten years later, Rose's recollection reveals resentment over not seeing strikes. "I was angry. Don't lay the ball down the middle, Garber. Hit the corners. Do what you want. But fight me man to man. Don't walk me."

Since Rose missed breaking the record by one, the game prior to the beginning of the streak carries equal significance with the one which ended it. On June 13 at the Reds' Riverfront Stadium, Cincinnati bagled the Cubs 1–0 behind four-hit pitching by lefty Fred Norman. While Yankee switch-hitter Roy White was homering from both sides of the plate for the fifth time in his career in New York (Pete would twice accomplish the feat before retiring), Rose was held hitless in three official at-bats by righthander Dennis Lamp and southpaw Dave Geisel. Although he was less prone to taking pitches in the late stages of his batting spree, realizing walks thwarted his chances, he was unconcerned about such matters that day and drew a pass in his other plate appearance. His leadoff position in the lineup would later prove advantageous in keeping the streak alive but was of no help in attaining an extra at-bat that day. Nor were Cub batters Dave Kingman and Manny Trillo, who stranded the tying run in the ninth, denying Rose a chance to hit in the home half.

Pete's collar that day aggravated a batting slump which had left him with 6 hits in his last 57 at-bats and a .267 average, prompting some to speculate whether the 37-year-old, ten-time All-Star was all but finished. Rose showed life the next day, however, with a single in the first inning off Chicago's Dave Roberts to start the streak and then added another in the 3–1 Reds victory. Interestingly, the streak might have been delayed a day had teammate Joe Morgan not suffered a groin injury before the game. Manager Sparky Anderson, who had planned to rest Rose, was forced to include him in the lineup.

After playing an exhibition game in Indianapolis on June 15, the Reds hosted the Cardinals the following Friday night. Former Met Tom Seaver, who started, was then in his 12th of 20 seasons of a Hall-of-Fame career. Seaver had already accomplished much, including five 20-win seasons, three ERA titles, five strikeout crowns, and three Cy Young Awards, and he was looking to notch his 8th win in 12 decisions that night. He would do better.

The Reds led 4–0 going into the ninth, thanks in part to Rose's pair of hits and RBIs, but there was tension among the 38,000 fans in attendance as Seaver prepared to face leadoff batter Lou Brock. Tom Terrific was three outs away from the one feat for which all great hurlers strive, a feat which had eluded him thus far — a no-hitter. Seaver said afterwards that he "always felt if I get one, I get one," a pragmatic philosophy inspired perhaps by his entering the ninth with a no-no thrice before, only to settle for one-hitters on each occasion.

Seaver retired Brock and then disposed of Garry Templeton. Righty-swinging George Hendrick dribbled a grounder to first baseman Dan Driessen, who stepped on the bag to begin the celebration. Seaver down-played the achievement in the clubhouse and also the following day, noting that, unlike a World Series victory, the thrill derived from hurling a no-hitter is "momentary, that's all." Still, Seaver "enjoyed the moment" enough to stay up talking with wife Nancy and well-wishers until four o'clock in the morning.

The next day Rose victimized the Cards' Pete Vuckovich for his third straight two-hit game, and his tally in the ninth was the decider in a 6–5 Reds win. Joked Rose to reporters afterwards: "It's nice to be talking to you all again. I knew you guys would be around before the year was up." What he didn't know was the extent of attention he would be receiving for the next six weeks.

Rose's streak was nine after he stroked three singles and a double off three different Los Angeles Dodgers pitchers on June 24. Mention of the streak was first made by the *Cincinnati Enquirer* when he lengthened it to ten in Los Angeles the next day, singling in his first two tries against the crafty lefty Tommy John. Pete then came to bat in the seventh with the tying run on second and was surprised to see Anderson flash the bunt sign. He reluctantly complied, and his successful attempt pushed baserunner Vic Correll to third, who scored the tying run on a groundout moments later. Although the Reds won 5–4, Rose was annoyed, saying afterwards, "I'm finally swinging the bat good and I got to be a sacrifice bunter."

The streak reached 14 on June 29 when Pete notched one of four Cincy hits in a 5–0 whitewash by the Astros' Floyd Bannister. Tommy John held him hitless through seven innings in the opener of a twin bill the next day, but Rose stayed alive with a hit off lefty Lance Rautzhan and then had another three off a trio of Los Angeles hurlers in the nightcap. The game featured shouting matches between Joe Morgan and a couple of disgruntled Riverfront spectators and between Rose and Dodger first baseman Rick Monday. Pete had made an unflattering remark to Bob Welch after grounding out in the sixth. When he took his position at third in the seventh, Monday began taunting him and Pete had to be restrained from charging into the Dodgers dugout. Peace prevailed, however, and when the game resumed, Jerry Grote hit the first pitch down the third base line, where Rose made a circus snare. His heroics that day weren't enough, however, to prevent another drubbing by the Dodgers, who surged past Cincy into second place behind the front-running Giants.

By July 5 the streak stood at 20. With a hit off the Astros' knuckleballer Joe Niekro that night, Rose celebrated his selection as the NL third baseman in the All-Star Game, one of four Reds to be chosen to start. "I might go forever," a cocky Rose remarked four games later when his streak was 2 away from the club record of 27 set by Edd Roush and Vada Pinson. Asked of his chances of reaching DiMaggio's mark, Pete surmised with tongue in cheek, "Right now, I'd say I've got the best chance of anyone."

On July 15 the Reds record was his after a seeing-eye single off Met righthander Craig Swan. He had another record the next day after his double to right-center in his last at-bat made it 29 straight, surpassing Red Schoendienst's streak for switch-hitters. "I wasn't too worried," Rose told reporters when asked how he felt being hitless as he went to the plate for his final turn. "I just didn't want to get any walks." Rose's next target was Tommy Holmes' modern record of 37 set in 1945.

On July 23 the Giants' Jack Clark extended a hitting streak to 25 games. Only Frisco fans knew or cared, for by then Rose's streak had reached 36, one away from Holmes' mark. Yet even Pete shared headlines the next day. The Yankees' brash manager Billy "The Kid" Martin had uttered his now infamous assessment of Yankee right-fielder Reggie Jackson and owner

George Steinbrenner, saying, "One's a born liar, the other's convicted." Martin was fired the next day.

Tommy Holmes was the Mets' community-relations director in 1978 and was at Shea Stadium when the challenger to his record came to town on July 24. New York starter Pat Zachry held Rose hitless in his first three tries, and by the seventh frame, a surprisingly supportive crowd of 39,000 fans were chanting "Pete! Pete! Pete!" hoping to be witnesses to history. Rose attempted a bunt on Zachry's first offering, fouled it off, took the next pitch for a ball, then stroked a changeup into left, precipitating an ovation which endured for several minutes. As Rose waved his helmet in acknowledgment, he might have considered the irony of the moment — such zealous plaudits coming in a stadium where only five years earlier he had been harassed unmercifully by hostile spectators infuriated over his manhandling their spirited shortstop, Bud Harrelson, in the NL championships.

Further irony was evident the next night, as Rose broke Holmes' record with a hit in the third inning off the Mets' Swan and then saw the Mets exec rush toward him, Tommy wanting to be the first to offer congratulations. The two hugged, and then Rose again raised his hat toward the delirious crowd in appreciation. A reporter in the clubhouse wanted to know when Pete thought the streak would end. His reply, "When I go 0 for 4 some night."

His new modern mark might have been sufficiently satisfactory to some, but the next night after making it 39 in a row, Rose took up another gauntlet. Brushing off the 41-game streak of George Sisler as well as Cobb's 40-gamer, Pete said, "The guy I want to pass is Wee Willie Keeler. He's got the National League record and even though people say it was before 1900, I'd like for people to say that I have the record before and after 1900."

Having set for himself this new challenge, Pete edged close with hits in both ends of a doubleheader against the Phils on July 28. The next day, as Steinbrenner was shocking an overflow Yankee Stadium audience with his Old-Timers' Day announcement that Martin would be back as Yankee skipper in 1980 (actually, he returned in 1979), Rose was surpassing Cobb and Sisler by extending his streak to 42 with three hits against Philly. On July 30, after being robbed of a hit in the third by right-fielder Jerry Martin, who made a running, lunging backhand grab of his third-inning line drive, Rose slapped a grounder off starter Larry Christenson past third sacker Mike Schmidt, making it 43 straight.

The Reds were in Atlanta the next night. With rain threatening to halt the proceedings, Rose hoped to get a hit early but was thwarted by Brave starter Phil Niekro, who walked Pete in the first and then retired him on a sharp line drive to short in the third. Batting in the sixth, Rose was feeling

Pete Rose takes a swing at a Phil Niekro delivery in the sixth inning of the Braves-Reds game on July 31, 1978. One moment later Pete had hit safely in his 44th consecutive game (UPI/Bettmann).

the pressure after taking two outside pitches. But with the game knotted at 1–1, the senior member of the knuckleball-specialist Niekro brothers was wary of walking the ledoff batter of the inning and gave Rose the opportunity to see a rare fastball. It led to a bouncer on the right side which at first appeared playable. Second baseman Rod Gilbreath made a diving lunge, but the ball scooted past his glove into right field. It was Pete's only hit of the game. "I gave it my best shot," Gilbreath said in defense of his defense. "If I had caught the ball, I'd have been standing on my head and couldn't have made a throw." As he stood at first base, Rose was honored for his record-tying feat with a bouquet of flowers (roses, of course) and fireworks which were ignited from the top of the center-field scoreboard.

There remained the matter of breaking Keeler's mark, which seemed merely a formality on August 1 for the millions of fans in support of Rose's quest. Again the Braves were the hosts, and since their team shared the bottom berth in the division standings, it can be assumed a large majority of the sizeable crowd of over 30,000 fans at Fulton County Stadium were there for the purpose of watching history in the making.

Towering rookie Larry McWilliams started for Atlanta. The lean lefty had made his major-league debut only two weeks earlier and had shown considerable promise in winning his first two decisions. Still, a green giant on a last place ballclub was an unlikely candidate to stop the streak. But luck, good or bad, plays a part in many endeavors, as it did that night. Pete saw a few hittable pitches his first time up before taking a walk on a full-count pitch. In the third, Pete drilled a low liner back to the box, but McWilliams' instinctive stab of the ball near his ankles prevented a sure single. Rose hit another on the nose in his third try but was thrown out by shortstop Jerry Royster.

By the seventh, McWilliams had been replaced by righty reliever Gene Garber. In the middle of a 19-year career marked with moderate success, the side-winding righthander had a reputation for being ornery and had once leveled slugger Bobby Murcer with a head-high heater after the Yank had rocked him for a pair of homers in a 1973 game. (Murcer arose and hit the next pitch into the right-field seats.) Garber's proud demeanor made him a formidable opponent for Rose.

For the third time, Pete hit the ball well, but his liner was corralled by rookie third baseman Bob Horner, who then doubled up Reds baserunner Dave Collins. (Horner, who joined the Braves in June, already had nine homers and would add another that night along with a single and double.) Over 30,000 fans stood applauding as Pete came to bat for his final chance in the ninth. He tried a bunt on Garber's first pitch, took two balls, and then fouled off the next toss. Garber then fooled the anxious batter with a changeup, and Rose whiffed, ending the streak.

Annoyed at Rose's implication that he had been trying too hard, Garber retorted in the clubhouse, "I had an idea he was hitting like it was the ninth inning of the seventh game of the World Series." McWilliams showed more compassion in remaining undefeated in his brief major-league tenure with the 16–4 victory; he sounded almost apologetic in describing his snare of Pete's liner: "It was just reaction on my part."

Following the snapping of the streak, Pete's average stood at .316, nearly 50 points higher than when it had begun. He had 70 hits in 182 plate appearances during the streak for a .385 average, hitting .364 against lefties and .397 against righties. Fourteen of his hits were doubles, while he failed to hit any homers or triples. He hit .404 at home and .359 on the road. Pete victimized the Dodgers more than any other club, gathering 13 hits in 30 at-bats for a .433 average.

Commenting on baseball's headliners of July, sportswriter Larry Merchant wrote on the thirty-first, "This would be a very dull world without the egos and neuroses and talents of the Steinbrenners, the Martins, and the Jacksons, but it needs the inspired accountants like Rose for ballast."

By the end of the season, the Reds didn't think so, not enough at least to offer the hard-working hit man a salary increase appropriate for one who could otherwise test the free-agent waters. Pete signed a four-year deal with the Phils worth three-and-a-quarter million, which at the time made him the highest paid player in baseball. He continued to run up the numbers in 1979, gathering over 200 hits for the tenth and final time of his career while hitting .331, good for second in the league. After a brief stay with Montreal in 1984, Rose returned to the Queen City late in the year as player-manager; he abandoned the player role in 1986.

In 1989, charges surfaced that Pete had gambled on baseball games. When legal battles over Commissioner Bart Giamatti's right to discipline him lingered for months, Rose finally agreed to drop the lawsuit in August and accepted Giamatti's ruling that he be permanently ineligible for employment in baseball, though the reason given was vague and made no mention of Pete's alleged gambling.

Despite supposedly overwhelming evidence against him, Rose continued to deny betting on baseball, suggesting in his autobiography that he had been framed by two blackmailing felons closely associated with bookies. Whether his allegation be fact or fiction, Rose's permanent banishment from baseball was unnecessarily cruel, a clear violation of the make-the-punishment-fit-the-crime principle. Comparing his infraction with that of the Black Soxers of 1919 is ludicrous. Joe Jackson and Company conspired to purposely throw ballgames. Rose may have bet on games but almost certainly never wagered against his own team. No better proof can be offered than his appetite for winning while a ballplayer.

How trivial his disappointment over the failure to break Keeler's hitting streak must seem to Rose today compared with that derived from the devastating decree denying one of the premier players his corner in Cooperstown.

Pete Rose's 44-Game Hitting Streak of 1978

No.	Date	Opponent	Ballpark	Pitchers Who Yielded Hits (lefty/righty)	AB	H	Avg. During Streak
1	6/14	Cubs	Riverfront Stadium	D. Roberts (L)	4	2	.270
2	6/16	Cards	Riverfront Stadium	J. Denny (R)	4	2	.274
3	6/17	Cards	Riverfront Stadium	P. Vuckovich (R) B. Schultz (L)	4	2	.277
4	6/18	Cards	Riverfront Stadium	S. Martinez (R)	4	1	.277
5	6/20	Giants	Candlestick Park	J. Montefusco (R)	5	2	.279
6	6/21	Giants	Candlestick Park	E. Halicki (R)	4	1	.279
7	6/22	Giants	Candlestick Park	B. Knepper (L)	4	1	.278

No.	Date	Opponent	Ballpark	Pitchers Who Yielded Hits (lefty/righty)	AB	H	Avg. During Streak
8	6/23	Dodgers	Dodger Stadium	B. Hooton (R)	4	1	.278
9	6/24	Dodgers	Dodger Stadium	D. Sutton (R)	5	4	.287
				C. Hough (R)			
				B. Welch (R)			
10	6/25	Dodgers	Dodger Stadium	T. John (L)	3	2	.291
11	6/26	Astros	Astrodome	M. Lemongello (R)	5	1	.289
12	6/27	Astros	Astrodome	J. Niekro (R)	4	1	.289
13	6/28	Astros	Astrodome	T. Dixon (R)	4	1	.288
14	6/29	Astros	Astrodome	F. Bannister (L)	3	1	.288
15	6/30	Dodgers	Riverfront Stadium	L. Rautzhan (L)	4	1	.288
16	6/30	Dodgers	Riverfront Stadium	B. Welch (R)	5	3	.293
				T. Forster (L)			
				C. Hough (R)			
17	7/1	Dodgers	Riverfront Stadium	R. Rhoden (R)	5	1	.291
18	7/2	Dodgers	Riverfront Stadium	D. Rau (L)	4	1	.291
19	7/3	Astros	Riverfront Stadium	F. Bannister (L)	5	3	.296
				B. McLaughlin (R)			
20	7/4	Astros	Riverfront Stadium	J. R. Richard (R)	4	1	.295
21	7/5	Astros	Riverfront Stadium	J. Niekro (R)	4	1	.294
22	7/7	Giants	Riverfront Stadium	V. Blue (L)	5	3	.299
				J. Curtis (L)			
23	7/7	Giants	Riverfront Stadium	J. Barr (R)	4	1	.298
24	7/8	Giants	Riverfront Stadium	J. Montefusco (R)	4	1	.298
25	7/9	Giants	Riverfront Stadium	E. Halicki (R)	4	3	.303
				B. Knepper (L)			
26	7/13	Mets	Riverfront Stadium	J. Koosman (L)	5	2	.304
				S. Lockwood (R)			
27	7/14	Mets	Riverfront Stadium	P. Zachry (R)	5	2	.305
28	7/15	Mets	Riverfront Stadium	C. Swan (R)	2	1	.306
29	7/16	Mets	Riverfront Stadium	P. Siebert (L)	5	1	.305
30	7/17	Expos	Riverfront Stadium	S. Bahnsen (R)	4	1	.304
31	7/18	Expos	Riverfront Stadium	H. Dues (R)	4	2	.306
32	7/19	Phils	Veterans Stadium	R. Reed (R)	4	1	.306
33	7/20	Phils	Veterans Stadium	J. Kaat (L)	5	1	.305
34	7/21	Expos	Olympic Stadium	R. Grimsley (L)	3	1	.305
35	7/22	Expos	Olympic Stadium	D. Schatzeder (L)	3	1	.305
36	7/23	Expos	Olympic Stadium	S. Rogers (R)	6	2	.305
				D. Knowles (L)			
37	7/24	Mets	Shea Stadium	P. Zachry (R)	5	2	.307
				S. Lockwood (R)			
38	7/25	Mets	Shea Stadium	C. Swan (R)	4	3	.311
39	7/26	Mets	Shea Stadium	N. Espinosa (R)	3	1	.311
40	7/28	Phils	Riverfront Stadium	R. Lerch (L)	2	1	.312
41	7/28	Phils	Riverfront Stadium	S. Carlton (L)	4	1	.311

No.	Date	Opponent	Ballpark	Pitchers Who Yielded Hits (lefty/righty)	AB	H	Avg. During Streak
42	7/29	Phils	Riverfront Stadium	J. Lonborg (R)	4	3	.315
43	7/30	Phils	Riverfront Stadium	L. Christenson (R) R. Reed (R)	5	2	.316
44	7/31	Braves	Fulton County Stad.	P. Niekro (R)	4	1	.316

Breakdown of Streak

Singles 56	*Doubles* 14	*Triples* 0	*Homers* 0

	Games	Hits	At-Bats	Average
Totals	44	70	182	.385
Home	25	42	104	.404
Road	19	28	78	.359

Average vs. Lefties	*Average vs. Righties*
.364	.397

Team by Team Breakdown

Team	G	AB	H	Avg.	Team	G	AB	H	Avg.
Cubs	1	4	2	.500	Mets	7	29	12	.414
Phils	6	24	9	.375	Expos	5	20	7	.350
Cards	3	12	5	.417	Braves	1	4	1	.250
Giants	7	30	12	.400	Astros	7	29	9	.310
Dodgers	7	30	13	.433					

Ten

The String Runs Short

Ted Williams was 31 years old following his near Triple Crown season of 1949, an age ushering in the twilight years for some modern athletes. Yet the Splinter continued to perform splendidly throughout the fifties, leading the league in batting and doubles twice, in slugging three times. With the exception of Mantle, he was probably the most productive AL hitter of the decade, as the chart on pages 186 and 187, comparing his combined stats with other junior-circuit stars, indicates.

Keep in mind that Ted missed nearly the entire 1952 and 1953 seasons while serving as a jet-fighter pilot during the Korean War. Recalling being drafted for the second time (he had served in World War II from 1943 to 1945), Williams wrote 17 years later in *My Turn at Bat*, "In my heart I was bitter about it, but I made up my mind I wasn't going to bellyache." Williams finished his career with a flourish in 1960, batting .316 with 29 homers, including a round tripper in his final at-bat, marking his Fenway farewell.

Williams's Combined Stats for the Fifties Compared with Other Notable American Leaguers*

Player	Years	Average	HR	RBIs	Runs
Williams	1950–59	.336	227	729	660
Mantle	1951–59	.311	280	841	994
Rosen	1950–56	.287	192	712	599
Doby	1950–59	.283	215	816	763
Berra	1950–59	.262	256	997	848
Minoso	1951–59	.306	145	790	898
Kaline	1953–59	.311	125	544	521
Sievers	1950–59	.263	199	682	576
Wertz	1950–59	.277	195	745	574

Includes those who played in at least five seasons of 100 or more game appearances

Jensen	1950–59	.281	186	863	746
Kuenn	1950–57	.314	53	423	620
Kell	1950–57	.308	60	521	490
Dropo	1950–59	.271	147	680	458
Fox	1950–59	.301	27	534	902
Vernon	1950–58	.291	107	716	612
Goodman	1950–59	.302	17	442	666
Woodling	1950–59	.286	110	603	606
Bauer	1950–59	.279	147	600	730
Boone	1950–59	.277	146	695	597

One of Williams' grandest achievements occurred in 1957. After being out of action for more than two weeks with a severe cold, Williams hit a late-game, pinch-hit homer on a 2–1 pitch off A's righty Mike Morgan on September 17 and then hit his only career homer to be yielded by Whitey Ford in the next game, again in a pinch-hitting role. In the lineup the following day, Ted was walked on four pitches in his first at-bat by Yank hurler Bob Turley. With the bags jammed in the second, Bullet Bob challenged Williams with a 2–0 fastball and paid the price. The grand slam was the 15th of Ted's 17 career slams (he would hit his final two the following season), and the Yankees took no chances in his final two at-bats, walking the sizzling slugger on four pitches both times to the chagrin of the Yankee Stadium fans.

Ted tied the still-standing major-league record of four consecutive homers with a drive off knuckleballer Tom Sturdivant after he had been walked in his first appearance. With a chance to break the homer mark in the sixth inning, Williams settled for a single and then drew a pass in the eighth, marking the 11th straight time he had successfully reached base. On September 23 the string was lengthened when Ted singled, walked three times, and was hit by a pitch. He was retired in his first at-bat the next day.

Reaching base safely in 16 consecutive appearances remains the major-league mark today, and as Williams wrote in 1969, "That might be a record to last forever." Some will, but none go unchallenged. In 1985 the Dodgers' Pedro Guerrero nearly duplicated the feat.

Guerrero was born on a hot summer day in June of 1956 in the small village of San Pedro de Macoris in the Dominican Republic, where sugar cane crops provide work, but not wealth, for most. (Manny Mota once noted, "There is no middle class. Just upper class and peasants.") Pedro was eight years old when he began playing ball, sharing bats carved from tree branches and worn-out gloves with the other kids. It was also about that time that his father abandoned his mother, two brothers, and him, forcing the distraught family into the already crowded one-room shack of

Pedro's grandfather, where a full belly and indoor plumbing were luxuries the youngster learned to live without. The family's destitute state necessitated Guerrero's discontinuing his education by age 11. He first earned two bucks a day as a cement mixer and then three per diem stacking cement-like sugar sacks.

The nearly insufferable conditions at home and exhausting workday didn't interfere, however, with Guerrero's baseball. He played amateur ball in a league headed by former Cleveland Indians second baseman Pedro Gonzalez. By age 16, "Pete" Guerrero's adept fielding and league-leading .438 average attracted a Cleveland scout, and though Gonzalez advised him to remain in the Dominican league a while longer, Guerrero couldn't afford to ignore a $2,500 bonus. As he recalled in an interview with sportswriter Mel Durslag many years later, "I kept $200 for myself and sent the rest to my mother, asking her to use a little of it to buy me a new bed. I couldn't sleep in the broken-down one I had."

Arriving at the Indians' spring training camp in Tuscon in 1973 with nothing more than one pair of pants and a shirt, Guerrero was also the youngest player there. His inability to speak or understand English made him uneasy and homesick, and he would cry at the mere mention of his family. Things got worse before they got better. Guerrero sprained his wrist attempting a slide, which put him on the sidelines. During his first year of pro ball playing for Sarasota in the Gulf Coast League, Pedro batted an alarming .235 and struggled when he was off the field as well in trying to overcome the language barrier. He came close to quitting and heading home but "had nothing to go home to."

Guerrero's first-year stats made the Indians organization nervous, so he was traded to the Dodgers in 1974 for a minor-league pitcher named Bruce Ellingsen. Pedro cried when he heard of the swap, thinking it would be harder to get to the big leagues with Los Angeles than with Cleveland. In the future, it would be the Indians executives who would be crying. As sportswriter Hal Lebovitz noted a decade later, "As I watched Pedro Guerrero lead Los Angeles in the National League playoffs, I kept thinking how smart that organization is. Which makes the Indians, to put it kindly, quite the opposite."

Ellingsen's major-league career consisted of half-a season's work with the Tribe in 1974. That same year Guerrero led the Northwest League in doubles while batting an impressive .316. More impressive were his stats the following year. Despite moving up a notch to the Midwest League, Pedro won the batting title with a .345 mark and made the Class A All-Star squad. He dropped to .305 in 1976 but catapulted to .403 in 1977, despite being sidelined with a broken ankle. His first taste of the majors came at the close of the following season; after an impressive showing in spring training in 1979, the 22 year old finally made the Dodgers roster. When he was informed in midseason that he was being sent back to the minors, Pedro nearly quit but was talked out of it by Dodgers batting coach and fellow Dominican Mota. Guerrero responded with a .333 average and 22 homers at Albuquerque, while leading the Pacific Coast League in RBIs with 103.

By 1980, Pedro was in the majors to stay. He began as a pinch hitter, but when Dodgers skipper Tom Lasorda was sufficiently impressed with his .448 average and second baseman Davey Lopes suffered an injury, Guerrero was inserted into the starting lineup. The rookie kept hitting, and despite Lopes' return, he kept playing — at third base, first base, the outfield — until he suffered knee-ligament damage while attempting a slide on August 21 which sidelined him for the rest of the season, except for four successful pinch-hit efforts in late September.

Finishing with a .322 average in 1980, Guerrero felt confident the following spring that one of the starting outfield positions would be his, until the Dodgers acquired the speedy Ken Landreaux. With slugger-outfielder Reggie Smith also in camp, Pedro was suddenly fighting for a spot again. Nevertheless, he would accumulate 347 at-bats in 98 games playing at third base, first base, and the outfield during that strike-shortened year. He was selected for the All-Star Game, his first, and finished the season with an even .300 average. His dozen homers were one fewer than team leader Ron Cey had, and his 48 RBIs were third-best in the club. In the division playoff against Houston, Guerrero's homer was the key to a Dodgers 2–1 victory in game four that knotted the series (which the Dodgers won the next day). He had another four bagger in the Dodgers' victory over the Expos in the championship series and had two homers, a double, a triple, two singles, and seven RBIs (including five in game six) in the Dodgers' conquest of the Yanks in the World Series.

Things were finally going well for Guerrero. Even his English was improving, though he would never completely master the language, as indicated by his late-career complaint that reporters "sometimes write what I say and not what I mean," a remark about as comprehensible as the daffiest of Berra's "Yogisms."

If it appeared the prospect had finally blossomed into stardom, there was no doubt at the end of the 1982 season. By then, coach Mota was labeling Guerrero "the most improved player in the National League." Playing nearly the entire season in the outfield, he again batted over .300, while belting 32 round trippers and attaining his first 100-RBI season. He lived up to Mota's boast by matching his homer and RBI stats the next year, but his output fell dramatically in 1984. As the season began in 1985, Guerrero found himself in the familiar position of having to prove himself in order to remain a regular on a formidable ballclub.

In analyzing his career, it would appear that Pedro thrived when challenged. By the All-Star break, he was among the leaders in most major offensive categories while being named to the National League squad for the third time (he had been selected in 1983 as well), though he was unable to play because of back spasms which had been bothering him for several weeks. As Los Angeles hosted the Pirates on July 23, it held a game lead in the National League West over the Padres, thanks mostly to traditionally superb Dodgers pitching but also to Guerrero's club-leading 21 homers (to Greg Brock's runner-up amount of 14), 48 RBIs (to Brock's 35), and .315 average (to Bill Russell's .280).

Orel Hershiser started for the Dodgers that day, pitching in his second year as a regular. He had been impressive as a rookie, winning 11 of 19 decisions with an admirable ERA of 2.66 and league-leading four shutouts, but 1985 was to be his first of several dominant seasons. As the 33,000 at Dodger Stadium watched Hershiser take his opening-game warm-ups, some may have been wondering just how good was this 26-year-old righty sinker-baller. Was his 9–3 mark a fluke? Would his 2.70 ERA remain as low throughout the season's tense second half? Were his one-hitter against the Padres in April and his two- and three-hitters that followed signs of greatness?

By season's end all Dodgers fans would have their answer, with Hershiser finishing with a 2.03 ERA in winning his final ten decisions. Three years later "the Bulldog" grabbed Cy Young honors by leading the league in victories (23), complete games (15), innings-pitched (267), and shutouts (8), while setting a still-standing major-league record of 59 consecutive scoreless innings. Although fate in the form of arm surgery interrupted what appeared to be a Hall-of-Fame career, Hershiser rebounded in the nineties and was arguably the key pitcher on the pennant-winning Cleveland teams of 1995 and 1996. Perhaps the Indians organization isn't quite so dumb after all.

For some Dodgers rooters, the question of Hershiser's potential was answered on that hot summer afternoon in July of 1985. But for a Jason Thompson wrong-field single in the second frame which fell a few feet in front of left-fielder Guerrero, Hershiser would have had a no-hitter. As superb as was Orel's one-hit masterpiece, Guerrero's performance at the plate that day was, in retrospect, more noteworthy.

After grounding out in the second and whiffing on a full-count toss in the fourth, Guerrero took his third swings against Pirates pitcher Rick Reuschel in the fifth frame and doubled to left, driving in the Dodgers' fourth run of the game. In the seventh, Pedro again doubled to left, this time off the Bucs' southpaw reliever Rod Scurry. That his doubles output was increased by two probably carried relatively little importance for Pedro (though he would be more conscious of his amount four years later in leading the league with 42). A few days later his strikeout of July 23 would carry major significance.

The next day Americans were shocked to discover that former heart-throb and longtime film and television actor Rock Hudson had for some time been suffering from the AIDS virus, though a spokeswoman's comment indicating that the actor was in remission and "cured totally" was reassuring. Sadly, as hundreds of thousands continue to do, including an alarmingly increasing number of children, Hudson succumbed less than three months later to what would become the fastest growing cause of premature death in America. Hudson was 59.

Life offers one tragedy after another, making recreation a necessity, not a luxury, a means of escape for an often harsh reality, a psychological reprieve, however brief. In Los Angeles that night, recreation took the form of 34,000 fans (from the word *fanatic*) at Dodger Stadium whose main concern was lengthening their game-and-a-half lead over the Padres. As on the preceding day, the Pirates were perfect guests. Leading by one in the sixth, Pittsburgh pitcher Don Robinson loaded the bases and then surrendered a grand slam to Brock. The Dodgers coasted to a 9–1 win, thus lengthening their lead over the losing Padres to 2½ games.

Guerrero's sole hit, an infield single, was attributable to caution on the part of Robinson, recently acquired Al Holland, and soon-to-be-traded John Candelaria rather than ineffectiveness with the bat. The trio of hurlers walked the dreaded Dominican in his other at-bats, stretching his consecutive successful plate appearances to six.

As arguments heated up the next day between union negotiator Donald Fehr and owner representative Barry Rona over a proposed player contract for the following season, Guerrero continued to sizzle with the stick when given the chance. After a base-on-balls against Cub lefty Ray Fontenot in the first, he appeared to be receiving yet another one in the fourth, but Fontenot's 3–1 pitch wasn't far enough outside. Pedro crushed it into the right-center-field pavilion for his first homer in two weeks, the power drought's end an indication that back spasms were no longer hampering his swing. Guerrero singled off Fontenot in the sixth and faced righty reliever Lary Sorensen in the seventh. With a runner on second and two outs and the game still close, Sorensen hastened the inevitable freebie by hitting Guerrero on the back on the first pitch. It marked the tenth straight time he had reached base safely.

If Guerrero was annoyed about being plucked by Sorensen, he didn't reveal his displeasure in the clubhouse, saying: "I keep getting my walks, and Brock keeps killing 'em. I'll take it." With his safety string approaching Williams' 16, Pedro's run was mentioned in the *Los Angeles Times* the next day. If the 41,000 spectators at Dodger Stadium that afternoon came to watch their team pull further from the pack and their hero get closer to history, they were disappointed in neither case.

Chicago manager Jim Frey would marvel after the game, "Guerrero — My God, he's really hot. It seems like every time he hits the ball, it goes in the seats." Some that do aren't always homeruns. Following a Landreaux single in the first, Pedro went with a Dick Ruthven outside slant. The drive appeared destined for the right-field stands, but destiny was in the hands of a 20-year-old fan eager for a souvenir who reached out and grabbed the ball prior to its clearing the barrier. First-base ump Bruce Froemming ruled fan interference, and Guerrero was credited with a double.

If at first you don't succeed, hit it farther next time. Although *Los Angeles Times* sportswriter Gordon Edes noted the difficulty of hitting at Dodger Stadium in the late afternoon, a Ruthven full-count curve that "exploded out of the shadows" had little effect against Guerrero, who parked the pitch over the right-center-field fence. Such displays of opposite-field power assured his being walked by Ruthven in his next at-bat in the fifth frame. Nor was reliever Warren Brusstar more willing to challenge Pedro in the sixth, despite a Dodger seven-run lead by then.

When the margin was extended to nine by inning's end, skipper Lasorda removed Guerrero, who was replaced by part-timer Candy Maldonado. Thus did Pete miss an opportunity to hit against southpaw reliever Ron Meridith, whose 53 hits, 24 walks, and 23 earned runs allowed in 46 innings' work that year would earn no votes for Cy Young Award but did make him a likely candidate to extend Pedro's on-base streak to 15. It should be pointed out that Meridith was able to retire Maldonado in the eighth, though Candy's sour average of .194 is equally noteworthy.

So the crowd would have to come again another day to watch the man who believed "there's no way they're going to get me out." They came. More than 46,000 fans jammed into Dodger Stadium on July 27, and as Edes surmised the next day, "It was Guerrero's hitting that many in the sellout crowd came to see." The job of thwarting the league's hottest hitter belonged to a righthander with a 90-mph fastball and a formidable curve, but a mediocre career.

Scott Sanderson had turned 29 five days earlier but still hadn't distinguished himself in the majors as much as some had predicted during his rookie year with Montreal in 1978. Nineteen eighty had been Sanderson's

Teammate Steve Garvey watches as Pedro Guerrero connects for a hit in a game at Wrigley Field (National Baseball Library & Archive, Cooperstown, N.Y.).

best year; he won 16 of 27 decisions with a 3.11 ERA. He was traded to the Cubs in 1984 but won only 8 of 24 starts. Scott had only a handful of wins in 1985 as he faced leadoff batter Bill Russell (who would replace Lasorda as Dodger manager in 1996) with a 1–0 lead in the bottom of the first.

Sanderson disposed of Russell but surrendered an infield hit to recently acquired Enos Cabell. Landreaux laced a double to center, Cabell stopping at third. Guerrero then stepped to the plate, hoping to give his club the lead and extend his streak to 15. Pedro later said he felt "no pressure. Why should I have pressure?" Why indeed? For one who had survived an impoverished youth and struggled to achieve virtually his entire life before finally attaining financial security in the form of a $600,000 contract, the reporter's question may have seemed amusing.

To his credit, Sanderson challenged Pedro rather than giving an open-base walk. Guerrero hung tough, fouling off four pitches before driving the next one to deep center. In some parks the drive might have carried, but not in Dodger Stadium that day. The catch was as routine for the speedy outfielder Bob Dernier as was the tag and score by Cabell. Like walks, sac flies aren't counted as official times at bat, but since Guerrero's streak involved consecutive times reaching base successfully, the sac fly marked its termination. Pedro made meaningless any arguments to the ruling by failing in his next try in the third inning.

Guerrero's reaching base in 14 consecutive at-bats remains the National League record, but he must have felt some measure of disappointment in failing to match Williams' 16, although he later said: "I got a couple of good pitches to hit. I hit it good. There is nothing you can do about it." The two streaks are actually remarkably comparable. Guerrero stroked 7 hits which accounted for 16 total bases, Williams 6 hits for 18 total bases. Guerrero had five extra-base hits (three doubles, two homers) to Ted's four, all being round trippers. Both players were hit by a pitch on one occasion.

Guerrero finished the 1985 season as the league leader in slugging (.577) and homerun percentage (one every 14.8 at-bats), second in batting at .320, and third in homers with 33. He fought back from surgery in 1986 (the surgeon was Dr. Frank Jobe, prompting broadcaster Tim McCarver to quip that "he's one of the patients of Jobe") and then belted 27 homers and batted .338 in 1987, second to Tony Gwynn's .370. Traded to St. Louis in midseason of the following year, the 32 year old responded to yet another challenge by finishing second in the league in RBIs (117), fourth in hits (177), fifth in batting (.311), while leading in doubles with 42.

Guerrero's output fell sharply in the nineties, and by the middle of the decade his playing career was over. No doubt the heroic Hispanic is currently seeking other challenges. As in his try at the record, he may not always succeed, but if determination overcomes obstacles, his chances are excellent.

Pedro Guerrero's 1985 14 Consecutive Times On-Base Streak

Date	Opposing Team	Opposing Pitcher	Outcome
7/23	Pirates (H)	Reuschel	double
		Scurry	double
7/24	Pirates (H)	Robinson	two walks, single
		Winn	walk
7/25	Cubs (H)	Fontenot	walk, homer, single
		Sorensen	hit by pitch
7/26	Cubs (H)	Ruthven	double, homer, walk
		Brusstar	walk

Ted Williams' 1957 16 Consecutive Times On-Base Streak

Date	Opposing Team	Opposing Pitcher	Outcome
9/17	A's (H)	Morgan	homer
9/20	Yanks (A)	Ford	homer
9/21	Yanks (A)	Turley	walk, homer
		Byrne	walk, walk
9/21	Yanks (A)	Sturdivant	walk, homer, single, walk
		Grim	walk
9/23	Senators (A)	Lumenti	single, walk
		Kemmerer	walk
		Minnick	walk
		Hyde	hit by pitch

Eleven

Eight Isn't Enough

Fame is the goal of youth; obscurity the reality of adulthood. Yet some beat the odds as a result of extraordinary skill and desire or fortuitous circumstances.

In baseball, eminence is achieved by those who consistently outperform their peers, but on occasion a mediocre player will gain everlasting acclaim with one exceptional performance. Would Sandy Amoros, a lifetime .255 hitter, be remembered today had he not made a brilliant running catch of Yogi Berra's fly ball to preserve the Dodgers' victory in game seven of the 1955 World Series? Mention to any baseball aficionado the name Al Gionfriddo, who played all of four seasons in the majors, three as a utility man, to arouse the mental image of Joe DiMaggio kicking the infield dirt near second base after the Dodgers left fielder robbed him of extra bases with a spectacular catch in the 1947 Series. Don Larsen never won more than 11 games in a 14-year career, but the perfect game the Yankees hurler pitched in game three of the 1956 Series is perhaps the most renowned performance in baseball history. The Giants' Bobby Thomson was a talented batter, but his lifetime stats don't warrant the excessive recognition he continues to receive, thanks to his game-ending, pennant-clinching homerun in the 1951 Giants-Dodgers playoff. Would Bill Mazeroski be as well known today had his long fly ball been caught by left-fielder Berra rather than landing in the Forbes Field stands, ending the 1960 Series? In 14 major-league seasons, Harvey Haddix won 20 once but gained immortality in 1959 by pitching a dozen innings of perfect baseball and then losing on an unearned run in the unlucky thirteenth.

By 1956, 30-year-old lefty first baseman Dale Long had spent 12 years in organized ball, mostly in the minors. Although the Missouri native had led the league in triples the year before, by May of 1956 he was fighting to preserve his spot in the Pittsburgh lineup, still in the doghouse with Bucs skipper Bobby Bragan, who had fined him a few weeks earlier for a defensive misplay. If not the least recognized regular in baseball, Dale Long was close, his playing for a last place club helping to ensure that obscurity.

Songwriters Richard Rodgers and Oscar Hammerstein weren't troubled by anonymity in 1956, with the musicals *Carousel* and *Oklahoma* still packing theaters by May. Mickey Mantle, already the talk of the baseball world after leading the league in homers, slugging, on-base percentage, triples, and walks in 1955, was furthering his renown in 1956 with major-league highs in homers, RBIs, and batting average by May 18, extending his lead in all three categories with a two-homer, four-for-four performance that night.

The next day Long doubled off Cub starter "Toothpick" Sam Jones to give the Bucs an early 2–0 lead. By the eighth, Pittsburgh had a 5–4 edge when Long drove a delivery from southpaw Jim Davis into the right-field seats. Long's four ribbies were admirable, but not worthy of an inordinate amount of media coverage. One week later, however, few newspapers around the country would be excluding his name from the front pages of sports sections.

The Pirates hosted the Braves the next day in a doubleheader. In the fifth inning of the opener, Long connected off righty Ray Crone for a three-run homer and then reached southpaw Warren Spahn for a four bagger in the opening inning of the nightcap. Adding a two-run single in his last at-bat, Long finished the twin bill with seven RBIs, giving him 11 ribbies in three games.

Long remained merciless when facing Cardinals pitching on May 22. In front of the largest night audience at Forbes Field in four years, Long singled, doubled, and drove in a run with his tenth homer of the season off Herm Wehmeier, raising his average to a league-leading .411. The following night, however, it seemed the Redbirds had Long stymied; he went hitless until his last at-bat in the seventh. Then he crushed a Lindy McDaniel forkball, sending the sphere sailing to straightaway center field. The drive cleared the 12-foot wall at the 436-foot mark for only the third time in the history of the then 47-year-old ballpark. The homer was good for another two RBIs, giving Long 14 in five games. Of greater significance was Long's having homered in each of those games. His streak was beginning to draw as much attention as that of Mantle, whose homer and five-for-five effort the next day kept him atop the American League leaderboard in the Triple Crown categories. (He would take the Crown at season's end.)

If Long was to match the major-league mark of homering in six consecutive games, he would have to do it on the road. The Pirates traveled to Philadelphia, where the Phillies shared Shibe Park (or Connie Mack Stadium as it was then called) with the A's, having forsaken cozy Baker Bowl

18 years earlier, to the chagrin of future Philly batters. Shibe Park's right-field fence wasn't as inviting as the famed Baker Bowl wall, which had stood 60 feet high but only 280 feet from home plate, but Long's target would still be reachable at 330 feet. In the fifth inning, Long faced lefty Curt Simmons, pitching in the middle of what would be an impressive, though not outstanding, career. As Long recalled for author Joseph Reichler in *Baseball's Great Moments*, "I had been feeling loose, but now it [the streak] was getting to me." It didn't prevent his 33-ounce bat from meeting a Simmons slant squarely as he homered in his sixth consecutive game.

The pressure was more intense the next day. After posing alongside seven bats for Philly photographers, Long tried to make the picture appropriate. Manager Bragan helped by moving him from the cleanup spot to third in the order, slightly improving his chances for an extra at-bat. Long recalled for Reichler that nervousness caused him to overswing that day. Newspaper summaries indicate, however, that he nearly hit one out in his first attempt, driving a Stu Miller changeup three inches from the top of the 32-foot right-field fence; it was good for a double. (It would have been a homer in Baker Bowl.) Then Long was robbed in the sixth frame when right-fielder Elmer Valo made a leaping catch of his deep fly ball.

Long stepped to the plate in the eighth knowing it would probably be his last chance to set a new homer record. Facing Ben Flowers, a towering, righthanded, journeyman reliever, Long blasted the first pitch over the right-field wall, the ball landing on a house porch across the street. It was corralled by a boy who in turn was corralled by ballpark officials and persuaded to trade his prize for a shinier one so that the historic baseball could be sent to Cooperstown. Meanwhile, Long was greeted by a mob of Pirate teammates at home plate and carried to the dugout.

The excitement lingered long after the clubhouse celebration. Rain postponed a scheduled doubleheader the next day, but Long was kept busy by phone calls from bread, milk, brewery, and cigarette companies offering commercial contracts, as well as an invitation to appear on the *Ed Sullivan Show*. Even more interesting was the $2,500 bonus he received from Pirates general manager Joe Brown.

Could Long lengthen his record streak to eight games? On May 28, few of the 32,221 gathered at Forbes Field (the largest night crowd in six years) were thinking of anything else prior to the start of the battle against Brooklyn. In the clubhouse, Long was visited by the Dodgers' Jackie Robinson, who was playing in the last of ten major-league seasons. Robinson congratulated the homer hero for his streak, though it's doubtful that Jackie wished Long luck in extending it.

The world-champion Dodgers would repeat as pennant-winners in 1956, thanks in no small way to pitcher Carl Erskine, who would win 13 that year. But Erskine was off to a slow start, having won two of five decisions before facing Pittsburgh that night. The Dodgers grabbed an early 2–0 lead, and Long's first shot at Erskine resulted in a weak groundout. With his team behind a run in the fourth and Bragan shouting encouragement from the third-base box, Long drilled a liner to right off Erskine that appeared playable to the slugger. The ball barely cleared the 375-foot marker in right. While rounding third, Long smiled at Bragan who was shaking his head in astonishment. Once again a Pirates party greeted their super slugger at home plate, and after disappearing into the dugout, Long was coerced into a curtain call by the 32,000 jubilant spectators.

Long's streak was finally snapped on May 29 by baseball's best pitcher that year — Don Newcombe. The tall, brawny, hard-throwing righthander would lose only seven while winning a major-league high 27 games, the most by a Dodgers hurler since Dazzy Vance's 28 in 1924. The former Rookie-of-the-Year was honored with the MVP and Cy Young Award in 1956, and remains today the only player in baseball history to have received all three prestigious awards.

Newcombe stopped the Pirates on seven hits en route to a 12–1 laugher. Long went hitless in four plate appearances, his collar partly a result of working on four-and-a-half hours' sleep, which had been interrupted at 4 A.M. by a phone call requesting an appearance on the *Today* show, which he had made that morning. Nevertheless, fatigue didn't prevent Long from giving the Tuesday afternoon crowd of 12,000 one last thrill. As if on cue, spectators rose in unison in the third inning, gazing hopefully at Dale's long fly which soared to the deepest part of the ballpark. Alas, Snider raced to the 470-foot marker and snared the ball at the wall. Had it been hit a couple of yards to the left or right of the barrier, Long would today own a still-standing homer streak of nine consecutive games.

Streak hitters try to stay in the groove as long as possible, knowing slumps often follow and can equally endure. Long "felt it coming" after failing against Newcombe, but he didn't realize mediocrity would characterize the remainder of his season, and his career. Batting .402 with 14 homers and 37 RBIs in the 32 games prior to the streak's end, Long followed the streak with only 13 homers and 54 RBIs in the remaining 119 games and finished the season with a .263 average. He was traded to the Cubs in April of 1957, where he belted respectable but not overly impressive totals of 21, 20, and 14 homers in three seasons before he was shipped to the Giants and then to the Yankees in 1960. (He played part-time for both clubs.) He rebounded with 17 taters as a regular for the Senators during the homer-happy year of 1961 and ended his career as a pinch hitter for

Dale Long, whose record for hitting a home run in eight consecutive games was matched by Don Mattingly and Ken Griffey, Jr. (National Baseball Library & Archive, Cooperstown, N.Y.).

the Yanks in 1962 and 1963, while rooming with the M&M boys, Mantle and Maris.

On the day it was snapped, Long's streak was praised in a speech on the Senate floor. Despite his lackluster career stats (.267 average, 132 homers, 467 RBIs), Long remains remembered today. The grand old game has oft honored homer heroes, with no other sports feat as wondrous as that of a ball being belted beyond a beckoning barrier. Not witnessing that event at least once can tarnish even the most thrilling game. What greater glory could any hitter achieve than to hit one out, not in one game, but in eight consecutive games? That honor belonged to Dale Long alone until a fellow first sacker forced a share of the record three decades later.

The Yankees weren't expecting many homers from 23-year-old Don Mattingly when he became a regular in 1984. In fact, the gifted gloveman might have been on the bench or in the minors that year had veteran pinstriper Bobby Murcer not called it a career in midseason of 1983. With a spot thus opened, Steinbrenner and his entourage decided it was a suitable time to test Mattingly, who was showing promise in the minors, though not in the power department. Mattingly finished the 1983 season batting a solid .283 in 91 games with the Bombers, hitting safely in 24 of 25 games during one stretch, while showing exceptional poise playing first base. It was enough to convince the obtrusive owner to issue orders that Don start the 1984 season as the regular first sacker, ahead of former Cincinnati star Ken Griffey. (Manager Yogi Berra heeded the order but was fired 17 games into the 1985 season anyway, despite Steinbrenner's preseason vow to retain him throughout the year. Berra reacted to the betrayal by promising never to return to Yankee Stadium, where he had played for 18 seasons and had managed for another three until Steinbrenner bid him adieu. To date, and unfortunately for Yankees fans who have since attended Old-Timers' Games at the legendary ballpark, Berra has proven a better man of his word than his adversary.)

Ironically, the veteran Griffey had been one of Don's idols when he rooted for the Reds as a youth in the Indiana town of Evansville. Born on April 20, 1961, the year M&M would mean more than a tidy treat, Don was the youngest of five children raised by Bill and Mary Mattingly. An average student, he became an all-around athlete at Reitz Memorial High School, lettering in football and basketball and showing exceptional ability in baseball. Scouts like the Yanks' Jax Robertson were attracted to Mattingly even when he was a freshman and showed intense interest after Don hit .500 as a junior and .565 as a senior in helping his school win 59 of 60 games, including an undefeated state-championship season in 1978. Recalled Robertson in 1985, "He's the best hitter I've ever scouted. He had great hand speed and outstanding hand-eye coordination. And he was intense, a fierce competitor."

Nevertheless, the Yanks waited until the 19th round of the 1979 draft before selecting Mattingly; the late pick was caused by concern over his inability to hit for power and pull the ball and a belief by ballclubs that he was college bound. Mattingly snubbed books for baseball, however, when the Bombers enticed him with a $22,000 signing bonus which, considering his lower-middle-class background and recent marriage to his high school sweetheart Kim Sexton, seemed far more attractive than the prospect of four years of campus life, even with the numerous scholarship offers and the fact that his weekly salary of $119 would necessitate their living with Kim's father during the off-season. (Remarked Mattingly in 1984 in regards to his meager first-year wages, "Then they wonder why ballplayers want money bad.")

Any second thoughts Mattingly or loved ones had about his pursuing a pro ball career probably vanished after Don hit .349 at Oneonta in 1979 and .358 at Greensboro the following season. He graduated to Double A ball in 1981, slowing down only slightly with a .314 mark at Nashville. Don edged closer to the majors in 1982 playing for Triple A Columbus, where he hit a healthy .315.

Although his stats were impressive, Don was wondering whether he would make the big club, especially with a Yank owner who preferred buying proven players over trying untested ones. Nevertheless, Mattingly appeared on the Yankees opening roster in 1983, earning the then minimum salary of $35,000 (the minimum soared to three times that amount ten years later), but he was shipped to Columbus when manager Billy

Martin decided he needed more polish playing first base. Murcer retired in June, however, and Mattingly returned.

Although the Yanks were happy with Don's defense in 1983, it's doubtful the impatient Steinbrenner would have remained satisfied for long with a lefty-swinging first baseman with a below .300 average who showed a preference for hitting in the opposite direction of the stadium's reachable right-field seats. Not exactly in the Lou Gehrig tradition.

But winning batting titles was in that tradition, and in 1984 Mattingly became the first Yankee to do so since Mantle's Triple Crown year of 1956. Despite an 0-for-17 slump in midseason, Don trailed league-leader and teammate Dave Winfield by a couple of points going into the final game. The underdog delighted Yankee Stadium spectators by outstroking Winfield four hits to one and finishing the year with a league-leading .343. Mattingly also displayed a perceptible increase in power in 1984; his 23 round trippers (compared with four the year before) were more appealing perhaps to the homer-conscious Steinbrenner than was the batting title.

Don would open wide George's eyes in 1985. Finishing the season with a solid .324 average, third-best in the league, the Hoosier homered 35 times, five fewer than champion Darrell Evans, and his 145 RBIs not only were tops in baseball but the highest American League total in over 30 years. Although New York lost the division title to Toronto that year, Mattingly grabbed MVP honors by taking 367 of a possible 392 points which, at the time, was the second highest total in the history of the prestigious award; he outdistanced runner-up George Brett by nearly 100 points.

Several factors contributed to Mattingly's emergence as a power threat. Upon entering pro ball, Don weighed 175 pounds, but by 1985 he had gained an additional 15 pounds of muscle from conditioning and weight lifting. Probably more significant was his learning to pull, thanks in part to hitting coach Lou Piniella, who altered Mattingly's batting stance and stride. A student of hitting, Mattingly's power production also improved as he became more familiar with pitchers' motions and velocities.

Was 1985 a fluke or could "the Don" approach the same kind of numbers in subsequent seasons? By October of 1986, Mattingly had answered the question for many with a .352 average (Wade Boggs led baseball with .357), the highest Yankees mark in 30 years (Mantle's was .356 in 1956), league-leading stats of .573 slugging average, 238 hits, and a still-standing Yankees club record of 53 doubles, and his second consecutive 30-plus homer season (he hit 31).

Although Mattingly continued to be impressive in 1987, as his .318 average and 47 RBIs by July 7 helped him attain a starting position in the All-Star Game to be played in Oakland the following week, his homer total of eight was disappointingly low. He would need to sock another 22 in the remaining 78 contests, an average of one every 3.5 games, to become the first Yankee to reach the 30-homer plateau in three consecutive seasons since 1962, Mantle's last year of eight straight and Maris' last year of three straight. That was assuming he could play in each of the remaining 78 games, not a certainty for a player who had already missed 18 games with a back injury, and also assuming he could stay focused at the plate, a task made more difficult because Kim was expecting their second child soon. At least finances wouldn't trouble Mattingly. Four years after a rookie salary of $35,000, Don was now earning $2 million for the 1987 season, thanks more to a preseason arbitration ruling in his favor than generosity on the part of the boss.

Baseball's beanballs and bench-clearing brawls were dominant discussions in early July. On the seventh, Chicago's Andre Dawson, whose 49 homers and 137 RBIs would win him the MVP by season's end, was hit in the face with an Eric Show fastball in the third inning of a Cub-Padre battle at Wrigley Field. Dawson charged the mound, inciting a free-for-all. Calm was restored until Cubs hurler Greg Maddux retaliated by nailing Padre Benito Santiago in the next inning, leading to his and manager Gene Michael's ejection. Three hundred miles east in Cleveland that night, benches emptied when Willie Wilson went after Indians starter Ken Schrom after the Royal center-fielder was sent reeling with a head-high heater.

While fisticuffs resumed in Cleveland on July 8 following a brushback of the Tribe's Brett Butler by Kansas City hurler Danny Jackson, Mattingly was putting some hurt on Minnesota. Don, who had improved his stats with three hits and an RBI against the Twins the night before, hit his ninth and tenth homers in leading the Bombers to a 13–4 win. With two aboard in the opening inning, Don drilled a delivery off righty starter Mike Smithson into the lower right-field seats and then duplicated the drive in the sixth. Mattingly used the same area of the stadium the next night when he homered off starter Richard Dotson during a 6–3 loss to the White Sox.

The Yankee slugger had accomplished much in the three years prior to the 1987 season but had yet to connect for his first career grand slam, a goal he finally reached on May 14 and repeated on June 29. Mattingly made it three slams when he homered in his third straight game on July 10. With the game tied, the bags jammed, and the hot Yank at the plate, Sox skipper Jim Fregosi yanked righty starter Scott Nielsen in favor of southpaw Joel McKeon. Hoping to break the deadlock with a fly ball, Mattingly looked for a pitch up, got one, and sent it up, up, and away into the right-field seats. Said Don afterwards, "All of a sudden, I'm hitting grand slams." He would hit more. Mattingly also remarked matter-of-factly that he felt as if he could "hit a homer every day."

On Saturday, July 11, 45,000 spectators in Yankee Stadium were somewhat disappointed with a 5–2 loss to the Pale Hose. They were nonetheless delighted by pregame Old Timers' Day ceremonies, Ron Guidry's fanning fourteen during the game, and the Hit Man homering in his fourth straight. With his three hits that afternoon, Mattingly was batting .520 in his last five games, including five homers and a dozen ribbies. He socked it to the Sox one last time on Sunday, his homer off Jim Winn coming in his final plate appearance before the All-Star Game of July 14.

In the five games during his homer stretch, Mattingly raised his average from .318 to .336, his RBI amount from 47 to 60, and his homer total from 8 to 14, numbers which inspired confidence for one looking for his first hit in All-Star competition. Nonetheless, he lengthened a hitless skein to six with two walks and a groundout in the National League's 2–0, 13-inning win in Oakland. (Tim Raines won it with a two-run triple.)

It was on to Texas for Don as he met his mates in Arlington for the start of a four-game series with the Rangers on July 16. The All-Star break, the road atmosphere, and a threatening thunderstorm were all factors which might have cooled his hot bat, but none did. After the weather cleared, Mattingly extended his homer string to six and his grand-slam total to four by timing a Charlie Hough knuckler in the second inning and parking it well over the 330-foot sign and into the right-field seats. Not satisfied with five RBIs (he had a ribby single in the fifth), Don reached a career-best seven with another blast off flaky lefty Mitch Williams, an opposite-field poke in the eighth frame.

Little mention had been made of Don's streak prior to the game. After his two in Texas, Mattingly had the media's attention. The *New York Times* noted his being two away from Dale Long's record homer streak, while acknowledging that Mattingly was only one shy of the major-league mark of five grand slams in one season, which was then held by Jim Gentile and Ernie Banks. Mattingly would establish a new record by season's end with a slam on September 25 and his sixth of the year four days later.

Mattingly's streak may have been on the minds of Yankees fans the next night but the Hit Man wasn't thinking about it when he faced the Rangers' Bobby Witt in the first frame. After taking ball one, Don drilled a fastball to straightaway center. Fleet-footed outfielder Oddibe McDowell raced back, stopped short, and watched. The ball struck a foot from the top of the fence 400 feet away, as Don coasted into second with a disappointing double. Admitted Mattingly later, "After I hit one that close, I didn't think I'd hit one tonight."

His next two tries made Don's prediction appear accurate. In the second inning, he pulled a Witt pitch to deep right that was pulled back into the ballpark and into Ruben Sierra's waiting glove by the swirling wind that pervaded Arlington Stadium. Facing lefty reliever Paul Kilgus in the third, Mattingly grounded out weakly to second. The record-chaser stepped to the plate against Kilgus again in the sixth. If he failed to connect, Don would have at least one more opportunity, but he wouldn't need it.

The count ran to two balls, one strike when Mattingly crushed Kilgus' next toss so forcefully that even a gust from behind the right-field stands couldn't prevent the ball from settling into the seventh row. Many of the 33,000 fans applauded in acknowledging the achievement of the new American League record-holder. Exactly 46 years before, Joe DiMaggio's famed 56-game hitting streak had come to an end. Mattingly's homer streak, now extended to seven, was still alive.

After the Yankees' 8–4 triumph, Mattingly discovered a bottle of sparkling wine aside his locker left there by clubhouse attendant Mike Wallace. No mob had met him at home plate following his homer, and as he walked amongst his teammates in the clubhouse, with wine in hand, many were wondering as to the source of the celebration. (Queried an incredulous Rickey Henderson, "We ain't won nothing, what happened?") Indeed, even Mattingly seemed somewhat oblivious. After being informed of the player who remained the sole obstacle to his owning a major-league mark, Don admitted never having heard of him.

Dale Long knew the name Don Mattingly, however. As the young Yank took aim at eight-in-a-row on July 18, the 61-year-old record-holder watched the game on television with some friends in an Albany restaurant. On the mound for Texas that night was hard-throwing righthander Jose Guzman, who faced Don for the second time in the fourth inning, having retired him previously. With the count two balls, one strike, Guzman challenged Mattingly with a down-the-middle, sinking fastball. As Mattingly swung, Long's initial reaction was relief since the ball was hit to the opposite field in left, normally not a slugger's homerun target. Mattingly, too, didn't believe the ball would carry.

Left-fielder Pete Incaviglia wasn't known for speed, but he managed to reach the fence in time to make a leaping stab for the ball. Barely escaping Incaviglia's outstretched glove, the sinking sphere settled in the small space separating fence from bleacher wall, where groundscrew member Denis Klein retrieved it. Not sure whether the ball had been caught, Mattingly hesitated momentarily at second base before commencing his home-run trot.

From the reaction of the 41,000 fans in attendance that Saturday night, one would have thought the Bronx ballpark was the setting. Even after Don returned to the dugout, the crowd continued cheering, prompting Mattingly, with some coaxing from Dave Winfield, to acknowledge the noisy accolade with a wave of the helmet atop the dugout steps.

Another bottle of wine was waiting for the new record-sharer near his locker, which Don again proceeded to share with teammates. "I know I talk about not caring about it but it does feel better after I hit one," he told reporters. "It's not like I'm worried about it one way or other, or I'm going to be disappointed if I don't hit one. It just keeps going on."

The question on everyone's mind Sunday night was whether it would go on for at least one more game and give Mattingly sole possession of the illustrious homer feat. Long was ambivalent, rooting for the likeable young Yank, while cherishing the prospect of "going down in history: Mattingly and Long." Countered Mattingly when informed of Long's hopes for a shared record, "That's OK, too. I'd be proud to be next to him."

But the Hit Man wouldn't willfully fail. Nor would Rangers starter Greg Harris succumb willingly. The seven-year veteran righty, normally a reliever, had a pregame plan. "I had one thing in mind," he would say later, "to keep runners off base against him," thereby enabling Harris to rely more on curves. His teammates would help remove any pressure by accumulating runs in bunches, leading to a 20–3 drubbing of the first place Bombers.

With two outs and none on in the first, Mattingly took a pitch, then grounded out second-to-first on a sinker. Harris again faced Mattingly with the bases cleared in the third and had some luck when Don fouled off a hittable high fastball (recalled Don, "I got it in the zone but just missed it"). Then Harris yielded a harmless single to center. Two innings later with two outs, Don fell behind two strikes before ripping a liner into the first baseman's glove.

With two outs in the eighth, Mattingly reappeared. Realizing it would probably be his last at-bat, he altered his normal hitting strategy, having in mind to swing for the seats. As he stepped in the box, the crowd showed their support by cheering and applauding, many while standing. Then they waited and watched as 25-year-old righty reliever Jeff Russell delivered.

A fastball. Mattingly fouled it back to the screen. The crowd groaned. Mattingly stepped outside the box to gather concentration. Russell stared at catcher Don Slaught's sign, nodded, and then threw an inside pitch for a ball. Good, Harris thought, now let's make him reach for one. Mattingly's eyes widened as the ball headed toward the outside corner. Going with the pitch, he lined a rope to left. Incaviglia had failed in his attempt to thwart Mattingly the night before, but on this night, Inky would end the last hopes of 31,000 spectators by retrieving the drive and tossing it to third. Amidst a standing ovation, which included many of the Rangers players, Mattingly stood somewhat satisfied at second, then showed appreciation with a wave of his helmet.

Mattingly's comments in the clubhouse, "I don't feel relief. It was no big thing," are characteristic of one known for being a team player, but belie what must surely have been a disappointing end to a glorious streak. To share a record is to be revered. To alone own one is even better. Mattingly must have, to some degree, longed for sole possession of the homer mark. What else would explain his late-game hitting strategy?

Whether or not Mattingly was perturbed by his failure, Long was obviously pleased. Sharing a record was better than losing one. When Long died in Palm Coast, Florida, in January of 1991, Mattingly and Long remained listed side-by-side in the books. Two years later a third name would be added to the eight-game-homer-streak club.

Mattingly was still a Yankee by 1993, but, although he was still the game's best defensive first baseman, he was a changed hitter. Although he finished the 1987 season with 30 homers, 115 RBIs, and a .327 average, Don's numbers dropped to 18 circuits, 88 ribbys, and a .311 average the next year, and though his power stats improved in 1989 with 23 homers and 113 RBIs, he barely became a .300 hitter for the sixth straight season (.303). The downward trend continued in the early nineties, and by 1993 it was evident to the most biased Mattingly supporter that the Yankees captain, though still superb in the field, would never again be bruising baseballs from the batter's box consistently.

It is characteristic of every profession that the old give way to the young, only it is more evident in sports. Mattingly's 32 years in 1993 wouldn't have classified him as over-the-hill in most jobs, and even in baseball he might be considered to be in his prime. Nevertheless, whether it was because of recurring back ailments or pitchers' successful strategy adjustments, Don was unable to compete with a talented crop of youthful hopefuls of the nineties — such potentials as Cleveland's muscular and moody Albert Belle, the Rangers' Puerto Rican prize, Juan Gonzalez, Chicago's hurtful homer-hitter Frank Thomas, and Motown's monstrous Cecil Fielder.

And Ken Griffey, Jr. Perhaps no other previous player prompted praise as often as had the son of the former Reds star during his rookie season of 1989, with expressions such as "can't-miss superstar" and "future Hall-of-Famer" usually included in any assessment of the slugging Seattle center fielder. Ken did little to discourage such talk, batting over .330 in the three years from 1990 to 1992 while driving in over 100 runs in each of the last two, though he had yet to display the consistent power that many were anticipating, accumulating respective homer totals of 22, 22, and 27. In the outfield, few balls escaped the speed and reach of the 6' 3" youngster, who would frequently frustrate opposing batters with leaping or diving catches following lengthy runs. Lou Piniella had managed one of the premier players of the eighties as Yankees helmsman from 1986 to 1988. As the Seattle skipper in 1993, it appeared he had, potentially, the best of the nineties.

The young phenom's fate could have been tragically different.

Born to Ken Sr. and Birdie Griffey in Donora, Pennsylvania, in 1969, Junior was a happy, likeable youngster growing up in Cincinnati during the seventies. Whether rubbing shoulders with Pete Rose, Joe Morgan, Johnny Bench, and Dad's other teammates in the dugout of the Big Red Machine or riding dirt bikes and skateboards and collecting bugs near his home or playing football with younger brother Craig, Junior's ever-present infectious smile revealed that he didn't have a care in the world.

But life would have its troublesome moments as well. As an 11-year-old playing Little League for the first time in 1981, Junior went through the entire season without making an out until his final at-bat; then he cried uncontrollably when his line drive was caught by the first baseman. That same year he and Craig were playing with their small racing car when they had the idea of sending it through a fire, à la Evil Knievel. Junior's resulting burns were fortunately superficial. In his first year at Moeller High in 1983, Griffey became ineligible for the baseball team in the spring because of poor grades (though he starred in football the following fall, once returning a kickoff 85 yards for a touchdown). Playing for the Mariners' Class A club at Bellingham, Washington, in 1987, Griffey struck out in his first at-bat and suffered through a batting slump before suffering an injury to his shoulder after crashing into the centerfield fence. He became so homesick that he seriously considered chucking his career before a phone call to a hometown girlfriend changed his mind. The next year Griffey missed much of the season at Class A San Bernardino because of back problems. During Seattle's spring training at Tempe, Arizona, in 1989, Griffey's hopes of making the roster were nearly ruined when a game of catch with a teammate resulted in his being hit in the eye.

Griffey's most serious problem came in 1988. After finishing the stress-filled 1987 season at Bellingham, the 17 year old returned to Cincinnati to live with his parents, but his late-night lifestyle soon created tension between his dad and him. In January, when Ken Sr. issued a change-or-get-out ultimatum, his son retaliated by storming out of the house. He drove to his girlfriend's home and swallowed a bottle of aspirin containing nearly 300 pills because he "was hurting and wanted to cause some hurt for others." Rushed to the hospital, Junior had his stomach pumped and then was placed in intensive care. A rash decision inspired by overwhelming emotions had nearly caused the demise of one of baseball's greatest prospects. As Junior admitted in 1992, "I'm living proof how stupid it is to try to commit suicide."

Griffey had luck on his side in 1988. He would need none in pursuit of a baseball career. High school coach Mike Cameron had tried tampering with Griffey's stride after watching him in the batting cage for the first time, but he wisely backed off when told, "This is the Griffey swing." Junior finished two seasons at Moeller with a .478 average and 17 homers, having wowed crowds often with mammoth blasts and over-the-shoulder catches. Rated by *Baseball America* as the top player in the 1987 draft, Griffey was scouted and signed by Seattle's Tom Mooney, slightly disappointing Ken Sr., who had hoped his son would go to college and thus become eligible for the Olympics in 1988. Junior's decision, however, would enable both to set a baseball first two years later.

Despite his talent, the odds were against the 19-year-old Griffey making the Opening-Day Seattle roster as spring training began at Tempe in 1989, but Jim Lefebvre planned to play him regularly in exhibitions in order to "take a good look at him." Junior displayed speed in the outfield and a better-than-average arm, once throwing out the Giants' rabbit Brett Butler who had tried to advance from first to third on a hit. He ran a hitting streak to 15, the longest stretch in Mariners spring-training history, and finished the Cactus League with a .360 average, while setting club marks for total bases, hits, and RBIs.

Despite the spectacular spring, Junior was apprehensive when Lefebvre called him into his office on March 29, but his "heart started ticking again" when he was informed he had made the big club. After his son signed a contract for $68,000, Ken Sr., who had been mulling retirement, decided to stick with the Reds one more year. The $320,000 annual salary was an inducement, but the fact that no father and son had previously played simultaneously during the same season was a bigger one. (When Griffey became a Mariner in midseason, they became the first father-son teammates, and they set another generational precedent on August 30 by stroking hits in the same inning.)

Griffey followed a mediocre rookie season of .267, 16 homers, and 61 RBIs with three solid ones and then took off in 1993. By midseason, he was among the leaders in most offensive categories and was the top vote-getter on the American League All-Star squad. He had the longest drive of the All-Star Monday Homerun Contest when he caromed a ball off the B&O Warehouse behind the rightfield wall at Baltimore's Camden Yards, an unprecedented feat.

Steinbrenner was expressing concern over low attendance figures prior to the opener of a three-game set at Yankee Stadium on July 19, warning on radio that the upcoming Mariners-Yankees series would "be a test" of whether fans continued to deserve the Bombers in the Bronx. "Tradition is a wonderful thing and I love it," he said, "But there comes a time when change is needed." (The Boss would refrain from moving his club, but renewed the threat during the world-championship season of 1996 before raising ticket prices in 1997.) Twenty-three thousand faithfuls showed up at Yankee Stadium that night, withstood a 70-minute rain delay to the start of the game, and then watched Mattingly extend a hitting streak to 14 with a single and double as the first place Yanks handled the Mariners 8–2. Griffey managed one hit in four trips, a double, and was fanned twice by right-hander Scott Kamieniecki, his limited production merely the quiet before the storm, or in this case, the hurricane.

The next afternoon, Griffey, who had been the only Mariner to take optional batting practice prior to the regular pregame warm-up, walked into Piniella's office. The manager had become visibly and vocally upset with his team's pathetic performance the night before. As reported by the *Seattle Times'* Bob Finnigan, Junior advised him to stop worrying, saying, "Skip, I'm going to take charge." Griffey made good his promise in the form of a key seventh-inning, two-run single and a homer off lefty Paul Gibson in the eighth, enabling the Mariners to overcome a 5–0 deficit with nine runs in the last three innings en route to a 9–5 victory. Griffey's single was yielded by veteran southpaw reliever Steve Howe, who had held him hitless in seven previous at-bats, the last being a double-play grounder in Seattle, which had sparked a shouting match between them. In regards to Junior's latest take-charge attitude, Finnigan speculated, "This may have been one of the watershed days in the notable career of one Ken Griffey, Jr." Considering Griffey's explosive hitting in subsequent games and seasons, Finnigan's statement may be the most prophetic in baseball history.

With a Sunday crowd of over 31,000 in attendance the next day (Steinbrenner had set between thirty to thirty-five thousand per game as his required average), Junior homered on a two-strike slider off southpaw starter Jimmy Key in the second inning to give Seattle an early lead, one which it never surrendered while winning in a breeze in the Bronx finale.

The transformed Griffey continued clobbering when the club traveled to Cleveland on July 22, homering in his third consecutive game, all coming off southpaws. The Tribe victim was Jeff Mutis, who was nursing a 1–0 lead when a 1–1 curve to Junior in the fourth frame tied the game, which was eventually won by Seattle 3–2. Albie Lopez had a 9–0 advantage the next day when Griffey tagged a fastball for number four in four games, igniting a comeback which forced the Indian off the hill in the sixth, though Cleveland eventually prevailed. Driving home with his mom that evening, Junior informed her of the record for most games with at least one homer. Responded Birdie, "It doesn't look good for you."

Junior was normally lethal against southpaw swingers, and lefty Matt Young's slider became his fifth-in-a-row and 27th of the season the following night, as he tied Juan Gonzalez for the major-league high in homers, and dealt a crucial blow in a 6–5 scalping of the Tribe. Seattle lost the getaway game on July 25, a wild shoot-out highlighted by five homers, two by Albert Belle. Griffey's came in the fifth on a fastball thrown by hard-throwing righty Jose Mesa. As Cleveland manager Mike Hargrove exclaimed after the game, "Griffey's so hot, he could homer off Superman."

Minnesota's Kevin Tapani wasn't a man of steel but was a respected starter by 1993, having been a winner in each of his previous three major-league seasons, including 1990, when he won 12 and lost 8 with the last place Twins. He was no match, however, for Junior. On July 27, in the opener of an extended Mariners homestand at the Kingdome, the Twins righty experienced a pitcher's worst nightmare — having to face baseball's most dreaded slugger with the bases loaded. Tapani tried an outside fastball, not a bad pitch," as he explained later, "just a good hitter." The ball landed on the tarpaulin in straightaway center 441 feet from where Griffey was standing and watching.

Others were in awe as well. "You get chills every time he hits a home-run," admired teammate Tino Martinez. "One of the top three, four players in baseball," rated the Mariner's Dave Magadan. Recalling Junior's promise the week before, Piniella told reporters, "We had lost four in a row. He comes in and tells me he's going to take over. And taking over he is."

Sweet Lou was referring to more than Griffey's slam. In the sixth, Minnesota's Dave McCarty hit an apparent cinch double toward the left-center gap. A galloping Griffey rapidly narrowed the distance between himself and ball, then made a desperate last-second dive, speared the drive, and made a belly-first landing on the punishing artificial surface. It saved at least one run and possibly the game, which was won by Seattle 10–8.

Afterwards, everyone was talking about Griffey's seven straight homer-games and his chance of matching the mark held by Long and Mattingly. Everyone but Griffey, that is. Junior showered and dressed, and not wanting to jinx the streak, he mutely bypassed reporters as he left the clubhouse. Besides, there were more important matters. His wife, Melissa, was four months pregnant with their first child. Junior wanted to be with her. (Mattingly's wife had also been expecting during his homer streak of 1987.)

It was back to the ballpark the next night, and 30,000 showed up at the Kingdome hoping to become eyewitnesses to history. Twin righty Willie Banks would try to spoil the fun. The 24-year-old Banks, in his first year as a regular starter, entered the game with an unimposing 6–7 record and 4.50 ERA. Nevertheless, he held Griffey homerless in his first three tries, surrendering only a harmless single. As Junior came to bat in what would be his last chance in the seventh, Banks was working on a two-hit shutout and had succeeded in subduing the once-exuberant throng.

The frenzy returned when Griffey caromed a first-pitch high fastball off the third-deck facade in right. Again Griffey watched from home plate, not so much in awe as in concern whether the ball would stay fair; then he circled the bases amidst a standing ovation. As he crossed home plate, he waved towards where Melissa was sitting, and she waved back. The next batter, Jay Buhner, took four pitches before Griffey finally acquiesced to the spectators, who were still standing and celebrating, by emerging from the dugout with cap held high.

The clubhouse wasn't characteristic of a team that had been beaten 5–1. While the record-sharer maintained silence, the Mariners were praising their superstar teammate and speculating on Griffey's chances of breaking the homer mark. "It wouldn't surprise me if he did," Buhner said. "He's so focused and mentally strong right now." Hurler Erik Hanson thought so too, believing "the ball must look like a beachball to Junior now." Catcher Dave Valle likened Griffey to hoop great Michael Jordan, "the best player in the game."

Minnesota's Scott Erickson was scheduled to start the next day. At first glance, that appeared to be an advantage for Griffey. Erickson was a righty and was hardly overpowering, his record for 1993 reading a dismal six wins, eleven losses, and 5.50 ERA. Junior had been successful in previous confrontations, collecting 12 hits in 23 at-bats against the tall, lanky hurler, including a king-sized Kingdome homer in May. Yet there were factors with which to be concerned. Erickson was no slouch at retiring batters. It had been only two years since he led the league in wins (20) and winning percentage (.714). His ERA in his three seasons prior to 1993 was a very respectable 3.20. In addition, Erickson was a low-ball pitcher, not conducive to the surrendering of long balls. As Banks noted, Griffey would "probably have his hands full if Scott keeps the ball down."

As Griffey stepped to the plate at 7:19 P.M., few of the 46,000 spectators were sitting. As the ovation subsided, Erickson fired a fastball. Somewhat nervous, Junior purposely took a big hack, hoping that if he didn't connect, he would at least release tension in doing so. He missed the pitch, but his healthy cut may have created some tension for Erickson, who didn't come close with the next delivery, to the annoyance of the jeering audience.

The Twins hurler tried another heater, but the more focused Griffey timed it well and ripped a liner to right for a hit, prompting a conspicuously subdued cheer in the Kingdome. In any other game a Griffey hit was welcomed, but more was expected of him that day.

So it was even more disheartening to Seattle spectators when, two innings later, Junior hit a belt-high fastball to the right-center-field barrier. The ball bounced off the 380-foot sign, was fielded by Kirby Puckett, and thrown in to the infield. Their hero was held to a double.

In the fifth inning, the Twins had a 3–2 edge, but the Mariners had a man on with one gone. With his team in a battle with five other contenders for the Western Division flag, Piniella ordered a steal of second. Mike Felder succeeded, and when Rich Amaral fanned, Minnesota skipper Tom Kelly had the option of ordering an intentional walk to the next batter, Griffey. Anticipating, perhaps, a hostile fan reaction if he did, Kelly elected instead to have Erickson go after Junior. The overly anxious slugger tried pulling an outside pitch and grounded out, second-to-first. Commented Piniella afterwards regarding his steal strategy, which could have cost Griffey an opportunity to swing the stick, "My first responsibility is to go out and win a ballgame. If we were up by four or five runs, it would have been different." Kelly defended his decision, saying, "You had a big crowd here wanting to see him hit. Hell, I wasn't going to deny him that."

Junior had had some good cuts against Erickson, and with one out in the seventh, walked to the plate for another try. As he did, Kelly ambled to the mound, left hand pointing. With Scott having already surrendered two runs in the inning, he was taking no chances. Griffey would be forced to face a southpaw.

Still, that wasn't Sandy Koufax running in from the sidelines. Prior to the 1993 season, the 6' 11" Larry Casian had pitched a total of 47 big-league innings and it was only the night before that he had recorded his first save. Casian's fastball wasn't Ryan's Express, and though he possessed a good curve and slider, mistakes from lefties often resulted in bleacher souvenirs, courtesy Mister Mariner.

As it turned out, Casian cooperated by throwing a slider for a ball and then hanging a curve which undoubtedly caused Junior's eyes to widen. Unfortunately, Griffey was a bit early with his stride, "off-balance" as Twins backstop Brian Harper recalled later. The popup was caught by second baseman Chuck Knoblauch.

An inning and a half later, Dave Winfield was out on a force at second, giving the Mariners a 4–3 victory. Winfield, who did some record-tying of his own that night with his 2,962d hit, matching Hall-of-Famer Wee Willie Keeler for 21st on the career total list (Winfield became a member of the 3,000-hit club a short time later), lingered near the second base bag as Griffey jogged in from center. Dave then congratulated Junior, who in the early eighties would frequent the Yankees clubhouse when Winfield and his dad were teammates.

By exchanging high-fives with other Mariners while walking across the infield, hugging his father (then a Mariners coach) near the dugout, and tipping his cap to the vocal unseated crowd who were offering a final salute, Junior was conceding failure to achieve the unprecedented, accepting instead a share of glory. With the streak snapped, Griffey could talk again, telling clubhouse reporters, "The streak was fun, but us winning meant more to me." Like Mattingly, Griffey wasn't disappointed by his failure, saying, "It was a long stretch. I'm happy with what I did." Then he showered, got dressed, and went home with Melissa.

Griffey's homer streak marked the beginning of his transformation from a player endowed with potential greatness to a bonafide superstar, as Finnigan had predicted. By season's end, Griffey had accumulated 45 homers, one fewer than major-league-leader Gonzalez. He led the league with 40 during the strike-shortened season of 1994 and belted 49 in 1996 despite missing many games because of an injury. As was noted by the Splendid Splinter in *Ted Williams' Hit List*, published in 1996, "If he remains healthy and committed to improving, God only knows what numbers this man may post in his baseball career."

Could those future numbers include another homer streak, perhaps one as long as nine consecutive games? Piniella believed in the possibility in 1993, saying, "He's going to be back in the same position again." Unlike predecessors Long and Mattingly, Griffey appears to have many great years ahead of him. (Mattingly left the game following the 1995 season and, amidst rumors that he might return, officially retired in January of 1997.) Nevertheless, it's rare that any player gets more than one crack at a long-standing record. As pertains to the consecutive game homer streak, the odds are Griffey won't either.

Dale Long's Eight-Game Homer Streak of 1956

Date	Opponent	Ballpark	Opp. Pitcher (lefty/righty)
5/19	Cubs	Forbes Field	J. Davis (L)
5/20	Braves	Forbes Field	R. Crone (R)
5/20	Braves	Forbes Field	W. Spahn (L)
5/22	Cards	Forbes Field	H. Wehmeier (R)
5/23	Cards	Forbes Field	L. McDaniel (R)
5/25	Phils	Shibe Park	C. Simmons (L)

| 5/26 | Phils | Shibe Park | B. Flowers (R) |
| 5/28 | Dodgers | Forbes Field | C. Erskine (R) |

Don Mattingly's Eight-Game Homer Streak of 1987

Date	Opponent	Ballpark	Opp. Pitcher (lefty/righty)
7/8	Twins	Yankee Stadium	M. Smithson (R)
			J. Berenguer (R)
7/9	White Sox	Yankee Stadium	R. Dotson (R)
7/10	White Sox	Yankee Stadium	J. McKeon (L)
7/11	White Sox	Yankee Stadium	J. DeLeon (R)
7/12	White Sox	Yankee Stadium	J. Winn (R)
7/16	Rangers	Arlington Stadium	C. Hough (R)
			M. Williams (L)
7/17	Rangers	Arlington Stadium	P. Kilgus (L)
7/18	Rangers	Arlington Stadium	J. Guzman (R)

Ken Griffey Jr.'s Eight-Game Homer Streak of 1993

Date	Opponent	Ballpark	Opp. Pitcher (lefty/righty)
7/20	Yankees	Yankee Stadium	P. Gibson (L)
7/21	Yankees	Yankee Stadium	J. Key (L)
7/22	Indians	Municipal Stadium	J. Mutis (L)
7/23	Indians	Municipal Stadium	A. Lopez (R)
7/24	Indians	Municipal Stadium	M. Young (L)
7/25	Indians	Municipal Stadium	J. Mesa (R)
7/27	Twins	Kingdome	K. Tapani (R)
7/28	Twins	Kingdome	W. Banks (R)

Twelve

Ending with
a Brilliant Failure

As the Mets' David Cone walked off the mound, having just struck out the Phillies' Doug Lindsey, the crowd of 30,000 fans who had gathered at Veterans Stadium in Philadelphia on October 6, 1991, realized the ninth inning would be climactic. What would make it so wasn't the fact that it was the season's final inning. Nor was it because their team would be competing in postseason play later. Both Philadelphia and New York had been hopelessly out of the pennant picture long before and would finish 20 games behind Pittsburgh. Even the outcome of the contest was no longer in doubt, with the Phils trailing 7–0 at the time.

What would make the Phillies' last at-bats significant was that Lindsey had become Cone's 17th strikeout. The righthander's total was only two shy of the National League record for most in one game and three away from the major-league mark. Cone could break one record and tie another if he could fan the side in the ninth.

Ironically, it had been a renowned Philly fireballer who had been the first major-leaguer to reach the 19-K plateau, with the Mets being the victims that day. Steve Carlton was throwing his beebees and slants for the Cardinals when New York entered St. Louis on September 15, 1969. Although Lefty was having an impressive season with a 16–9 record, his greatest years awaited him in the seventies with Philadelphia, including his first of five strikeout titles and six 20-win seasons.

The defending-champion Cards were a distant 10 behind in the pennant race that day, with only 16 games remaining. In contrast, the Amazing Mets had made believers of nearly all fans by then, and in four weeks their miraculous season would end with a catch of a fly ball hit by the Orioles' Davey Johnson in the final game of the Series. Their initial world championship, following seven tormenting years in which the club finished in last place five times and ninth place twice, would become the most talked-about news event of the year, dominating even such explosive stories as the Kennedy calamity in Chappaquiddick, the My Lai massacre, and the U.S. moon landing.

For Cards catcher Tim McCarver, it couldn't have taken long to realize his hurler had extra heat on the fastball. After waiting out a 20-minute rain delay, Steve opened the contest by fanning the first three Mets, including Amos Otis, who would fan four times before the game ended. After showers again interrupted play, with Carlton forced to sit in the clubhouse for another hour, he returned to the mound and performed another strikeout hat trick, giving him six K's in two innings.

In the bottom of the second, the Mets' Gary Gentry was reached for a run on a walk to Lou Brock and singles by Vada Pinson and Curt Flood. When Flood's club attempted to trade him to the Phillies the following year, he challenged baseball's reserve clause, and this led to a revolutionary change in the game's power structure. Although the Supreme Court ruling of 1972 once again legitimized baseball's right to exemption from antitrust laws, owners were pressured into amending the reserve clause and this paved the way for the free-agency era which followed.

Carlton fanned Gentry in the third and began the fourth by blowing away Otis and Tommy Agee for his eighth and ninth victims. Steve then lost Donn Clendenon, issuing his first of two walks in the game. The next batter was Ron Swoboda. Carlton threw the first pitch by him. Swoboda swung and missed the next one. On an 0–2 pitch, Lefty may have been feeling cocky, a mistake too often made by Mets' opponents that year against a team which they thought deserved little respect. Swoboda had him right where he wanted. Carlton tried another fastball, but Rocky hit it into the left-field seats, giving the Amazins a 2–1 lead.

Carlton had already started to think about the record of 18, then held by Bob Feller, Sandy Koufax, and Don Wilson, before he ended the inning by whiffing Ed Charles. "When I had nine strikeouts, I decided to go all the way," Lefty declared later. "But it cost me the game because I started to challenge every batter." Swoboda's homer, which came following Steve's ninth strikeout, was proof that a pitcher can't think about strikeouts when trying to win a ballgame. The Mets slugger would offer further proof of that axiom later.

Carlton's admission afterwards that "I always pitch a game looking to strike out as many men as I can" may explain why he didn't become a consistent winner until later in his career. Still, though he trailed in the game, the 24 year old was feeling good about his chances of breaking the record. He furthered those hopes by fanning two more in the fifth, raising his total to a dozen. With four innings and twelve outs remaining, Carlton needed six more whiffs.

When the Cards scored a pair of runs to take a 3–2 lead in the bottom half of the fifth, the satisfied crowd prepared themselves for an exciting final four frames. They were hopeful that the home-team hurler would not only put the Mets' pennant drive on hold but would badly embarrass the upstarts in the process. Gil Hodges' crew had other plans.

By the eighth, Carlton had added another 2 Mets to his list of K victims, which numbered 14. He would need 4 more in the final 2 frames to tie Feller and Koufax. Tommy Agee began the inning with a single, but Steve overpowered Clendenon for the first out and 15th strikeout, bringing Swoboda to the plate. Lefty had successfully avenged himself by fanning the muscular outfielder on three pitches in the sixth. Now it was Swoboda's turn.

Again after getting two strikes, Carlton challenged Swoboda, who deposited the fastball into the same left-field area as before. The two-run shot enabled the Mets to regain the lead. The fans, who moments before had been cheering Carlton's every throw, were silenced.

It didn't take long for Lefty to raise their spirits. He rocketed three heaters past Charles for his 16th whiff. While in the dugout waiting to throw in the ninth, Steve glanced at the scoreboard. "They flashed the message that I had 16 strikeouts to tie my own personal high," Steve said after the game. "I just wanted to get out there and go for the record. I wanted to strike everyone out in the ninth."

The tall, slender Floridian got off to a good start by fanning Mets' reliever Tug McGraw. Bud Harrelson, who would become the New York manager 20 years later, was next. He quickly fell behind in the count and then looked at a third strike. Carlton shared the strikeout mark. The 13,000 spectators rose to their feet in anticipation of a new record. It remained for Amos Otis to try to stop him. "I wanted to do it so bad," Steve told reporters. "I put every ounce of energy into those last pitches to Otis."

When the count went to two strikes, it was as if Otis' fate was out of his hands. By waving and missing the next pitch, the rookie played his part in history. An elated Carlton walked to the dugout, amid wild cheering from an appreciative crowd. "It's all like a dream now," the new strikeout king commented. "I was thrilled with the standing ovation the fans gave me. I knew I'd done something that had never been done before."

It was hard for the crowd to accept that such an overpowering performance should end in failure, and they hoped their heroes would rally to win in the last of the ninth. They almost got their wish. Ed Charles dropped a fly ball, and Brock singled, putting the tying run on second with one out. The fans then waited for the come-from-behind victory that never came. Tug McGraw, whose shouts of "Ya Gotta Believe" became the battle cry of the Mets and their fans, made believers of the Cards and their supporters that day, getting the final two batters to end the game.

If Carlton was ecstatic in owning the record for himself, it was a short-lived exuberance. The following season a hard-throwing righthander from those same World Champion Mets would force Lefty to share the honors. Tom Seaver had been the ace of New York's staff for several seasons. Just one year before, he had come within two outs of a perfect game. He had a career-high 25 victories en route to his Cy-Young-Award-winning 1969 season. Yet Tom Terrific's greatest accomplishment may have come on a cool, spring afternoon in 1970, when he not only matched Carlton's strikeout output for one game but set a mark for the most consecutive K's as well.

The season was only a dozen games old when Seaver took the mound on April 22. A modest crowd of 14,000 gathered at Shea Stadium on a chilly day, but those in attendance had reason to celebrate. Before the game against San Diego, their hurling hero was presented with the Cy Young trophy. Seaver accepted it graciously and then took the mound and showed why he deserved it.

What would become Tom's masterpiece in moundsmanship began in mediocre fashion. Staked to an early 1–0 lead, he yielded a long poke to Al Ferrara in the second to knot the game at one. His mates helped by tallying in the third, with Harrelson's triple driving in the go-ahead run. By the sixth, Seaver had found his strikeout groove. Ferrara's whiff to end the inning boosted Terrific's K total to ten. Still, only the most fanatic Tom Seaver fan would have given him any chance of tying Carlton's record at that point. With three frames remaining, he would have to strike out the final nine Padres' batters.

Mets catcher Jerry Grote explained later that the cool weather had helped Seaver and during the final innings "he was stronger than ever." Tom fanned the side in the seventh and then the first two batters in the eighth. As Carlton had done the year before, Seaver glanced at the message board, which indicated he had tied the team mark of 15 strikeouts, set by Nolan Ryan just one week earlier. "I didn't know I had 15," he said in the clubhouse later. "But when I knew I did, I tried for 16 ... and then 19."

Due to bat was Jose Arcia, the only Padre not yet set down on strikes. He was an adept contact-hitter, and Seaver's string of six consecutive K's appeared in danger of being snapped. As New York's Kenny Boswell told reporters, "That Arcia don't swing hard enough to strike out." Fortunately for Seaver, the closeness of the contest worked to his advantage. San Diego was trailing by a run with only four outs remaining and had to use a pinch

Tom Seaver's powerful legs seem ready to burst through his uniform as he delivers.
Note the exaggerated knee bend (National Baseball Library & Archive, Cooperstown,
N.Y.).

hitter for the light-hitting Arcia. Ivan Murrell was more capable of tying
the game with one swing. He was even more capable of striking out. Tom
finished Murrell off in quick fashion to break the club record.

While the Mets prepared for their swings in the eighth, Seaver accepted
congratulations from his teammates. The game's outcome was still very much
on his mind, however, and he recalled afterwards, "All I could think of was
Carlton had struck out 19 of us and still lost." He hoped his club would provide him with a couple of insurance runs. They failed, and as he toed the
rubber in the ninth, Seaver had to concern himself with winning the game,
extending his strikeout streak, and matching Carlton's 19 K's.

Van Kelly opened the Padres' ninth by swinging at three fastballs from
terrible Tom, missing each one. Seaver's eighth straight strikeout tied the
record then held by four previous major-leaguers. When Clarence Gaston
followed by looking at a heater for strike three, Seaver had the record for
himself.

The question remained whether Seaver could extend his string to ten
and tie Carlton's single-game total in the process. Ferrara, who had connected
earlier in the game was the Padres' last hope. Tom worked a slider on the

outside corner for a strike. When he missed with another slider, it became the first ball he had thrown in the inning and he lost a chance to become the tenth National Leaguer in the century to fan the side on nine pitches. (Six others have since succeeded.) That Seaver cared or was even aware of the missed opportunity is doubtful.

Tom then hurried a fastball past Ferrara for strike two, and the stage was set. Those in the crowd not already on their feet arose. Their hero glanced at Grote for the sign, and while preparing to throw, he thought about the disappointment he once felt in coming close to glory and then failing. "I missed the perfect game last year," Seaver said. "But I wasn't going to lose this one. I just let the fastball rip."

When Ferrara homered in the second inning, the Mets' moundsman hadn't found his groove. By the ninth, the San Diego slugger was overmatched. By swinging at strike three, he put an end to the game and put Seaver in the record books. Said pitching coach Rube Walker of the ten straight strikeouts, "That's a record that's going to stand a long, long time." So far, no player has proven Rube wrong.

One can't help wondering how many more consecutive whiffs Tom could have strung together if the Mets hadn't knotted the score in the third and the game had been forced into extra innings after the ninth. It's also possible the future Hall-of-Famer could have accumulated more than 19 strikeouts that day had he adopted Carlton's philosophy of "striking out as many batters as possible" throughout the contest. Still, a share of the major-league record was a high enough honor to satisfy anyone, even Seaver.

While David Cone threw his warm-up tosses in the City of Brotherly Love, preparing for his shot at glory, he knew that fanning the side would ensure him of setting a club and National League record. He was also aware that a rival strikeout artist from the junior circuit had established a new major-league mark five years earlier. Boston's Roger Clemens laid claim to the title King of the K's when he set down 20 Seattle Mariners on strikes.

As a cloud of radiation from Chernobyl in the Soviet Union and news of the world's most notorious nuclear disaster were spreading, the Mariners prepared to do battle in Beantown on April 29, 1986. Seattle sluggers Phil Bradley, Ivan Calderon, and Gorman Thomas must have been eager to test the inviting left-field wall at Fenway Park. The expansion club's lineup was just as inviting to the hard-throwing Clemens. Entering the contest, the Mariners were averaging 9.2 strikeouts per game and had struck out 32 times in their previous two games.

The contest began predictably enough, with both Clemens and the Seattle hitters doing what they did best — accumulating K's. The Rocket excited the partisan Fenway crowd by striking out the side in the opening inning. The 23 year old repeated the feat in the fourth frame, with a little help from teammate Don Baylor. Facing the Mariners' Thomas, Clemens fired a fastball. Gorman made contact, but the ball went no farther than first base. Baylor settled under it in foul territory but dropped the can-of-corn for an error. With both Clemens and Thomas being given a reprieve — Thomas another chance to hit and Clemens a chance for an additional strikeout — Roger benefited by zooming a third strike past the dazed power-hitter.

The Boston fireballer retired the Seattle side on strikes again in the fifth. When he fanned Steve Yeager to begin the sixth and followed by firing a third one by Dave Henderson, Clemens stretched his strikeout string to eight. He failed to get closer to Seaver's consecutive K record, however, when Spike Owen lifted a fly ball to center. This one was caught. Since Roger's eighth straight did tie a still-standing American League mark, it's important to remember it wouldn't have occurred without Baylor's miscue. Clemens' second-chance strikeout would prove to be even more consequential to baseball history by game's end.

Although Clemens' mound opponent wasn't throwing in as spectacular a fashion, Mike Moore was nevertheless proving to be as effective in helping his club. Said Clemens afterwards, "I was trying to keep it close, trying to battle a guy that's throwing a good game against us. The strikeouts just kept on coming."

The game entered the seventh scoreless. With two outs, Thomas, who in 1982 won the homerun title, showed he was still a threat, especially in a park which favored righty swingers. He pulled a Roger rabbitball over the wall for the game's first run. Dwight Evans quickly came to his teammate's rescue, however, with a three-run Boston pop in the bottom of the inning. Clemens had a 3–1 lead. Could he get the strikeout record? It was a thought just beginning to materialize in the mind of the Sox hurler. "Late in the game I knew something was happening because the fans were all behind me."

Rocket increased fan frenzy in the eighth when he led off the inning by fanning Ivan Calderon for his 17th whiff, matching the club mark set by Bill Monbouquette in 1961. Five minutes later Monbo's record was history, with Clemens finishing the eighth by throwing three past Dave Henderson. The phenom fireballer was within one of the major-league mark that was shared by three others. (In 1974 the Angels' Nolan Ryan had joined Seaver and Carlton with a 19-strikeout performance against the Red Sox.) The night crowd of over 13,000 fans talked enthusiastically prior to the ninth, anticipating a fabulous finale to the day's drama.

Spike Owen was first to bat. It was Owen who had prevented Clemens from extending his strikeout streak earlier, so it was fitting that Clemens made him his 19th victim. With at least a share of the record already assured, Roger had two more chances. Phil Bradley was the next hitter, or nonhitter to that point. He had fanned in three previous trips for a total of 19 whiffs in his last 23 plate appearances. The perfect pigeon for Clemens never took the bat off his shoulders. The Sox fans cheered wildly for Clemens who, with the record now secured for himself, retired the final Mariner, Ken Phelps, on a comeback grounder to end the game.

The Rocket was lauded in the clubhouse. "I saw Catfish Hunter pitch a perfect game [in 1968]," Sox skipper John McNamara stated. "I've seen Mike Witt [who threw a perfecto in 1984], but this has to be one of the tops." Catcher Rich Gedman described the reactions of Mariners at the plate. "They looked like they wanted to say something but just didn't know what to say." Pitching coach Bill Fischer exclaimed, "I almost had tears in my eyes. It was the best game I ever saw pitched."

Had Fisher been around ten years later, he might have changed his mind. Incredibly, the 34-year-old Boston ace again struck out 20 on September 18, 1996. Clemens fanned the side in three innings and entered the ninth needing two to break his own mark. Alan Trammell popped up and, following a Ruben Sierra single, Tony Clark skied to left before Travis Fryman whiffed for the fourth time to end the game. The 4–0 four-hitter was the Rocket's 30th career shutout, matching Cy Young's record for most blanks by a Red Sox hurler. Clemens had thanked the man upstairs for helping him reach the 20-mark in 1986. His needing to throw over 150 pitches to repeat the feat near the end of a season in which he would comfortably lead the majors in innings pitched, and at an age in which many hurlers would be calling it a career, left few doubting that he was blessed with a superhuman arm.

Perhaps the man upstairs was behind David Cone as well as he readied himself for his shot at immortality, but the fans clearly weren't. Unlike Seaver and Carlton, and Clemens in his first effort, Cone had accumulated his K's on the road. That the game was in Philadelphia, where baseball followers are known for being uncharitable, made his task even more difficult. Even in Clemens' second masterpiece, most of the 8,779 spectators at Tiger Stadium were cheering for the Rocket to shoot down the Bengals because they were hungry for excitement after watching their club struggle in the basement all season and were especially ravenous following the trade in August of their longtime slugging superstar, Cecil Fielder, to the Yankees. Not many in the crowd of nearly 30,000 at Veterans Stadium were eager, however, to see David Cone become a Goliath against their hometown heroes.

But Cone was used to adverse conditions. He was born in 1963 in a tough working-class neighborhood in Kansas City, an area where "if you didn't stand up for yourself, you got eaten alive," as he recalled decades later. Cone once bloodied the face of a basketball teammate at Rockhurst High for taunting him and then stood up to the dean afterwards. A Royals fan during his youth, Cone became ecstatic after he was picked by Kansas City in the third round of the 1981 draft. He made 11 relief appearances as a rookie in 1986, but he was traded to the Mets the following year because of the conservative organization's antipathy to his inclination for "candor," as he later asserted. Cone's independent spirit soon made him the choice of the Mets players for union representative.

Having to handle hostility, both as a youth and as a player, Cone wouldn't be perturbed by the Philly crowd during his attempt to break the K mark. Nor would the game's outcome be a concern during the final frame. Uncharacteristically, his mates had provided him with seven runs, more than enough against a team being held to three hits. Cone had struck out the side in the first two innings while New York was tallying three times. They added another run in the third and Cone an additional strikeout. He notched three more K's in the fourth, two in the fifth, and another trio in the sixth. With 15 strikeouts and four innings in which he struck out the side, the Met was more overpowering than any of the other three record-holders had been through their first six innings' work. Cone was then in a perfect position to break the mark.

In the seventh, however, the strikeout artist had faltered. He retired the side in order but without any strikeouts. Suddenly the tiring hurler's chances appeared slim. Cone needed five more K's for a share of Clemens' mark with only six outs left. He remained in contention in the eighth by fanning Braulio Castillo for his 16th of the game and setting down Doug Lindsey for number 17.

In the dugout awaiting the last inning, the would-be record-setter reflected on his chances. "I knew I had to strike out the side to get 20," Cone admitted afterwards. "It was just a thrill to be in that position." It became even more thrilling for Mets fans watching the televised game in New York when David threw three strikes past the first Philly batter, Kim Batiste, to open the ninth. Although that chore seemed simple enough because Batiste had failed to make contact in his previous three at-bats, the next batter, Mickey Morandini, would be a more difficult challenge. The spray hitter had one of the two Philadelphia hits to that point and was the only regular in the lineup not to have fanned. With the record so near, however, Cone was up to the challenge, and Morandini joined his mates as one of his 19 strikeout victims.

Cone was one strikeout away from owning the National League mark by himself and forcing his greatest strikeout rival to share the major-league record. His chances seemed excellent. Not only had his strikeout groove been revived, but the next Philly batter hadn't put the ball in play in three previous tries. Commented Wes Chamberlain after the game, "His fastball was so good, it was on you before you realized it."

The count against Chamberlain quickly went against him as Cone fired a called strike. The Phil's outfielder then surprised Cone, and probably everyone else in the ballpark, by putting the following fastball in play. The drive was out of right-fielder Howard Johnson's reach, and when Chamberlain happily pulled into second with a double, Cone was undoubtedly just as pleased that the ball wasn't caught and the strikeout record was still a possibility.

Slugger Dale Murphy was next, one of the all-time great homer-hitters, but he was prone to striking out and had been set down twice already. Perhaps because he was thinking about preserving his shutout with a runner in scoring position, Cone pitched too carefully to Murph and fell behind 2–0. Cone came back with a strike and then tried a slider. The long-armed swinger reached out and touched the ball, with a resulting grounder to second ending the game — and Cone's dream.

The hurler was philosophical in the clubhouse about his season-ending failure. "Am I disappointed by missing 20? No. I realize one doesn't get in the position often, even ever. But the silver lining is that 19 is still a record for the National League. I'll be in the book." That he is, along with Carlton and Seaver.

While Cone was smoking in Philly, his American League counterpart was also throwing in Boston's last game. Over 30,000 fans showed up at Fenway, almost three times as many as had witnessed Clemens' masterpiece five years earlier. The game meant nothing to the Red Sox, who were already assured of a second place finish, but Bostonians had by then understood the possibility which existed of a record-smashing performance whenever the Rocket was firing.

When Clemens struck out ten that day, it upped his season total to 241, tops in the junior circuit. Coincidentally, Cone's 19 whiffs had lifted his league-leading amount to 241. During the winter, David could console himself with the fact that he shared the major-league strikeout title with Clemens that season, despite his failure to equal Roger's prestigious record for most in one game.

Cone could also be satisfied in knowing that of the four record-K performances, his was perhaps the most overpowering in that he allowed no runs. With that exception, the pitching feats were quite similar. Cone threw

141 pitches, Clemens 138, and Seaver 136. All four hurlers' control had been sharp, with Seaver and Carlton walking only two, Cone one, and Clemens none. The games were played either at the very beginning or end of the season, in rather cool temperatures, and with no pressure of being in a pennant race. Finally, each moundsman faced a rather weak-hitting club filled with batters prone to striking out frequently.

The brilliant three-hitter by Cone ended what had been a mediocre season for the Mets' righthander, who finished with a 14–14 record. Said Cone, "It doesn't make up for the season, but it gives you something to look forward to." Still, it was a bittersweet end to the year. Cone could point to the seventh inning, when he failed to fan a batter, as his downfall. Just as harmful to his chances at a new strikeout record was the comfortable, early lead given him. It resulted in his seeing a pitcher as a batting opponent only once in the contest; he faced pinch hitters the rest of the way. When Cone was unable to strike out the Phils' hurler Andy Ashby in the third inning, it probably didn't bother him at the time, but by the end of the game, his missed opportunity had come back to haunt him.

Ironically, Cone's overpowering outing would be his final appearance as a Met. Despite four outstanding seasons, the outspoken hurler was traded to Toronto in 1992, part of the reason being a midseason televised shouting match with manager Bud Harrelson. Cone had shaken off a pitchout sign ordered by Harrelson and complained loudly after the inning about the wisdom of the strategy. Harrelson became so livid that he began shoving Cone before the pair were separated.

In a game against Texas on June 17, 1996, Cone once again flirted with immortality by coming within two outs of a no-hitter before a clean single ended his quest. He was traded by the Blue Jays and pitched for the Yankees the remainder of the season and in the division championships. The following year he began experiencing numbness in his right hand. In May, doctors at Columbia Presbyterian Medical Center diagnosed the problem as a "very small aneurysm" in his right shoulder. Aneurysms, which can be life-threatening, are also often correctable. Surgery and rest enabled Cone to return to the mound a couple of months later in Oakland. He astonished everyone by pitching seven innings of no-hit ball before he was pulled from the game by a cautious Joe Torre. Although he was disappointed, Cone admitted afterwards that Torre had made the proper call. (Torre made many in 1996, as the Yankees won the division, the pennant, and the World Series.)

Cone's failures have been outweighed by a career that has included a 20–3 mark and 2.22 ERA in 1988, a 17–10 record and 2.81 ERA in 1992, five seasons with more than 200 strikeouts, including two K-crowns, and five

David Cone authored many masterpieces during his career, but none as superb as his season-ending gem of 1991 (National Baseball Library & Archive, Cooperstown, N.Y.).

appearances in postseason play. When he retires, most experts will probably place him among the top ten pitchers of his era.

Still, being the best at blowing away batters has been a much-coveted goal of hurlers since the untouchable tosses of Cy Young and Amos Rusie in the 1890s necessitated that the distance from the pitching mound to home plate be lengthened from fifty feet to its present span of sixty feet, six inches. Consequently, fanning more in one game than any other hurler in history would go far to legitimizing the claim to King of the K masters. With his two 20-strikeout performances, Clemens deserves that regal title today. Yet how less worthy is Cone, having come within one in 1991 of His Majesty's mark?

Perhaps Keats was correct in writing, "I would sooner fail than not be among the greatest."

David Cone's 19-K Game Compared with Other Outstanding Performances

Pitcher	Date	Opponent	Ks	H	BB	R
David Cone	10/6/91	Phils (A)	19	3	1	0
Roger Clemens	4/29/86	Mariners (H)	20	3	0	1
Roger Clemens	9/18/96	Tigers (A)	20	4	0	0
Tom Seaver	4/22/70	Padres (H)	19	2	2	1
Steve Carlton	9/15/69	Cards (H)	19	9	2	4

(Note: On May 6, 1998, the Cubs' rookie righthander Kerry Wood fanned 20 Astros batters en route to a 2–0, one-hit victory at Wrigley Field. Wood is the new holder of the NL record for most strikeouts in a game, and he shares the major-league mark with Clemens.)

Bibliography

Newspapers and Periodicals

Albany Times Union
Baseball Hobby News
Baseball Magazine
Baseball Quarterly
Baseball Research Journal
Boston Herald
Cincinnati Enquirer
Cleveland Plain Dealer
Collier's
Dallas Morning News
Houston Post
Kansas City Star
Los Angeles Times
National Pastime

New York Post
New York Times
Philadelphia Inquirer
St. Louis Post-Dispatch
San Francisco Chronicle
Saturday Evening Post
Seattle Times
Sport
Sporting News
Sports Collector's Digest
Staten Island Advance
Staten Island Register
USA Today

Books and References

Alexander, Charles C. *John McGraw*. New York: Viking, 1988.
_____. *Our Game — An American Baseball History*. New York: Holt, 1991.
_____. *Rogers Hornsby — A Biography*. New York: Macmillan, 1990.
Anderson, Dave. *Pennant Races — Baseball at Its Best*. New York: Doubleday, 1994.
The Baseball Encyclopedia. 9th ed. New York: Macmillan, 1993.
Blake, Mike. *Baseball Chronicles — An Oral History of Baseball Through the Decades*. Cincinnati: Betterway, 1994.
Bonavita, Mark, and Sean Stewart, eds. *The Sporting News Baseball Register*. Rev. ed. St. Louis: Sporting News, 1997.
Broeg, Bob. *Superstars of Baseball*. Reprint. South Bend: Diamond Communications, 1994.
Carney, Gene. *Romancing the Horsehide*. Jefferson, N.C.: McFarland, 1995.
Carrieri, Joe. *Searching for Heroes — The Quest of a Yankee Batboy*. Mineola, N.Y.: Carlyn, 1995.

Carter, Craig, ed. *The Sporting News Complete Baseball Record Book.* 1995 edition. St. Louis: Sporting News, 1994.

Cataneo, David. *Peanuts and Crackerjack — A Treasury of Baseball Legends and Lore.* Nashville: Rutledge Hill, 1991.

Charlton, Jim. *The Who, What, When, Why, and How of Baseball.* New York: Barnes and Noble, 1995.

Creamer, Robert W. *Babe — The Legend Comes to Life.* New York: Simon & Schuster, 1974.

_____. *Baseball in '41.* New York: Penguin, 1991.

Curran, William. *Big Sticks — The Batting Revolution of the Twenties.* New York: Morrow, 1990.

Daniel, W. Harrison. *Jimmie Foxx — Baseball Hall of Famer, 1907–1967.* Jefferson, N.C.: McFarland, 1996.

Debs, Victor, Jr. *Baseball Tidbits.* Indianapolis: Masters, 1997.

_____. *Still Standing After All These Years.* Jefferson, N.C.: McFarland, 1997.

_____. *They Kept Me Loyal to the Yankees.* Nashville: Rutledge Hill, 1993.

Dewey, Donald, and Nicholas Acocella. *The Biographical History of Baseball.* New York: Carroll & Graf, 1995.

Dickson, Paul. *Baseball's Greatest Quotations.* New York: HarperCollins, 1991.

Dittmar, Joseph J. *Baseball's Benchmark Boxscores.* Jefferson, N.C.: McFarland, 1990.

Edwards, Bob. *Fridays with Red — A Radio Friendship.* New York: Simon & Schuster, 1993.

Eisenhammer, Fred, and Jim Binkley. *Baseball's Most Memorable Trades.* Jefferson, N.C.: McFarland, 1997.

Fisher, Jim. *The Lindbergh Case.* New Brunswick, N.J.: Rutgers University Press, 1994.

Gorman, Bob. *Double X.* New York: Goff, 1990.

Gregory, Robert. *Diz.* New York: Viking Penguin, 1992.

Halberstam, David. *Summer of '49.* New York: Morrow, 1989.

Honig, Donald. *Baseball in the '30s — A Decade of Survival.* New York: Crown, 1989.

_____. *National League — An Illustrated History.* New York: Crown, 1987.

Isaacs, Neil D. *Innocence & Wonder — Baseball Through the Eyes of Batboys.* Indianapolis: Masters, 1994.

James, Bill. *The Bill James Guide to Baseball Managers from 1870 to Today.* New York: Scribner, 1997.

Katz, Lawrence S. *Baseball in 1939 — The Watershed Season of the National Pastime.* Jefferson, N.C.: McFarland, 1995.

Kelley, Brent. *The Case For: Those Overlooked by the Baseball Hall of Fame.* Jefferson, N.C.: McFarland, 1995.

_____. *In the Shadow of the Babe — Interviews with Baseball Players Who Played With or Against Babe Ruth.* Jefferson, N.C.: McFarland, 1995.

Laird, A. W. *Ranking Baseball's Elite — An Analysis Derived from Player Statistics, 1893–1987.* Jefferson, N.C.: McFarland, 1990.

Lewis, Allen. *Baseball's Greatest Streaks.* Jefferson, N.C.: McFarland, 1992.

Liebman, Glenn. *Baseball Shorts — 1,000 of the Game's Funniest One-Liners.* Chicago: Contemporary, 1994.

Lowry, Philip J. *Green Cathedrals.* Rev. ed. Reading, Mass.: Addison Wesley, 1992.

Mead, William B. *Two Spectacular Seasons: 1930— The Year the Hitters Ran Wild; 1968 — The Year Pitchers Took Over.* New York: Macmillan, 1990.

_____, and Paul Dickson. *Baseball— The President's Game.* Washington, D.C.: Farragut, 1993.

Murdock, Eugene. *Baseball Players and Their Times— Oral Histories of the Game, 1920–1940.* Westport, Conn.: Meckler, 1991.

Oakley, J. Ronald. *Baseball's Last Golden Age, 1946–1960.* Jefferson, N.C.: McFarland, 1994.

Okkonen, Marc. *Baseball Uniforms of the 20th Century.* New York: Sterling, 1991.

Okrent, Daniel, and Harris Lewine. Eds. *The Ultimate Baseball Book.* Boston: Houghton Mifflin, 1991.

_____, and Steve Wulf. *Baseball Anecdotes.* New York: Oxford University Press, 1989.

Perry, Daniel, ed. *We Played the Game.* New York: Hyperion, 1994.

Rader, Benjamin G. *Baseball— A History of America's Game.* Chicago: University of Illinois Press, 1992.

Reichler, Joseph. *Baseball's Great Moments.* Rev. ed. New York: Bonanza, 1982.

_____. *The Great All-Time Baseball Record Book.* Revised by Ken Samelson. New York: Macmillan, 1993.

Ritter, Lawrence S. *Glory of Their Times.* Enlarged ed. New York: Morrow, 1984.

Rose, Pete, and Roger Kahn. *Pete Rose— My Story.* New York: Macmillan, 1989.

Rust, Arthur, Jr. *Legends— Conversations with Baseball Greats.* New York: McGraw-Hill, 1989.

Seaver, Tom, with Marty Appel. *Great Moments in Baseball.* New York: Carol, 1992.

Shulman, Arthur, and Roger Youman. *How Sweet It Was.* New York: Bonanza, 1966.

Thorn, John, and Pete Palmer, eds. *Total Baseball.* New York: HarperCollins, 1993.

Ward, Geoffrey C., and Ken Burns. *Baseball— An Illustrated History.* New York: Alfred A. Knopf, 1994.

Will, George. *Men at Work.* New York: Macmillan, 1990.

Williams, Ted, and Jim Prime. *Ted Williams' Hit List.* Indianapolis: Masters, 1996.

_____, with John Underwood. *My Turn at Bat.* New York: Simon & Schuster, 1988.

Index

Numbers in **boldface** refer to pages with photographs.